A Deadly Thaw

by the same author

IN BITTER CHILL

A Deadly Thaw

SARAH WARD

FABER & FABER

First published in 2016
by Faber & Faber Ltd
Bloomsbury House
74–77 Great Russell Street
London WC1B 3DA

Typeset by Faber & Faber Ltd
Printed and bound by CPI Group (UK) Ltd, Croydon CR0 4YY

A CIP record for this book
is available from the British Library

ISBN 978-0-571-32102-5

2 4 6 8 10 9 7 5 3 1

For Dad and Andy Lawrence

Sunday, 19 September 2004

Lena felt his emotional withdrawal before the physical. He rolled away from her and reached for his phone. 'You could've waited at least five minutes before checking that thing.' She kept her voice light but could feel his irritation. He kept his face turned away from her, and, in the gloom, she could only see the curls of his too-long hair reflected in the meagre moonlight coming in through the window.

'I've got a lot of things to do before I leave the country. Loose ends to tie up. You wouldn't know, but it's not easy moving anywhere. Especially overseas. I need to be on my phone twenty-four seven.' He turned onto his back without looking at her, still clutching the mobile in his hand, and listened to his messages. The white incandescent light from the device threw a pallid glow across the blankets. She slid out of the bed and padded to the bathroom.

The cold porcelain tiles chilled her feet. Sitting on the toilet, she heard the murmur of a hushed conversation. She eyed the shower nozzle over the ancient bath and, getting up, turned it on to its full strength. The water was hot, although the spray took time to splutter into life. When the steam rose from the floor of the bath, she stepped into it and allowed the scalding water to drench her skin.

By the time she returned to the bedroom he was asleep, snoring softly on his back, his face turned into the pillow. He had placed his phone on the bedside table. She went over to it and scrolled through the calls made. A set of random digits. No names attached. She stared at the numbers for a moment and then put the phone gently back on the table and joined him in bed. He continued to snuffle in his sleep, and she turned away from him.

On the white wall opposite she followed the light of the phone, measuring with her eyes the shape thrown by the pale glow. It was distended at one end, the light merging from a sickly green into a pale red. She squinted at the image to bring it into focus and frowned. It wasn't a trick of the eyes. The red hue suggested a source of light other than the phone she'd just examined.

In the darkness, she got up to track the origin of the other light and went softly towards the leather jacket that he'd thrown over the chair in his haste to join her in the bed. Inside the jacket, she found another phone, with a light indicating a low battery. Her fingers fumbled over the keys. After two minutes, she placed the mobile back into the jacket's top pocket and went over to the bed. He was still on his back, his chest rising with each snore. She picked up the pillow from her side, which gave off the unfamiliar odour of her new hairspray. She placed it over his head and pushed.

Detective Inspector Francis Sadler looked down at the rigid corpse of the ashen man lying on the stone slab and swallowed the bile that had risen in his throat. The corpse had a solid muscularity that death hadn't yet robbed it of. Sadler noted the large biceps visible through the thin cotton of the man's grey T-shirt. It was a good place to focus his attention, because his eyes were irresistibly drawn to the bloom of red that spread out from the chest. The poppy-red stain suggested the victim hadn't bled as much as Sadler would have expected for a gunshot wound. Death had come quickly; the pumping heart stilled in a beat. Someone with a good aim or a lucky chance.

His eyes moved upwards. It was the face of all the dead he had seen. Devoid of expression. If you could tell how someone had died by reading their faces, it was an art that Sadler had yet to master.

'Great place for a body. A morgue. I'd have never thought of looking there.'

Sadler looked across at the pathologist, Bill Shields, who was typing something onto his tablet with one finger. Bill's eyes met his, and he shrugged. 'Simply stating a fact. A first for me. I still have the capacity to be surprised, you know.'

A slight noise from the doorway alerted Sadler to the fact that Detective Constable Connie Childs had arrived. She was sweating slightly, small drops of moisture scattered across her temple, which she brushed with her sleeve. She looked around the room, and Sadler could see her assessing the paint hanging in strips off the wall and the cracked stone tiles steeped in damp. Only when she had taken this in did she finally look at the man lying on the stone block.

She turned to Sadler with a glint of amusement in her eyes. He could feel his mood darkening. 'Bill's already made the joke, thank you Connie.'

'I haven't said anything.' She shot Bill a conspiratorial look, and Sadler saw the pathologist smile into his computer. 'Sorry I was late. I had to leave the car on the road and follow the track up here on foot. Like everyone else it seems. There are no signposts at all, you know.'

'I'm not surprised. The only visitors here these past fifty years, I suspect, have been ghouls looking to visit a place that should be left to history. It was one of them that found the body. An *urban explorer* he called himself. He seems genuine enough though. Even has his own website.'

'It is a morgue, isn't it? Who would build something like this in the middle of nowhere? What's the name of this place again?'

'Hale's End Mortuary. It must be coming up for its centenary. It was built during the First World War to help process the casualties that were being shipped back from France. It's got an interesting history.' Sadler felt another urge to leave the dank building.

Connie had perked up. 'The First World War! Why would the casualties end up in Derbyshire?' She sounded curious. Really they should have been looking at the body behind them, but Sadler welcomed the distraction. He looked at the green algae-covered floor as a beetle scurried in front of him, seeking refuge in the deeper darkness of the room's recesses. 'You need to read up on your history. There were over thirty-eight million casualties in that war. They ended up where there was room, including here in Derbyshire. There were three hospitals at one time in Buxton looking after the injured. They requisitioned buildings for the war effort and converted them into temporary hospitals.'

'But this looks permanent.'

Sadler could feel the bile rising again. 'A lot of the injuries were severe. People more often than not died from their wounds. So you needed a mortuary. They built this place to prepare the bodies to be sent to wherever for burial.'

Connie was looking at him now, her focus shifting from the room onto him. 'You know a lot about it, if you don't mind me saying.'

Sadler did mind. The place had been a regular haunt when he'd been a bored teenager looking for an evening's recreation. He could remember breaking into the building a couple of times with his friends. They would scale the ageing wire fence and, with torches in their hands, scare themselves by larking around in the chilled building.

Once, he remembered, he had lain on one of the two cold trays and pretended to be dead. His friend, Michael, had made a more convincing corpse with his hands pressed primly together. Sadler could remember his heart thudding in his chest and the cold finger of fear on him. To Connie, he simply said, 'It's well known locally.'

'First time in a long while it's seen a dead body, though,' said Connie.

Bill Shields put his tablet into a supermarket carrier bag and tied a knot in the top. 'I'm done. I'm not doing the PM here, as much as I'd like to for historic purposes. You know, to see what it used to be like.' He must have seen Sadler's face because he winked at Connie and walked out.

Sadler looked after him and wished that he could follow him into the clear air.

Connie was leaning over the body. 'We should be able to get a positive ID, though. He looks like a recent one. Did Bill give you an estimate of the time of death?'

'Within twenty-four hours, he thinks. That would go with your more prosaic way of guessing these things.'

Connie looked downcast, and Sadler felt a sharp pang of regret. Wasn't it a good thing that one of his colleagues wanted to make her own conclusions based on the evidence before her?

'Any ID?'

Sadler shook his head. 'No. But there's no need. I know who he is.'

She swung around with a look of shock on her face. 'You know him? Why didn't you say so when I came in?'

Sadler looked at the ground. 'His name's Andrew Fisher. Same age as me. Same school, even.'

Connie moved away from the body and joined him. 'Did you know him well?'

'Not very. I saw him around Bampton occasionally. I didn't even know him well enough to say hello. Maybe a vague nod of recognition. That was it.' Sadler could feel her eyes on him.

'If you don't mind me saying, you look a bit shocked for someone you didn't know well.'

He turned to her. 'Shocked? Yes, you could say that.

Andrew was murdered in 2004. Asphyxiation.'

'What?'

'His wife was convicted of his murder. She served a long stretch in prison. Less than the statutory fifteen years minimum, I heard. She was a model prisoner and pleaded guilty. She's now out on parole.'

'You're kidding. This guy's not been dead for twelve years. Unless he was kept in a freezer.'

Sadler, irritated, wanted to smoke one of the cigarettes he had given up twenty years earlier. 'I'm not suggesting he was kept in a freezer. The body was positively identified in 2004 and a funeral was held. I'd only recently joined CID. I remember the case well because, as I said, I knew Andrew.'

'And this person has turned up dead in Hale's End morgue.'

She was baiting him. He recognised it and could do nothing to quell the irritation. 'We clearly identified the wrong person.'

'That's not possible, is it? These days, I mean.'

Sadler turned to look at the body of his childhood contemporary. 'Possible or not, over there I'm pretty sure is the body of Andrew Fisher. Who was supposedly killed in 2004.'

'And who identified the body? I mean, we're looking at a miscarriage of justice here if his wife served time for his murder. Who gave the positive ID?'

Sadler let the weariness wash over him. 'His wife, Lena.'

3

Kat was fascinated by the scar on Mark's face. His right cheek had a narrow perpendicular mark that, in a previous session, he'd revealed was the result of his mother throwing a vegetable knife at him when he was ten. His reflexes hadn't, at that stage, advanced to the degree they'd reached by the time he left home when he was fifteen. He had ducked the flying blade, which, a doctor later suggested, had prevented it piercing his windpipe. But it sliced through his cheek, which bled with a profusion of crimson that had alarmed his mother so much that she had driven him to the A&E department with a warning to say that he had tripped and fallen onto the sharp edge of the kitchen counter.

At the hospital, a young registrar from the Sudan had played enough childhood games with knives to recognise a blade wound and, after sending Mark's mother away with a nurse to get a cup of tea 'for her shock', had asked him what had happened. Mark, yet to develop the sheen of protection that had served him so well up until six months ago, had told him. The doctor had said nothing, patched him up and wished him good luck.

'What should I say to her in my reply?'

Kat shifted in her seat. Mothers and sons. It had fascinated the Ancient Greeks, and sometimes she wondered how little had changed. Mark possessed the strength of character to leave when he could, going to stay with an elderly uncle whose fundamental dislike of women had extended to his niece. His financial support of Mark had been as much to do with his distrust of all things female as with a desire to stand up to his niece's abuse of her son. Yet Mark, at thirty-five, was once more being tormented by his mother.

'What would you like to say to her? Say out loud what you really want to write in your response.'

It was an old counselling trick. People rarely wrote what they wanted to say in the same way that they rarely said what they wanted to. Therapy was a way to air unspoken grievances. Kat let the silence settle around them.

'I want to say, "Thanks for nothing for getting in touch. I made my decision to sever all ties with you when I was fifteen. I've never regretted it for a moment. So, whatever the reason is for getting in touch with me, thanks for nothing." That's what I want to say to her.'

Kat waited, but nothing else came. Mark had returned to that fifteen-year-old self, his arms folded and refusing to look her in the eye. She tried another tack. 'Do you know why she's decided to contact you now?' She watched him shake his head. 'Do you want to try and guess?'

She glanced at the clock. The hour was nearly up. Mark had dropped the news about his mother's email in the last fifteen minutes. She had seen his agitation build up in the preceding forty-five, but gentle questioning hadn't revealed anything until he had suddenly blurted out the reason for his tension. 'We're going to have to stop shortly. Are you going to be okay until the next session? We can always meet later in the week if you want.' Now that the session was coming to an end, Kat allowed herself to relax with her client. Despite his agitation, he was smiling across at her, and she felt like grinning back at him.

'It's fine. I like my routine, you know.'

Kat didn't know. He was her first client who had served in the army. He'd seen action too, in Iraq, although it was his childhood that had sent the demons to him, not those days in the heat of the Middle East. She showed him to the door, but he didn't leave straight away.

He was standing in front of her. A little uncertain. She felt she should move away from him, give him more space, but she was enjoying his proximity. 'Is everything okay? I have another client in half an hour.' She looked up again at the clock. 'But if there's something you want to talk about now . . .' He was shaking his head. 'Until next time then.'

4

'My God, it's the House of Usher.'

Detective Sergeant Damian Palmer smirked next to Connie but said nothing in response. It was officially his day off. He'd been grumbling the day before about a shopping trip to Sheffield with his wife, Joanne, but as soon as he heard about the body on the local radio, he hotfooted it back to Bampton, and Connie picked him up from the train station.

He didn't look very happy, but Connie couldn't tell if it was because of his disturbed leave or the fact he'd missed seeing the body. Probably both. She looked up again at the house, shocked that so dilapidated a building had been able to survive the gentrification of Bampton. It was a huge Victorian edifice, made from limestone probably quarried from the nearby hills and erected in the days when the purpose of your residence was to overwhelm and impress. But creating an imposing home also required money to keep up appearances, and Lena Fisher clearly didn't have the cash to spend on the façade of the house. Or, if she did, she wasn't spending it where it was needed.

The house wasn't in a much better state than Hale's End Mortuary, and at least that was boarded up. Here was a building being lived in. The stone was solid enough. There wasn't much that years of neglect could do to limestone. However, the wooden windows were another matter. They were not only rotten, it looked like someone had attempted to repair them with strips of cardboard and tinfoil. Some roof slates had slipped out of their fastenings and were lying in a heap near the rusty wrought-iron gutter. At the top of the building, set into the stone under one of the eaves, was the house's name, Providence Villa.

Connie would have believed the house to be abandoned if it weren't for the line of washing hanging to one side. It suggested that the address Lena had given to the Probation Service was the correct one. Although, if appearances were anything to go by, God knows what state she would find the occupant in.

They walked up to the front door. The old brass knocker was strangely comforting in its solidity. Connie noticed with surprise that the face in the rusting metal was a Green Man. He leered out at her from the metal oak leaves. Palmer lifted and dropped the brass ring, and Connie listened to the sound echo around the house. It appeared empty, and she wondered how much furniture was on the other side of the door. She was about to peer through one of the grubby windows when the door opened, and there stood a woman.

Connie had long ago learnt that starting an investigation with a set of assumptions was a sure-fire way of making things more difficult for yourself. People rarely reacted in the way you expected, could look unmarked by the vicissitudes of life and could surprise even the most experienced copper.

But Lena was still a surprise. Given she had served a long stretch inside Styal high-security prison, Connie expected at least a visage of shame and possibly guilt. Instead, the woman standing in the open doorway was looking at her with cool detachment. 'What have I done now?'

Connie wasn't surprised. Although people rarely identified

her as a copper straight away, her tiny frame and fragile appearance lulling suspects into a false sense of security, there were two of them presenting themselves at this woman's front door. She reminded herself that here was a woman used to the criminal justice system. 'I'm Detective Constable Childs, and this is Detective Sergeant Palmer. Can we come in?'

She saw, for the first time, a flash of concern in the woman's expression. She stood aside to let them into the house. As Connie had suspected, the large hall was bare, with only a small side table filled with a jumble of letters and keys, too meagre for the cavernous space. An effort had been made to brighten the interior. The painted walls might have been stained, and a smell of damp assailed her nostrils, but a bunch of hydrangeas was floating in water on the table, their colourful orbs providing a splash of brightness in the dark hallway.

The woman noticed her looking. 'You like flowers?'

Connie shrugged. 'No. Well, yes, of course I like flowers but I particularly like hydrangeas. They remind me of my grandmother. She used to have two large bushes growing in her front garden. I don't remember them being out in spring though.'

The woman stroked one of the heads. 'They're the first blooms of the year. The garden is full of the bushes. The flowers are supposed to symbolise vanity and boastfulness. I can't see the connection myself.'

Connie looked at the flowers and stifled the urge to touch them too. 'You are Lena Fisher?'

The woman winced. 'I'm Lena Gray now. I went back to my maiden name. Come through to the living room. Forget about the bloody flowers.'

The lounge was huge, with picture windows at either end.

The one looking out towards the front garden was almost obscured by an oak tree whose branches tapped against the glass. The back window at least gave a partial glimpse of the rear garden but was so dirty that all Connie could see was the ghostly outline of her own reflection in the glass as she stared across the room.

She and Palmer sat on one of the sofas, and Lena took the one opposite them. She had long dark hair, streaked with fine threads of silver, pulled up into a French knot. She wore an old white shirt over a grey T-shirt and jeans ripped at the knees. She looked both untidy and effortlessly chic. Connie glanced down at her scuffed shoes and promised herself a shopping trip as soon as the sales started.

'Ms Gray. You were released from prison in April last year having served ten and a half years of a life sentence. Is that correct?' The woman nodded but said nothing. Connie carried on. 'You were convicted of the murder of your husband, Andrew Fisher, in a trial that took place in March 2005. You agree this is the case?'

Again the woman nodded.

Palmer was silent next to her. Watching them both.

Connie could feel her blood pressure beginning to rise. She took a deep breath. 'When Andrew Fisher was found dead in September 2004, it was initially thought to have been the result of a heart attack. You positively identified him as being your husband. Is that correct?'

The woman's expression was unreadable. But still she nodded. Connie had had enough. 'And at what point did you realise he wasn't, in fact, your husband?'

Silence.

'And why didn't you think to mention it when you were subsequently arrested and tried for his murder?'

The woman's amused expression had gone.

'Aren't you going to say something?'

Lena put her head in her hands. Connie waited, giving her time to compose herself.

There was a scraping noise of metal hitting metal, and then the sound of the front door opening and closing. A woman walked into the room, so resembling Lena that Connie had to look back opposite her to make sure what she was seeing wasn't an optical illusion caused, perhaps, by the shadowing glass.

'What's going on?'

Lena stood up but didn't move away from the sofa. 'These are . . . detectives.'

As the other woman approached, Connie could see that the resemblance between the two women was superficial. They both had long dark hair and thin-limbed bodies, but whereas Lena Gray was calm self-containment, this new woman had a restless energy which, Connie thought, she was making an attempt to suppress.

The similarity hadn't gone unnoticed by Palmer. He was looking at the two women with a puzzled frown on his face.

'I'm Kat Gray. Lena's sister.'

Sadler hadn't mentioned anything about a sister. Perhaps she hadn't been around at the time of the killing.

She walked over to Lena's sofa and sat down next to her. Two pairs of pale-blue eyes fixed on Connie, and she was suddenly aware of an undercurrent of strength emitting from these two women. She leaned forward. 'So, Lena. I was asking you at what point you realised that the man you identified as your husband in 2004 wasn't in fact Andrew Fisher.'

That shocked the new woman. 'What?' She swivelled around to look at her sister, who was still staring at Connie. 'What's she taking about, Lena?'

Lena shook her head, and Connie, for a moment, let the silence settle over the dusty living room.

'In 2004, you positively identified a body found in your bedroom as your husband, Andrew. However, given that you had been married to him for five years and that the injuries that the dead man had sustained had not particularly affected his facial features, you must surely have realised that the man you were identifying was not your husband.'

Kat was pale with shock. Her sister, wary. 'What makes you so certain that the man I identified wasn't my husband?'

Connie looked at the two sisters. 'Because earlier today the body of a man was found which we believe to be that of Andrew Fisher. So the question I'm putting to you, Ms Gray, is who did you kill on the nineteenth of September 2004?'

5

After the police had gone, Kat went into the kitchen and put the kettle on the hob. She hunted around for matches and finally located them under a damp tea towel on the kitchen counter. It was useless to complain to Lena. Especially now they had more important things to discuss. Nothing could be forced into the open. Ever since she was a teenager, Lena had responded only to words of encouragement and enticement. Any criticism, implied or otherwise, would be met with withdrawal and distance.

As the kettle spluttered to life, Kat thought back to the other time when the police had come to the house. She hadn't been living here then. She'd taught English abroad for most of the 1990s, returning in 1998 to retrain as a therapist. She'd used her savings to rent a modern loft in the old textile mill at Litton. Although housed in a Victorian building, it was aeons away from the draughty wreck that this place had become.

Then, one day in 2004, she had a call to say that her brother-in-law was dead, and she'd gone back to her childhood home to support her sister. And she had. At least for a short time. But then the police had come to arrest Lena, and, after that fateful visit, Kat had never, really, ever left. Because Lena had gone with them. No denials, no protestations of innocence. The same through the trial. Pleaded guilty and had done nothing to help herself. It had been left to the solicitor to try to present any mitigating circumstances.

Kat's phone pinged, and she picked it up to look at the message. It was from Mark Astley. 'Thanks for the support today.' Her heart jumped. Of course he had her mobile number. She'd given it to him during the first session in case either of them needed to change their appointment times. She'd never said that it was okay for him to contact her otherwise, and certainly not via text message.

She thought about replying. Something neutral and innocuous but encouraging. Professional but a reply all the same. Discretion got the better of her, and she deleted the message.

After pouring the hot water into the teapot, she put everything on a tray and carried it through to the living room. Lena hadn't moved. Kat carefully placed the tray on the table and sat opposite her, taking the seat where the detectives had been. 'Is it true?'

Lena turned to look out of the far window. 'I can't tell you.'

Kat could feel her face turning red. 'What do you mean you can't tell me? What can't you tell me?'

Lena stood up and walked towards the window. 'Don't ask, because I can't tell you.'

'Can't or won't?'

Still facing away, her sister spoke to the window. 'Does it matter? I'm not able to say.'

Kat looked at the brewing tea and felt the urge to pick up the pot and hurl it at her sister. She willed herself to stay calm. 'Can you at least tell me if the man you identified in 2004 was actually Andrew?'

'No.'

'No what?' Kat was shouting, the frustrations of the day suddenly to the fore. 'No, you can't tell me, or no, it wasn't Andrew?'

Lena remained silent.

'Aren't you going to say something?'

Finally, Lena turned to her sister. 'Not everything can be told. You, of all people, should know that.'

6

Palmer deposited three Styrofoam cups of coffee onto Sadler's desk. 'Hot off the press, as it were.'

Connie gave him a sour look. 'You're mixing your metaphors. I thought we were boycotting that place.' A well-known chain of coffee shops had recently opened a branch in Bampton despite vociferous opposition. Some of the smaller cafés that had been in the town for generations predicted their own demise as they struggled to cope with the competition.

Sadler forced his attention back to the voice on the phone.

'I like the coffee there.' Palmer picked up one of the cups and took a long swig. 'I'll have yours if you don't want it.'

'Coffee is the least of our worries.' Sadler put down his phone, got up and shut the door to the office. 'That was Superintendent Llewellyn. For the third time this evening. We're getting a media strategy together before the details of the victim's identity get into the press. Because once the body that was found at Hale's End Mortuary is confirmed to be that of Andrew Fisher, we're going to be bombarded with questions. I need to go through with you what we're going to have to cover. Let's start with 2004.'

Connie opened her notebook. 'I've had a chance to glance through the old files. On the morning of the twentieth of September 2004, a Monday, Lena Fisher, now Lena Gray, awoke to find her husband, Andrew, dead in bed. She called an ambulance, which arrived at the house twenty-two minutes later. He was taken to hospital and pronounced dead on arrival.'

'That was certainly what we believed to be the initial sequence of events,' said Sadler.

Connie nodded. 'According to her later statement, following her arrest, she changed the story slightly to say that they had sex when he got into bed, and then they both went to sleep. I'm telling you this because it might be relevant to helping us identify who the man was. It was someone she was willing to admit she'd had a sexual relationship with.'

'But why did the sex come out in the later statement?' asked Palmer. 'Why didn't she tell us at first?'

Sadler picked up his coffee and frowned at the logo emblazoned on the cup. 'Because when Lena Gray was first questioned, it was as a woman whose husband had died in the night of natural causes. Whether or not they had sex the previous evening was none of our business.'

Connie was looking disapprovingly at her notes. Sadler guessed that she would have asked the question. He felt the prickle of irritation. 'In any case, the question wasn't asked.'

Connie, always quick to pick up on his mood, turned the page of her notebook. 'Given that Andrew Fisher had been positively identified by his wife and death wasn't considered to be suspicious, no further DNA proof was obtained or required. This is standard procedure in cases of natural causes.'

Sadler could feel Palmer's eyes on him.

'However, an autopsy was carried out two days later by Dr Shields – Bill – and he concluded, given a small amount of bruising around the mouth and some evidence of burst blood vessels in the ocular orbit (that's eyeballs, in layman's terms), that death was, in fact, most likely due to asphyxiation.'

'And no further checks were done on the man's identification, even though the cause of death was now considered to be suspicious?' asked Palmer.

There was silence in the room.

'That's what's going to be investigated. We would have done identity checks and I'm pretty sure these were carried out,' said Sadler. He could see them both looking doubtful. 'I have to say that I strongly suspect that the correct procedure was followed. However, I don't want you to get involved in any mistakes that might have been made over the misidentification of the body. The case has been referred, by us, to the Independent Police Complaints Commission. There'll be an investigation, and we can't let that hinder what we're having to do now.'

Palmer looked concerned. 'You'll be all right, though, won't you? You said you weren't directly involved in the case.'

Sadler made a face. 'It's a small team here. We all got involved one way or another. I may need to look at my own actions in relation to how we policed this.'

'Hold on,' Connie's face was indignant. 'First of all, as you said, you weren't the investigating officer, so I hardly think you should be doing too much mea culpa. Second, let's not forget that the body had already been positively ID'd by his wife. It's not you that the press are going to go for when they find out about this. It's her.'

Sadler looked at the two members of his team sitting across the desk and wondered, not for the first time, what he had done to deserve such loyalty. 'Which brings us on to Lena Gray. What do we know about her?'

Palmer opened his mouth to speak, but it was Connie, once again, who got in first. 'Lena and Andrew Fisher had been married for five years, no children. It was his second marriage. Lena's first. Andrew worked as a consultant for one of the big City accountancy firms. By rights, they should have been living in a house in the London commuter belt. However, Lena, by her own admission, didn't want to leave the family home, Providence Villa, where she is, in fact, still living. So she stayed in the house all week while her husband rented a flat in London, paid for by the company, and joined his wife at weekends.'

Finally, Palmer was able to interrupt. Sadler noted that he'd clearly skimmed through the file too. 'The marriage was, by all accounts, a happy one, as far as these things go. Neighbours hadn't reported any domestic disturbances, and both persons were under the police radar. However, subsequent scrutiny of Lena's medical records revealed that she had, on a number of occasions, sought medical help for stress and depression. No other information was held on her medical file so it's only guesswork as to what caused these illnesses.'

Connie turned to Palmer. 'Mental-health problems aren't simply a question of cause and effect. Lena could well have suffered from stress and depression without any direct cause.'

'Did Lena talk about any problems in her interviews?' Palmer asked.

Sadler rubbed his face. 'She didn't talk about anything, from what I can recall. When the results of Bill's autopsy came in, she was arrested on suspicion of her husband's murder. It was strange really. You're not going to be able to hide the physical evidence of asphyxiation. She was always going to be found out after the PM.'

'What was she like?' asked Connie. 'During the court hearings, I mean.'

'She was calm. I assumed it was because of the trauma but clearly we underestimated her, because all the time she was hiding a much larger truth from us all.'

'That the man in her bed, suffocated with a pillow, wasn't her husband at all. He was, in fact . . . ' Connie let the words hang in the air.

Sadler put down his pen. 'That is the first of many questions we're going to have to answer. It's been quite a day. I can safely say, without a doubt, that it's been a first for me. There's going to be a lot of fall-out tomorrow. Let's call it a night.'

7

Kat woke the following morning and listened to the rain splatter the window next to her bed. Spring hadn't decided whether it had completely arrived. They'd had a week of true warmth where she had felt the chill of winter lift from her bones. But it had been followed by a cold snap, and winter and spring were still battling it out for ascendancy in Derbyshire.

The sash window had an inch gap at the top where the wind tried to whistle through the packing tape she'd put up over the winter in anticipation of the usual cold bite. It was the problem with having a room at the top of the house. In summer she overheated in the stuffiness as not only did the window not close properly, it also failed to open to its full extent. But it was the room that Kat had slept in since she was a teenager, when she had finally been allowed to move out of sharing the large bedroom below with Lena.

At the time, Lena had been exultant at being in the bigger bedroom, hers by right because she was older by one year. Kat had preferred this room, with its faded rosebud wallpaper which would now be known as shabby chic. It was to here she had come back after Lena's arrest.

The door eased open, and Charlie marched into the room, his tail upright, a sign he was hungry. To emphasise his deprivation, he jumped on the bed and began to meow at her. Kat looked longingly at the hardback book she'd treated herself to the previous day but thought also of the warm tea that would take the chill off the bedroom. She found her slippers and padded downstairs after the swaying tail of the ecstatic cat.

In the kitchen, she tipped some dried cat food into the bowl and went to fill the kettle. It was cold, an unusual sign, as invariably Lena would be the first to wake and make a cup of tea to take back to bed. While the cat crunched in satisfaction, Kat made her way back up the stairs to her sister's room. 'Lena?'

Even before she entered, Kat could sense the emptiness behind the door. Lena's presence could always be felt, but Kat knew she would not find her in the room. The bed was made, the smoothness of the duvet suggesting that care had been taken.

She moved over to the wardrobe and opened the door. Clothes hung on neat hangers, the trousers together, next to shirts, then woollens. She looked inside the bedside table drawer. Her sister's passport, still bearing her married name, sat among the jumble of pens and hairgrips. She made her way along the landing to Lena's studio, the smell of oil paint and turpentine growing in intensity with every step. As usual, she was surprised by how much light entered the room through the windows. It was their parents' old bedroom. Lena had been adamant that this was the room she wanted for her painting. At the time, not long after their mother died, it had seemed an act of sacrilege to remove the huge marital bed and heavy oak wardrobe. They had given the furniture to a local charity as neither of them could bear to sell it.

The studio was empty. Kat ran her hands across the brushes and palette boards. It didn't look like anything had been taken, but she wouldn't have been able to swear to it. There was a half-finished painting on the easel, one of Lena's signature flower pictures. This one was of a blue iris against a black background. The flower's petals were daubed with spots of pink pollen. It was a powerful image, but also nauseating, the bright splashes reminding Kat of blood. She turned away from the picture and went back down to the kitchen to think.

8

The man known as Andrew Fisher had been cremated on the twenty-ninth of November 2004, which saved the police having to apply for an exhumation order. This, in Connie's eyes, was the first blessing of the case. Graveyards gave her the creeps at the best of times, and, deep down, she dreaded the time she would have to attend an exhumation. Once, on a training course, she had confided her fears to another of the attendees. The roaring laughter that her words had produced meant that Connie had never again spoken of her deep-seated fear of the buried dead.

Of course, Connie knew that procedurally this was, in fact, a disaster. It gave them nothing tangible to test for the victim's true identity. This meant that the only person who knew the identity of the man for sure was Lena. Which would mean more questioning.

Connie had got nowhere with Lena the previous day, so Sadler had decided to try himself. Connie would be concentrating on the investigation into the murder of the man found the day before, the man they now believed to be Andrew Fisher. There would be no more mistakes. A visual identification had been made by Sadler. Given Lena's role in the deception over the first body, she would not be called upon to make an ID. Rather belatedly, in Connie's view, Andrew's dental records had been sent to Bill Shields, along with the medical records held by Fisher's GP. It was to the pathology unit that she was headed.

Tucked away from the main hospital building, the grey plastic-cased pathology unit looked bleak and uninviting. Given that grieving relatives often had to visit the building to see loved ones, they could have made the building more presentable. Connie thought back to Hale's End morgue with its lovingly crafted stonework and wondered how the world had changed in such a short period of time.

'You coming in, or are you going to stand there gawping all day?'

Bill Shields was loitering in the entrance with what looked like a cup of tea in his hands. He was a heavily built man whose clipped accent disguised his Derbyshire roots. He and Connie had hit it off from the start. Her mother had been a pharmacist, and she had grown up amid the accoutrements of the sick.

'I was just wondering where we went wrong. You know, between Hale's End and this place.'

Bill Shields shrugged and went back inside. As she followed him, she saw Scott, his assistant, hunched over a computer screen. 'You looking at dodgy sites again, Scott?'

He didn't lift his eyes from the monitor. 'The dental records are a match. There's a slight gap between the central incisors. The measurements match an X-ray on the patient's file, as do the details of dental work. Do you want to take a look, Bill?'

Bill made a face. 'I better had, hadn't I? We don't want any more mistakes.'

'Hey! It was before my time,' said Scott.

He was smirking at Connie, and she resisted the temptation to stick her tongue out at him.

Bill sat down heavily in the chair. 'What are you here for anyway? We did the PM this morning. I was going to phone the results through to Sadler.'

She took the chair opposite him. 'He's on his way to interview Andrew Fisher's wife. He's going to take her to the station and question her under arrest once we confirm that ID. Can you give me the gist of what you've found?'

'I don't see why not.' He pulled a file towards him. 'Although I'm sure you worked out the cause of death yourself. Massive trauma to the chest cavity as the result of a gunshot wound. What was interesting, however, was that the bullet I extracted didn't come from a rifle as I expected. It's what you would assume around here. Given the hunting community.'

'Go on.'

'What was used was a pistol. I haven't seen that for a long while. Not that easy to get hold of these days. I'm surprised.' Bill's eyes flickered.

'What is it?' asked Connie.

'I'd prefer not to say. Not at the moment. I've sent the bullet off to Ballistics for more information. Let's wait for their report, shall we? There's been enough problems with this case already. You don't need me blundering along with something I'm not confident about.'

Connie decided to leave it. He clearly wasn't going to be telling her anything before the report came in. 'It's my first shooting, you know. I wonder how you'd get hold of that sort of gun around here. Anything else?'

Bill shook his head. 'He was a physically fit, large man. "Well-nourished" is perhaps the best phrase. Like me, I suppose. He had a slightly enlarged liver, probably liked a drop or two every evening but nothing that should have killed him.'

'That's it?'

'For now. I've taken blood samples to send off to the lab. They'll be about a week, unless you want me to ask them to speed it up. There didn't seem much point given the clear cause of death.' Bill shut the file and rubbed his hands on his trousers. 'Any idea how old I am?'

Connie started. 'Bill, I've never given it a thought. You're timeless, I mean . . .'

She saw him smile and look pleased. 'I'm fifty-five. I know I look older. I've got a good ten years before retirement, and, ideally, I'd like to see them out. No other hobbies to speak of, although my wife keeps nagging me to join her badminton group.' It was the first Connie had ever heard of his wife. Where was this conversation going?

He read her thoughts. 'The thing is, if we misidentified the body in 2004, and it's certainly looking that way, then it's a monumental cock-up. They could have my head on a platter.'

First Sadler and now Bill. Connie felt queasy at the thought of the men in her professional life lining up to take the blame for what appeared to be a genuine mistake in the way that bodies were identified. 'Look, if you woke up tomorrow and told me that your wife was dead in your bed, I'd take your word for it. That it was her. I mean, you're the one who would know her identity. Especially if we initially thought it was a natural death.'

The pathologist smiled. 'Don't worry, Connie. I harbour no malicious thoughts towards Jill. But you know it doesn't work like that. And Jill may well be seeing more of me around the house. We'll see. Let's hope I can ride out the storm.' He turned back to Scott, who handed him a large pink folder. Bill cast his eyes over the results. 'At least we've got the right bugger this time.'

9

Superintendent Dai Llewellyn shut the office door behind him, feeling old. The meeting had been short and to the point. Orders had been given, and he was long enough in the tooth to know when it was pointless arguing. Some things were negotiable; others weren't. The problem was that some things were forgivable and some things not, too. He had a horrible feeling that a line had been drawn and that he was on the wrong side of it.

He wanted a drink and thought briefly of the glass of Bushmills that he would have before bed. He desperately wanted to bring that drink forward but old habits are hard to break, and he had come to rely on habit. His eyes fell to the files on his desk. Now he had something else to deal with: the misidentification of a body from 2004. Another old case.

A knock, and his secretary, Margaret, put her head around the door. 'Fancy a coffee?'

He thought again of the Bushmills. 'That'd be great.'

'Are you okay?' She'd been working with him for ten years. It hadn't started off well – his inexperience in the superintendent role, her brisk efficiency, which, he later discovered, was hiding the trauma of a messy divorce – but they'd settled into a routine that suited them both. *Routine*, he thought again. *Why is it that I can draw so much comfort from it these days?*

There were limits to their relationship. He smiled up at her.

'Everything's fine.'

Her eyes dropped to the files on his desk. 'DI Sadler's called three times this morning. He wants to see you. He's gone out to reinterview Lena Gray but he'd like to see you as soon as he gets back.'

Llewellyn picked up the file and opened it. 'Right.'

The loud knock echoed around the house, waking Kat from her reverie. She looked down, aware that her frayed dressing gown had a large coffee stain down one side. She rebelted the garment to hide the spatter and walked to the front door. Behind the coloured glass she could see the shadow of a figure leaning against the stone arch. She frowned and opened the door, taking in with a glance the tall man with pale hair and blue eyes.

He showed her his warrant card. 'I'm Detective Inspector Sadler. It's Kat, isn't it? I'm not sure if you remember me from 2004. I wonder if I could have a word with your sister?'

Kat stifled the impulse to shut the door on this man. She felt shabby and dowdy and, although his eyes hadn't left her face, was sure that he had taken in the state of her undress. 'She's not here. Come in while I get changed.' She took him through to the living room and left him examining the books in the shelves covering the side wall.

Back in her bedroom, she leant against the door and closed her eyes to gather strength. She could hear nothing downstairs, but the silence felt different. A presence within the walls of this too-solid house. She opened a drawer and took out her underwear, surprised to see her hands shaking. She lifted the jeans that she had slung over a chair yesterday and then scrabbled through her wardrobe for a clean jumper. The heap of clothes in the wicker washing basket told her what she needed to do when she had got rid of the policeman.

When she got back to the sitting room, the detective had settled on the sofa. She crossed the room and sat next to him, noting his surprise. 'Sorry. Sitting opposite you would seem too much like a therapy session.'

He shifted his body towards her. 'You're still working as a counsellor then?'

'It's an ideal job, really, given everything that happened with Lena. Counselling allowed me to work to my own timetable, which gave me the chance to visit her in prison when I could.'

'You went often? To the prison, I mean.'

'Twice a month. I would have gone more but that was the allowance we were given. An hour every two weeks.'

'Did anyone else visit her? Friends, for example?'

Kat leant forward and dug around on the messy coffee table in front of her. She found a packet of cigarettes with two left inside and lit one, offering the other to Sadler. He made a face and shook his head. 'Don't approve of smoking.'

She smiled. 'Don't worry, neither do I. The problem is that once I stop, something happens to make me start again. I'd made six months until today.'

'The cigarettes—?'

'Lena's. She started inside. I don't think there was much to do. Except read and smoke.'

'And you say she's not here.'

Kat turned her face away and blew out a stream of smoke, resisting the impulse to cough. Her lungs, unused to the tobacco, were aching in protest. 'I woke up this morning, and she'd gone. I wake up quite early anyway. It was about half six. She left before then.'

'What time did you go to bed?'

'Lena went first – about eleven, I think. I was around midnight.'

'You still woke up at half six? That's not much sleep.'

'You don't know the half of it. I was awake at quarter past two, then three and again at twenty past four.' She stole a glance at him.

'Insomnia?' Something flickered in his eyes. 'You have my sympathy.'

Kat stubbed out her cigarette. 'You too?'

He didn't answer her. 'Do you think Lena could have left after you'd gone to bed? Or do you think she left early this morning? If she knows you suffer from insomnia, when are you most likely to be sleeping?'

Kat was impressed. It was a good question. 'I never have any trouble getting to sleep. I'm usually dog-tired when I go to bed. It's just that it doesn't last. I'm awake after a couple of hours.'

'So if Lena wanted to leave the house without you knowing, the best time would be between, say, twelve and two a.m.?'

Kat felt a spurt of anger. 'Yes.'

The exchange seemed to have unsettled Sadler also. He stood up and went over to the far window that looked out onto the lawn. Kat was glad that she had heaved the old mower around for the first cut of the year.

'I'm not surprised you're having trouble sleeping. My colleague, DC Childs, tells me you looked shocked when we told your sister that we found the body of her husband yesterday.' He turned around to face her. 'It was a surprise, wasn't it?'

Kat, shockingly, felt like crying. 'A complete surprise. I just couldn't believe it.'

'But you think she did lie? About the man we found dead? You haven't asked how sure we are that the body we found yesterday is that of Andrew Fisher.'

Kat shrugged and reached for the remaining cigarette. 'I'm a therapist, and she's my sister. I'm not bad at reading people. When you came to the house yesterday, whatever Lena may have been feeling, it wasn't surprise. She knew what your colleague was saying was possible.'

'Was she unsurprised that we know that the man found dead in her bed in 2004 wasn't in fact Andrew? Or was she unsurprised that Andrew had now been found dead? Which of these, in your opinion, was she already aware of?' Again, he knew which questions to ask, and, once more, she was impressed.

He was looking at her with his pale-blue eyes, and Kat found it difficult to meet his gaze. She lit her cigarette, giving herself time to think of a reply.

He looked impatient. 'Kat. I know this is your sister we're talking about. Whatever happened in 2004, it's going to be horrendously complicated to untangle, especially now your sister seems to have gone missing. So I need to ask you. Of course she would have been aware that the man in her bed wasn't her husband. So I need you to tell me: was she surprised that he had now been found dead?'

Kat's eyes locked with Sadler's once more. 'I'm sorry. With Lena you never can tell.'

11

Connie left Bill staring at his tea and contemplating the future. As she was leaving the prefabricated building, she heard running footsteps behind her. She turned to see Scott panting towards her.

'You need to get more exercise.' She took in his face, decorated with a myriad of silver piercings, and his long blond hair tied back in a ponytail. 'Do you actually do any?'

'What's exercise?' He grinned at her and then looked down at himself. 'What do you think?'

'Did you want something?'

'It's hit him harder than you realise, you know. What's happened.'

Connie quelled the irritation rising in her. 'I *am* aware of that. I'm not a complete dimwit.'

'Isn't there anything you can do?'

She saw his miserable expression and took pity on him. 'Look. There's been a huge error made. A body's been misidentified.'

'But you said in there, to Bill I mean, that if someone identifies a person in their bed as their spouse, then we take their word for it.'

'In case of natural causes, yes. Because the next of kin has identified the person, we just do a double-check through birth certificates, NHS numbers and so on. It's not usually a problem.'

'So—'

'Well, that was okay for the first two days, until the post mortem was completed. The problem is that once it was discovered that a crime had been committed, then checks should have been made to confirm the identity of the victim.'

'Should Bill have done that?'

'I don't know.'

'But—'

She put up her hand. 'Look. I can't tell you any more. I wasn't doing this job in 2004, and I don't know what the procedure was.'

'But you told him in there that it wasn't his fault.'

Connie rubbed a hand across her eyes. 'I don't think it's his fault initially but something's gone wrong, and I don't know what. I was giving what reassurance I could. We've been warned by Sadler not to take any notice of the inquiry into how a misidentification was made.'

'You don't think it's relevant to now?'

'It might be, but that's what we've been told. Bill needs to stop worrying. I suspect there are going to be more culpable people than him. What about Lena Gray's lawyer, for example? He or she didn't do their job in relation to identity checks. Can you see? It's not just about Bill.'

Scott looked unhappy. 'I've worked with him for five years. Ever since I left school. I came here for a lark, to be honest. Someone mentioned there was a job going in the pathology department at the local hospital. It appealed to my goth instincts.' He caught Connie's expression. 'I don't mean anything weird to do with the dead bodies. I was brought up a Catholic. I've got a lot of respect for the dead. I just thought it'd be an interesting place to work.'

'And is it?' She wouldn't fancy it. Connie didn't like the dead at all. The smell and the waxen bodies repulsed her.

'I suppose. There's a lot of admin, to be honest, and also, although Bill would never admit it, a lot of down time. That's how I've got to know him. In the quiet periods between the autopsies we chat and drink a lot of tea.'

'About what?' Connie was genuinely curious. She'd been privy to the tea and conversation too. But, now she thought of it, the chat had been desultory, and she doubted if she could remember a single topic that they had discussed in any depth.

Scott looked downcast. 'We talk about life. And the past. What it was like in the old days when forensics were in the early stages. He was, I mean is, interesting. He loves his job. Cares about the process and the way things are done. Which is why he's so gutted that he got things wrong.'

Connie flopped down on the wall next to Scott and fumbled in her bag. She screwed the lid onto the base of her electronic cigarette and gave a deep puff. Scott looked at her with amusement. 'It's hardly Lauren Bacall in *The Big Sleep*.'

Connie snorted. 'This is hardly LA. Look, Bill's one of the good guys. He needs to ride this one out. I'm going to give you the benefit of something I've learnt since I became a copper. Don't look at me like that. I've developed this theory. I've tested it in other cases, and I think it's going to hold up in this one too.' She looked at him and was surprised to see he was eager to hear what she was going to say next. She took a deep breath. 'When someone, like Lena, wants to deceive you – I mean, really deceive you – there's absolutely nothing you can do. It takes a fluke or complete luck to catch them out. I've seen it time and time again, and the simple fact is, Lena Gray wanted us to think that the man she found dead in her bed was her husband, and it would have taken a mind-reader to have worked out what she was up to.'

She saw that Scott was looking relieved. He should be. Because she was damned if she was going to stand by while Sadler and Bill took the blame for the deceit being pulled by Lena Gray. 'Look, let me give you my mobile. What's your number?'

He rattled it off, and she typed it into her phone. 'This is mine. Call me if you think Bill is getting seriously stressed about this case. He needs to know we're with him on this.'

'Will do.' Scott was looking at her in amusement and, unless she was mistaken, with a familiar glint in his eye.

She decide to ignore the expression. 'Can you give me directions for the quickest way back to Hale's End Mortuary? I only just managed to find it yesterday. I want to take another look at the place where the real Andrew Fisher's body was found.'

*

Even with the dead man's body gone, Hale's End was a grim place. Connie could smell rotting foliage that was out of place in the spring sharpness. Five crime-scene investigators were still combing the area for clues, and, as she ducked under the tape, she shouted at one of them: 'Anything interesting?'

He shook his head but walked over to her. 'There are footprints everywhere. Considering how bloody difficult this place is to find, it seems half of Bampton has walked down here at some point. Well, maybe not half, but I've counted at least twenty different feet at the front of the building. I'm about to go around the back now.'

Connie could feel her phone vibrating in her bag. By the time she retrieved it, it had clicked off. She looked at the ID. Sadler. When she tried to call him back, he was engaged. Damn, he was probably calling Palmer. Her competitive instincts kicked in, and she dialled Palmer's mobile. He was engaged too. Subduing the urge to get back in her car and drive down to the station to see what Sadler wanted, she walked up to the stone building and peeped inside.

The crime-scene investigators had finished with the interior. Stepping into the space, Connie was assailed with a pressure in her ears. She walked over to the stone slab where Andrew Fisher had been found. Why murder him here? Was Hale's End just a place to lure the victim to his death, or was there a more deep-seated reason for killing a man considered by everyone to be dead in a place for the deceased?

Her mobile vibrated again.

'It's Palmer. Where are you? Sadler's been trying to get hold of you.'

Connie dropped her bag in irritation, which made her jump. She grabbed it and walked out of the mortuary. 'Well, he clearly found *you*. What's the problem?'

'Lena Gray's gone missing. Sadler's just been around to the house to interview her. The only person there is her sister Kat, who claims that Lena must have left in the middle of the night. Sadler says her story rings true.'

'Does she have any idea where she might have gone?'

'Apparently not. Sadler wants us back at the station pronto. This case is becoming a can of worms. First he has to see Llewellyn. Let's hope by the time we get back it's still Sadler we're reporting to.'

43

12

Kat's professionalism was being stretched to the limit. She couldn't afford to cancel on any clients, but, at the same time, she needed to ensure she didn't lose any through inattentiveness or being generally useless as a therapist.

It was Theresa's first time with her, but, as she had assured Kat at the beginning of the session, she'd seen therapists before. For Kat, this always brought out mixed feelings. People tended to stick with their therapists if they were any good, and Theresa's ready admission that she had been through a few suggested either she'd been unlucky with her previous counsellors or she had unrealistic expectations as to what she would get out of the sessions.

Sweeping her eyes over the information sheet that her new client had filled out, Kat could see that she would be fifty next month. Her marital status was down as divorced, and she wanted help with 'anxiety'. Bare bones of information, and yet you could develop a set of assumptions on such meagre pickings. Kat noticed the unease as soon as Theresa showed up at the door. Small lines radiated from her eyes, although Kat could also detect a hint of wry amusement when she introduced herself.

She suspected that Theresa might well be a more complex client than the bald tag of 'anxiety' could cover. But, again, speculation. *Stop it*, she thought. Her training kicked in, and she smiled. 'What brought you here today?'

At the end of the session, Kat rose from her chair and showed Theresa out. So her assumptions had been wrong. *Idiot*. She should have known better. In fact, she did know better. Behind the calm façade and anxious eyes had been a story. Not merely sad or depressing, like some clients' tales. No, a traumatic event that had given Theresa a very real reason to fear the world. Nor was it commonplace. Surely the story wasn't commonplace? Kat searched her tired brain. She had never heard anything similar in her years of practice. No, not a run-of-the-mill story.

She thought about Lena. Kat had suggested counselling when she'd come out of prison but her sister had given her a closed look, and the matter had never been referred to again. The events yesterday had shattered that façade. Behind it all was a secret so monstrous that her sister had absented herself from the house.

Well, she'd got through the morning. First, the meeting with the policeman and then a new client. She frowned again at the thought of Theresa's story.

Theresa had assured her she would come back next week. Kat thought the likelihood was that she would, but she wasn't one hundred per cent sure. She wouldn't have bet her life on it, but, chances were she'd be seeing Theresa again.

13

Sadler sat in front of Llewellyn, curiously moved. He'd gone into his office expecting a tantrum, warnings of dire things to come but, as he reminded himself, he always underestimated his boss. Underneath the bluff insensitivity of his public profile was a decent person and an experienced policeman. It wasn't the first mistake that he'd seen. What made the difference was how you managed it.

Blame. Something goes wrong, and the first thing you do is look around for someone to hold to account. He'd forgotten that Llewellyn shared his dislike of this reaction. Llewellyn would want to sort it out first. Holding someone to account would come later, if necessary.

'So,' Llewellyn said, looking at Sadler over the top of his glasses. 'An almighty cock-up is what we've got here. In fact,' he smoothed a hand across his desk, 'what we've got is cock-up on top of cock-up. First, the misidentification of a body we thought was Andrew Fisher, then the murder of the real Andrew. And now you tell me that Lena has disappeared. Which makes it cock-up number three.'

'You think we should have arrested her when we went to question her about the body in Hale's End? We were, at that time, relying on a visual identification of the dead man. *My* identification. It was hardly grounds for arrest. Especially as she had already served a ten-and-a-half-year sentence for his murder.'

Llewellyn sighed. 'It's damn lucky you weren't the investigating officer in 2004. In fact, I've gone back through the files. Your input was fairly light. A mere DC. You've not done too bad in the intervening time.'

'It's been nearly twelve years. I wouldn't be much good if I hadn't.'

Llewellyn grunted. 'The main thing is that you're okay to head up this case. I've had to approve it with the Chief Constable, though. Second time I've spoken to him today.'

A note in his voice made Sadler look up but Llewellyn didn't elaborate.

'Everything we do from now on is going to come under scrutiny. All of us. In fact, only those who weren't around in 2004 are likely to escape attention. You need to make good use of Palmer and Connie. Their inexperience is going to be an asset here.'

'Will I need to get involved in the review into what happened?'

Llewellyn sighed. 'I want you to keep out of that, Sadler. Of course, you'll be interviewed. It's going to be painful for us all. I intend to take full responsibility for this. I'm going to see Andrew Fisher's mother myself after this meeting.'

'You're not going to break the news to her yourself?'

'Of course not. She's already been informed of the discovery. We did it as soon as we had official ID but I need to see her myself. Explain what we're going to do. As I said, Sadler, I'm taking responsibility for this one. I'll let you know what she tells me.'

'Do you want to take someone with you? Connie, perhaps?'

Llewellyn shook his head. 'The family-liaison officer will be

there. You'll be following it up with an interview, of course.'
Sadler's face reddened. 'Don't look at me like that. I know she
might be involved in this. Where the hell has Andrew Fisher
been for the past twelve years? But that's not our only worry.
You know what you need to do, don't you?' Llewellyn counted
the list off the fingers on his left hand. 'First, find out the identity of the man found in Lena Gray's bed in 2004. If she was
having an affair, which it certainly looks like, then someone
must have known about it. A friend possibly. Second, we need
to open an investigation into the killing of the real Andrew
Fisher. Not least, why he was killed at Hale's End. I'd forgotten
all about that place. Why murder him there?'

'And third, you want me to find Lena Gray.'

Llewellyn left his hand up in the air. 'Well, she does appear
to be the one with all the answers, doesn't she?'

14

Kat stood outside Providence Villa and looked up at its bleak façade. They were mad trying to hold onto the place. It was crumbling around their ears. A cavernous void that consumed whatever money she and Lena managed to scrabble together – Lena from her paintings and she from her clients. She tried to view the place with an outsider's eye, but it was impossible. Too much of her childhood and teenage years were bound up in the house, and she could only see the vestiges of the family home it had once been. It hadn't always been so drab. Only in the past ten years or so. Since Lena went to prison, certainly.

Walking into the house, she could sense it was still empty of Lena's presence. She called out to make sure, but her voice just bounced off the walls. She knew she should cook herself something to eat, but the knot in her stomach filled the gap where food was needed. She ignored the kitchen and climbed the wide stairs, past Lena's room and up into her attic bedroom. She sat on the high bed and wondered if this was all that life had to offer her: shelter in the bedroom of her teenage years, a non-existent love life and a career that continually threatened to collapse through the sheer difficulty of scratching a living.

Something thumped against her window, and she crossed over to it, peering into the gloom. She was too high up to be scared of an intruder. It was probably a bird or, possibly, a bat. A bat, a creature of the supernatural. Kat frowned. The town that was most associated with the Gothic in England was Whitby, a favourite place of Lena's. During the dark days of her late teens, times she would refer to as being chased by the black dog, Lena would often take herself out of Bampton and drive east until she reached the coast. Derbyshire, for all its wild and untamed beauty, lacked the ingredient that could calm Lena's perturbation. The sea.

Lena and Kat, growing up in the limestone dourness of their Victorian villa had, perhaps inevitably, been fascinated by all things dark. In Kat, this had manifested itself in a love of horror films, especially those produced by Hammer in the sixties and seventies. Lena had initially embraced the Gothic seventies kitsch with gusto but had suddenly declared them too childish. And that had been that. But she hadn't forsaken the Gothic completely. A trip to Whitby when she was in the sixth form had led to a lifelong attraction to the place.

Another thump. This time outside her door – and a sound that Kat recognised. She got off the bed and opened it. Charlie strolled in and jumped up onto the bed before curling up into a circle, his tail wrapped around his head. Kat reached out to stroke him, and he purred obligingly.

Whitby. Could Lena have gone there? The problem was that she'd left the house in the middle of the night, possibly just after midnight according to DI Sadler. She wouldn't have been able to go far on foot at that time. They shared a car between them, and it was still parked in front of the house. It was the first thing that Kat had checked when she discovered Lena missing. The police would presumably be checking the local taxi firms. Would she have gone all the way to Whitby by cab?

Lena had always been protective when it came to her privacy. Kat had never accompanied her to Whitby and had little idea where her sister stayed during her visits. In a hotel, perhaps. Only once, when their mother was sick, dying in fact, had Kat shouted at her sister over her secrecy. 'It's all very well you needing your space but what about me? How am I going to contact you if you never answer your mobile phone?' Lena would talk to you only when she wanted and not before. Calls constantly went unanswered.

Kat frowned, trying to recall a fragment of memory. Lena had, after the argument, given her something. She could recall a piece of paper. An address hastily scribbled down. Where would she have put it? In the drawer of the hall table was the family's address book. It had been used by their parents since sometime in the early seventies. Long-dead relatives vied for space among half-remembered acquaintances.

Kat went downstairs to the book and tipped it upside down. A confetti of notes, letters and cards dropped onto the dark wood. She rifled through the detritus, trying to find something that resembled what she remembered. Eventually she opened out a lined scrap, torn from a notebook. There it was, written in Lena's impatient swirls: 43 Crowther Terrace, Whitby. No postcode. No directions. But an address.

Kat picked up the car keys and weighed them in her hand. Lena, having run away at the news of her husband's death, would surely be prime suspect for his murder. Despite the fact that Lena had already gone to prison for his killing. Kat's head ached with the sheer impossibility of it.

She pulled back the curtain of the hall window. Rain was lashing against it, and the sashes strained against the wind blowing at the window pane. It was a wild night; winter hadn't yet finished with Derbyshire. From behind her she heard Charlie come clattering downstairs as if to remind her of his presence. Taking a packet of cat biscuits from the shelf, she shook out his daily allowance. She also changed his water and went upstairs to take a bath before having an early night. The weather was too malevolent to be going anywhere this evening. She would make a start first thing. She needed to find Lena before the police did.

15

Saturday, 14 December 1985

Kat leant forward to push the video into the player. She could hear Lena munching on a packet of crisps behind her. The sounds of a hand being delved into the packet and shovelled straight into Lena's mouth. She didn't need to turn around to know that they would be nearly finished. 'Your breath will stink.'

'I'm not planning on kissing anyone, so it doesn't matter.'

She heard Lena twist the packet into a tight ball and saw it, out of the side of her eye, hurtling towards the corner of the room. It made a popping sound as it bounced off the wall before landing in the wicker bin. 'The whole point of film snacks is that you eat them during the movie. Not scoff the lot beforehand.'

Lena shuffled off the sofa and, with a blanket over her shoulders, sat cross-legged on the floor next to Kat. 'Which one are you putting on?'

She showed her the thin white strip on the cassette. *The Kiss of the Vampire* was written in Lena's impenetrable loops.

'Ooh, one of the good ones.'

Kat felt Lena snuggle into her. 'I bet Jennifer Daniel's breath doesn't smell of barbecue crisps.'

'Don't be cross, Kat. There's more in the bag. Cheese and

onion. Your breath can smell as bad too.'

Despite herself, Kat sniggered. She pushed the cassette into the player and leant back against the sofa, feeling her sister's arms around her as she reached for the crisps. 'It's a good one this. Really scary.'

16

Connie had grown up ten miles, as the crow flies, from Bampton. In many respects, she and the Gray sisters had a lot in common. Connie's mother had been a pharmacist, a good one, and the family were well known in Matlock. Lena and Kat Gray were the children of GPs, who, according to interviews given to the police at the time of Lena's arrest, had been well respected in the community.

Connie's upbringing had been solidly working-class. Tea at half five as soon as her mum came back from the pharmacy. The house spick and span, no books but the TV constantly on. They'd never have been able to afford a house like Providence Villa and no way would her mother have wanted the creaking old building.

Connie quickly read through the file, looking for any inconsistencies. She could find none, but there could easily be something there. She was an expert in family secrets, because her mother, despite the respect given her by the community, had hidden a dark secret. When the pharmacy shut at 5 p.m. every evening, her mother would come home and start drinking, often late into the evening. Everyone had turned a blind eye. No reason was offered when she would walk rather than drive to the pharmacy in the mornings. Nor were her mysterious ailments, which culminated in an early death from a heart attack, ever alluded to.

Whatever secrets the family might be hiding, Connie wouldn't find them in the files. The information there seemed innocuous enough, although there were plenty of questions to be answered. The social status of the parents' job would explain the large house but not why Lena had chosen to stay there after her wedding. Both parents were deceased by the time Andrew Fisher and she had married. The house, surely, should have been sold and the proceeds divided between Kat and Lena.

As Sadler had said, Andrew Fisher was from Bampton too, but with ideas beyond the constraints of the Derbyshire town. After university in Leeds, he'd married a local girl, but it hadn't lasted. Following his divorce, he'd transferred from the consultancy firm he worked for in Leeds to their London head office and had stayed there. He had a flat in the City and returned home, or rather to Lena's home, at the weekends.

Connie inwardly groaned. She really did hope that she wouldn't have to take a trip to the capital. She didn't like London. She mistrusted its busyness and was wary of the conspicuous wealth it shrouded itself in. She hoped Palmer would be assigned the task if they were forced to follow that line of enquiry. It wasn't her decision to make, of course, but surely Palmer would relish a trip to London.

Of Andrew Fisher's next of kin, there was just his mother, Pamela, still living in Bampton. He had an elder sister living in Australia. Another one keen to spread her wings, by the look of it.

Connie frowned and looked around the room. Damian Palmer was leaning over his desk, flicking rapidly through a report and frowning. She shouted over to him. 'Do you know who told Andrew Fisher's mother about the discovery of her son's body? The recent discovery I mean. There's no note on the file yet. I want to read her reaction to the news.'

Palmer lifted his head and took his time to focus on her. He looked like he was in another world. 'Sorry, mind else-where. She was told by a family-liaison officer but Llewellyn's also been to see her. Damage limitation and all that.'

'Oh.'

Palmer looked across at her. 'He's just come back and is in a foul mood according to his secretary. I wouldn't go chasing him for a report if I were you.'

'As if I would. Interesting, though. I wonder what her reac-tion was.' She walked across to him. 'What are you so engrossed in anyway?'

He sat down, as if staking claim to his chair. 'I've been going through the post-mortem file of the man we thought was Andrew Fisher in 2004. We need to give him a name, and I've thought of one. How about Joe Tagg?'

'Joe Tagg?' said Connie. 'What's wrong with John Smith? It's what we usually use.'

Palmer looked defensive. 'Joanne and I went to a folk night in a pub a few days ago. The band played some local tunes, and one of them stuck with me. It was about a Derbyshire man named Joe Tagg.'

Connie stared at him. 'Are you taking the piss? We're not a bunch of yokels around here to be laughed at.'

Palmer was smirking at her. 'Don't be so touchy. It was only a suggestion. John Smith gives us no idea about his personality. I think my choice is better. Gives us something to help con-struct a real person.'

'And you think Joe Tagg sounds better? Suit yourself. I'm

not sure Sadler will go for it though. Anyway, what did you discover from the PM?'

'Well, Joe Tagg's physical description is very similar to that of the real Andrew Fisher. Listen.' He picked up the report and started to read. 'Muscular build, height five foot ten, weight 201 pounds, and so on. Virtually identical to Andrew Fisher, in fact.'

'You think it was deliberate? An intention to deceive by killing a physically similar man?'

Palmer was peering at the report again. 'Well, maybe. But listen to this. On the deceased's right arm is a scar indicative of excision.' He lifted his head. 'That's surgical removal at some point in the past.'

Connie rolled her eyes. 'I know what excision means, thanks, Palmer. Do you think I've never read an autopsy report before?' She snatched the file out of his hand. 'You think it's important? The fact that at some point he had something removed? A tattoo maybe? It could have been a suspicious mole or something.'

Palmer calmly took the report back from her. 'I don't know. It's the only thing I can find that might help with identification. I'm going to run with this for the moment. Try to find an ID. Can you give me a hand? You know, with the database?'

Connie pulled a face and looked at the clock. Time to go home. She thought of her empty flat. 'Of course.'

17

Kat set the alarm for 6.30 a.m. and reached for the phone after stumbling out of bed. Her eyes were gritty from the lack of sleep, and there was a heavy pressure behind them. It was a bad sign. If she started the day with a headache it was unlikely to clear until the next morning. She looked to see if there were any messages on her phone from Lena. Nothing. Charlie was curled up in the middle of the landing, and she stepped over him to check Lena's room one final time. The space was devoid of her presence, and there was an unfriendly chill to the air.

Bampton that morning was covered in a shroud of mist waiting for the pale spring sun to rise. The first part of the drive was slow. She could see nothing further than a few feet in front of her, and, although she knew the roads well, the speed of other drivers hurtling towards her made her fearful. As she left Derbyshire behind, the promise of sunshine proved to be false. The day opened out into a bleak morning, clouds gathering and darkening in the grey sky.

She switched on the radio and let music soothe her frayed nerves. By the time she had reached North Yorkshire, the rain was pelting fat blobs onto the windscreen.

The sky reflected the black hues of the moor in the final miles to Whitby. As she drove down the narrow streets, she was suddenly aware of the futility of what she was trying to do. She knew that Lena came regularly to the town, but the only clue was an address she knew her sister had stayed at years ago.

Parking was clearly an issue in Whitby. When she finally found a space and hunted around for enough change to pay for a few hours, she retrieved the piece of paper she had from her pocket. The ink had faded only slightly, and Lena's swirls were still legible on the yellowing paper. Crowther Terrace. Kat took out her phone and found the street on the map. She had parked on the wrong side of the river. She not only had to go down the steep incline, her ankles groaning in protest at the unfamiliar pull, but then puff up the hill on the other side. When she got to the street, she quickly found number 43. One look at the house, and she sighed. It was a holiday cottage now. Or perhaps it had been all those years ago. A card in the window was advertising Whitby Holiday Homes with a mobile number underneath.

Her call was answered by someone with a husky male voice, his Yorkshire accent immediately apparent. Kat plunged in. 'I'm standing outside 43 Crowther Terrace, which I'm thinking of renting at some point in the future. I just want to know, has it been on your books for long? I'm looking for something with an up-to-date interior.'

There was a short silence. Then a cough. 'Hold on. I can check.' Silence, and then he came back on. 'It's been with us since 1995. Not that recent, I suppose. I've just called up the property on the computer. The rooms are traditionally furnished with—'

'Fine, fine.' Kat was making some mental calculations. Lena must have rented the house off this company when she stayed here. 'Do you have a list of people who have used the cottage over the years?'

It was a long shot, and too much for the man at the other end of the phone. 'Hang on, who are you?'

Kat cut the connection and stepped into the road to take a good look at the house. It was a traditional fisherman's cottage, built in the days when houses and shops were jumbled together on the same street. Next door was its mirror image, the brick whitewashed less recently, though.

Kat went to the house and rang the bell. The door opened immediately. 'I thought you were a potential burglar staring at my house like that.' He was a tall man with a black beard, roughly trimmed. A thick-ribbed green jumper was half-tucked into his jeans and his feet were bare.

'I wondered if you could tell me something about the cottage next door? My sister stayed there, I think. A few years ago.'

'You're Lena's sister? It gave me a shock when I saw you outside. I thought you were her for a moment. You look like her, you know.'

Kat sighed. 'I do know. I'm Kat Gray and I'm trying to find Lena. Have you seen her? This week, I mean?'

'Lena?' The man stared at her. 'I haven't seen her for years. That's why I was surprised to see you standing there. It would've been nice if it *was* her. I miss her. You okay?'

Kat suddenly felt exhausted. The three-hour drive, conducted in nervous tension, had drained her of all energy. She wondered if he would invite her in, but he made no move to open the door any further. 'Can you remember when you last saw her?'

'Lena? Like I said, years ago. She used to come here all the time.'

'Can you remember what years?'

The man looked at her in amusement. 'You're kidding, right? Of course I don't know what years. She was always by herself. She used to come a lot. It's how I got to know her.'

'You were friendly?' She wondered if he'd tell her his name, but, standing over the threshold of his home, he was revealing nothing about himself.

'Fairly. It's not a huge amount of fun living next to a holiday cottage. Some people can be noisy and, of course, people rarely come more than once. But Lena was different. She came back again and again. Until—'

'Until?'

The man shrugged. 'I don't know. She just stopped coming. A long time ago. It was a shame, us not getting to say goodbye.' He looked at her in consternation. 'She's all right, isn't she?'

Was Lena all right? wondered Kat. It was difficult to say for sure. Her abrupt disappearance from Whitby must have been a result of her arrest and imprisonment. 'I haven't seen her for a while, that's all. You know how it is with families sometimes, don't you?'

The man looked like he did. 'Sorry I can't be any more help, Kat. When you track her down, tell her from me that it'd be nice to see her.' And without saying goodbye to her, he shut the door gently.

18

Andrew Fisher had either hidden himself away since 2004 or had been hidden. This was the only indisputable fact that Sadler's tired head was able to crystallise. He'd slept badly, waking at approximate half-hourly intervals and checking, pointlessly, his alarm clock. He'd never overslept in his life and yet the fear was always there – the possibility that one day he would miss the shriek of his bedside alarm.

And yet what if he did? As a detective inspector he had some flexibility with his hours. It wouldn't be a complete disaster if he turned up late once in his professional career. The thought made his head ache even further.

The thing giving him the biggest headache was where Andrew Fisher could have been since 2004. Twelve years was a long time to hide yourself these days. Even overseas there were ways of tracing you. Although, Sadler suspected, if you weren't being looked for, why would anyone find you? But until the identity of the dead man had been uncovered, and Lena Gray found, Andrew's whereabouts would be an area of focus.

Connie walked through the door with her usual bustle of energy, remembering to knock only as she was three-quarters into the room. 'There's something I want to run past you, if that's okay?'

Sadler gestured to the chair in front of his desk.

She flopped down and sat with one foot over her knee.

'Palmer's concentrating on the identity of our original dead man. There's a distinguishing feature in the PM report that he wants to investigate. A possible surgical procedure on his arm. He's looking at an ID that way and I've been giving him a hand by researching persons reported missing around the same time. But something else came up while I was going through the database.'

'Go on.' Sadler reached into his drawer and took two tablets from a blister pack, swallowing them with the remains of his cold coffee.

'Well. In 2012, a report was made by a member of the public who claimed to have seen Andrew Fisher while she was on holiday in Whitby. She's from Bampton and was visiting Whitby as part of a coach tour.'

'A coach tour? How old was the witness?'

'The report doesn't say but I would guess over retirement age. Doesn't mean she's not reliable though, does it?' Connie held out the report to him. 'Would you like to see it?'

It was a few lines. A Jane Reynolds, resident of Curlew Road in Bampton, had called the station in the summer of 2012 to say that she had seen Andrew Fisher alive in Whitby while she was there on a weekend trip to the area. The officer, PC James Walker, had recorded the action but had done nothing to follow up the report.

Connie saw him looking at the name. 'I rang him. Before coming to you. He remembers the call but only in vague terms. He thinks the woman began by being positive that it was Andrew Fisher she had spotted but by the end of the call had talked herself into believing it was a case of mistaken identity. So he made a note of the call and filed it away. I'm sure I'd have done exactly the same.'

Sadler smiled. 'Me too.' He handed her back the report. 'Whitby? Interesting mix of Dracula, chip shops and early Christian religion. Don't we have enough on our plate?'

'It seems not. She'll need checking out. Jane Reynolds lives on the other side of Bampton. It's not far.'

'Go and see her and get a proper statement from her. Then let me know how you get on. Whitby? What the hell would Andrew Fisher be doing in Whitby?'

Connie left the room, and, in the silence, Sadler thought back to his teenage years. He had shared many classes with Andrew Fisher while at Bampton High. They had been in the top set for most of the subjects and had progressed through school in the classrooms, thrown together by a shared capacity for doing well in exams. But they'd never been friends. Sadler had liked reading and cricket, and that was about it until he was fifteen. Then he had discovered music, and he and a group of friends would travel to Sheffield to see the latest bands.

Andrew Fisher had been sporty but was a rugby-playing drinker, even as a teenager. He would come into class hungover, smelling of stale beer and teenage sweat. Then they had gone their respective ways to university, and Sadler had seen him only very occasionally.

As Sadler had climbed the ranks of the police, the casual acquaintances of his childhood could basically be divided into two reactions. Those who were impressed by the status that the job of a police inspector afforded, and those who gave him a wide berth. Sadler had long learnt not to make any assumptions about the latter group, which had included Andrew. People steered clear of the police for a variety of reasons, not all of them criminal. Not all. But some.

Another knock on the door. This time it came in advance of the person entering. It was Llewellyn. Sadler stood up, but his boss waved him back to his seat. 'Needed to stretch my legs. Get out of the office. You know how it is.'

'I do. I'm about to go out myself. How did the visit to Mrs Fisher go?'

Llewellyn sat down in the chair opposite and clasped his large hands together behind his head. 'She'd already had the news broken to her, of course. The family-liaison officer was still with her. She seemed to be taking it okay, though.'

'She was surprised? His mother, I mean. About her son being alive all these years?'

'I'd say she'd had the surprise of her life. I think she was still in shock when I left her. I mean, let's face it, it's a lot to digest, isn't it? Your son's alive, then he's killed, then he's alive because it was someone else who was killed, but actually you can't see him because he's now dead.'

It was almost comical, thought Sadler, and it was unsurprising that Llewellyn could see the humour in the situation. 'So we can rule her out as an accomplice? That's interesting in itself. Whatever made Andrew Fisher disappear, it was enough to make him determined not to speak to his mother.'

'We're missing something, Francis. I don't want us pissing about just looking for Lena Gray, wherever she may have got to. Don't look at me like that. Of course I want you to *look* for her. What I mean is there's something gone on, that's still continuing. We need to find out what it is.'

Sadler exhaled a deep breath. 'You think this is part of something bigger? Connie's investigating a possible sighting,

66

and Palmer's looking at the identity of the original victim. Do you have anything in mind?'

Llewellyn stood up to leave. 'Take my advice. Start with the affair. That man was found in Lena Gray's bed. What do you think he was doing there? Having a kip? This case revolves around sex. That's where you need to start.'

19

The pale sunshine lifted Kat's spirits as she drove to the small studio she rented for her therapy sessions. She opened the door and went to put some flowers in a glass vase in an attempt to brighten the place. When she'd first qualified, Lena had suggested Kat use one of the downstairs rooms of their house for her practice. Kat had swallowed the retort that had come to her lips and merely said that she wanted to split her professional and home life. Which, in a sense, was true. But the idea of meeting clients in one of the rooms with peeling wallpaper and shabby furniture was laughable. Anyway, it was Lena who had always identified with the house. At some point Kat would need to make her escape. Perhaps sooner rather than later. When she found Lena, she would have it out with her. It was nonsense holding on to the place.

Kat's first client of the day was Miriam, who was invariably late. Kat kept rigidly to her slots. Miriam's appointment was at 9.30. If she turned up at 9.40, the session would still finish at 10.30. In this regard, Miriam had run the gamut of emotions, from outrage at paying for a shortened session to pleading for a bit of tolerance. Now she faced the routine with a calm acceptance. At no point had she considered changing her behaviour.

Kat glanced at the clock. Ten past. She had at least twenty minutes to wait, almost certainly longer. She pulled out her iPad and looked at some of the online sites. News of a body at

Hale's End was being reported, but that was it. The coverage was sober and, to her mind, uninterested. Even the location of the body was failing to spark much interest from journalists looking for an angle for sensationalism. A middle-aged man wasn't providing that for them. For the moment. She wondered how things would change when news of his identity was revealed.

She shut down the news page and opened up her diary. There was little point. She knew she would be seeing only three clients today. She could have recited the appointment times in her sleep. It was another reason for her childhood room in Providence Villa. She was barely keeping her head afloat. She had known counselling wasn't lucrative from the first time around but she'd anticipated more clients than she had been able to muster.

The last person she would be seeing today was Mark. When she had written up her notes from the previous session, she had emphasised the unexpected email he had received from his mother. She had made no mention of his subsequent text.

She heard a rattle on the door and looked up in surprise. The clock said twenty past. Surely Miriam wasn't early? Kat got up and opened the front door. Standing in front of her was a boy wearing a grey sweatshirt and jeans. His white Converse trainers were grubby. The hood of his top was pulled up and underneath Kat could only see the pair of brown eyes and pale skin. He looked young – mid-teens, she guessed.

'You Kat?' He was softly spoken, his voice barely above a whisper. He was holding out something in his hand. A small package wrapped in newspaper. She looked behind him at the cobbled courtyard. It was empty, although she could see one of the shops to the left had its lights on. It comforted her that there was help nearby. She took the parcel from him, and he turned and walked off. Not fast.

'Hold on!' She ran after him. 'What's this?' She held out the package to him, afraid to open it. 'Who are you?'

He tugged at his hood, pulling it further down over his eyes. 'A friend of Lena's.'

'Lena's?' Kat couldn't hide the incredulity from her voice. How would Lena know this boy?

He looked hurt at her tone and turned away. Over his shoulder, he shouted, 'I know her better than you,' then broke into a run. As he turned the corner, she saw Miriam pass him and come towards her. For once, she was on time. Kat swore silently to herself and waved a hand at her client. She assessed the package in her hand. It was heavy, about the weight of a bag of sugar and not dissimilar in dimensions.

Miriam came puffing up. 'Broken a habit of a lifetime. I'm on time.'

Kat, sharper than she'd intended, said, 'You're early actually.' Seeing Miriam's face, she backtracked. 'I'm sorry. You're a few minutes early. I'll let you into the room, and you can make yourself comfortable.'

Miriam relaxed. 'Sure. Why not? I need a bit of time to catch my breath.'

Kat led the way into the room and watched distractedly as her client settled herself into the chair. 'Will you excuse me for a minute?'

In the hall, she peeled the newspaper off the package. Underneath there was wadding, which looked like it had been pulled from a Jiffy bag, closely bound together with Sellotape.

She tugged fruitlessly at the binding, then went into the small kitchen and pulled a knife from a drawer. She sliced away at the tape until one side was completely open. Gently she slid the contents onto the counter, and started in horror.

20

Connie was in the part of Bampton that made her heart sink. During the Second World War, there had been a revival of the town's fortunes due to the need for textiles. Soldiers returning from the fighting, buoyed from victory and wanting to start a family or add to their existing ones, were seeking new housing for their expanding broods. The properties that had sprung up must, once upon a time, have seemed appealing. However, years of wear and tear and a haphazard approach to maintenance in this largely working-class area had given the street a hotchpotch look. It was an estate 'known to the police', that catch-all phrase used in these politically correct times to indicate trouble.

She made her way towards one of the nondescript houses that ringed the cul-de-sac. The woman who answered the door looked like she was eagerly expecting her visitor. Connie wondered if it had been a good idea to call ahead, but turning up without warning and asking someone to remember an incident four years earlier was hardly playing fair.

Jane Reynolds was styled perfection. The money she had clearly went on her own upkeep. She had coiffed blonde hair in curls that licked her face. Her face was heavily made-up, and Connie could smell her face powder, which she found repellent. Her living room was frozen in the 1950s. It presumably had been furnished when she had bought the house and had never been updated. The sofa was comfortable but the springs worn, and Connie felt her small frame sink so low that her bottom was almost touching the floor.

Over a cup of hot tea and bourbon biscuits, she confided to Connie what she had seen. 'I was on the coach tour to the North Yorkshire coast with my neighbour. You know, Robin Hood's Bay and the moors. Anyway, one of the days, we stopped off at Whitby to see the abbey and have fish and chips in the town. It was while we were having lunch in one of those chip shops that I saw him.'

'The man who looked like Andrew Fisher?'

Jane Reynolds took on a hurt expression. 'Looked like Andrew Fisher? It was definitely him. His mum went to Women's Institute with me. I've known him since he was a little lad. It was definitely him.'

'But if you were so sure, why didn't you make more of a fuss when reporting it to the police? The officer I spoke to thought you weren't at all sure.'

Jane Reynolds smoothed down her skirt. 'Have you ever tried to report something? Of course you haven't. You're police yourself. It's different for you. The man who answered the phone treated me like I was an idiot.'

'In what way?' Connie made a mental note to have a word with him.

'It was a case of "There, there dear. We've all got a lookalike somewhere." And I said to him, "It didn't just look like him. It *was* him." But it didn't make any difference, and by the end of the call it was just easier to agree with him. He treated me like I was a daft old bat. It's what happens when you reach a certain age. You've got that to look forward to.'

Connie laughed. 'You should see the way my colleague treats me. I think I've reached it already.'

Jane Reynolds narrowed her eyes. 'You haven't.' And then smiled.

Connie changed tack. 'How did he look? Andrew Fisher. Did he look well? Or like he'd been sleeping rough?'

The woman considered the question with the tip of the bourbon biscuit between her teeth. 'He looked well. Relaxed. I was surprised at how well he looked. Considering he was supposed to be dead.'

Connie laughed again, and Jane Reynolds laughed too and then stopped abruptly. 'I've heard about the body at Hale's End. Is that why you're asking me all these things? And I know it's him. The boss in your place went round to see Andrew's mum yesterday. We all know.'

Nothing stays secret around here, thought Connie, and then realised how completely untrue that was. 'Any idea why he would be in Whitby? There's not much of a connection to the area. It's a good three-hour drive from here.'

The woman shrugged. 'No idea. He was always a funny one, Andrew. A real mummy's boy. You wouldn't have thought it to look at him. Big chunky lad that he was but he adored his mum. What did she say about Andrew being alive all these years?'

She was looking at Connie with a sharp expression. Should she tell her that Andrew's mother had been kept in the dark too? Connie wondered what this must have cost a man who was so close to his parent.

Jane Reynolds was good at reading other people's expressions. 'You don't think she knew?' Jane Reynolds sniffed. 'I wouldn't be so sure about that if I were you. We're good at keeping secrets round here. That's as much as I'm going to say. But you won't get far taking what everyone says at face value.'

21

Kat managed to get through most of the morning harnessed to adrenalin and caffeine. The fruit she'd brought for a snack lay in her bag untouched, but she'd made serious inroads into the packet of coffee she kept in the small kitchen fridge. Her head was buzzing in anger at the infliction she had put on her body, but the loud thud of her heart had as much to do with what was nestled in her handbag, wrapped in her scarf.

She sat in her therapy room and waited for Mark's knock. The thought of his solid presence was both comforting and thrilling. Underneath that was a profound fear when she thought of what she had been given.

He was, as usual, exactly on time. She opened the door, and he smiled down at her, his scarred cheek puckering lopsidedly. 'Come in.' The relief washed over her. She let him enter the room first, and he strolled over to the seat at the far side of the room and settled himself in.

'How are you?' It was always him first. Asking after her welfare.

'Fine. How are you?' Her stock answer. Fine was all her clients ever got from her.

'Not bad. I've been thinking about some of the things you spoke about in our last session. I'm sorry for texting you, by the way. I just wanted to thank you for giving me something to think about.'

He didn't look sorry at all. Kat smiled, pleased, but said nothing.

'When you said that not everything deserves a response. I appreciate you telling me about that. I've been thinking about it all week and I've decided not to reply. I've been mulling it over, and I think you're right. *She's* the one who chose the time to get in touch with me. Then suddenly I'm expected to drop everything and reply. I don't have to do that, do I?'

Kat shifted in her seat. 'Not if you don't want to but, then again, if you wanted to reply, I would also encourage you to do so. It's about taking control of your life.'

'I don't want to reply. It's what I've decided. Thank you for supporting me in this.' He looked closely at her. 'Are you all right?'

'Yes, of course, I'm fine. How have you been sleeping?' As he talked, Kat watched as his foot, crossed over his leg, jigged up and down. His repressed energy both repelled and fascinated her. He noticed her looking and stilled his foot for a moment. Then carried on with his narrative, his foot resuming its syncopated rhythm.

She forced herself to focus on his words and not on the object that lay in her bag. It was pointless. Mark, for all his dysfunctional childhood, or perhaps because of it, was an expert at reading people's moods. He was also adept at carrying the blame for other people's problems. 'I'm sorry. I feel that I'm boring you. I know you've heard it all before.'

Kat had hardly been listening, but her professional training kicked in. 'I'm so sorry, Mark. It's not you at all. Would you excuse me a minute while I get myself a glass of water?' She wanted to burst into tears, hold on to him and cry like she'd once seen him do when he'd talked about his childhood. Instead, she escaped to the kitchen and laid her hot forehead against the cool wall tiles for a moment. Then she poured some water from the tap into a mug and swallowed the tepid liquid in one gulp.

When she returned to the counselling room, Mark was standing. 'Are you sick? We can do this another time, if you want.'

She should have lied and said that she was ill. Professionally, it would have been the best thing to do. But the turmoil of her thoughts meant that all she could focus on was the package she had been handed earlier. 'I've got a few problems that I need to sort out. It's completely unprofessional of me. I think we should stop this session and rearrange it. As soon as possible, of course. These things do occasionally happen but it's the first time for me.' Kat felt tears prickle at the back of her eyes and stood up to hide them from him.

But Mark's instincts were on full alert, and he crossed the room towards her. 'I've heard about the body. There's a rumour going around Bampton that it's Andrew Fisher. Is that true? His wife is your sister, isn't she?'

He was standing in front of her. She could smell soap – a citrus tang. Kat took a step back. 'The Bampton rumour mill. I should've guessed it'd be in full swing by now.' There was no chance of anonymity in this small town.

'I thought you might cancel our session, what with everything that's happened. I wouldn't blame you but I was hoping you wouldn't. Because I wanted to see you.' He reached out a hand, and Kat braced herself. There was no further step away that she could make in this small room. Now was the time to tell him to go. That she'd call him to rearrange the session. He'd given her an opt-out by mentioning Andrew Fisher, but the monstrosity that she'd been given this morning needed, in its horror, normalising in some way. And here was a man who would recognise its significance. She took a deep breath. 'Mark. Will you help me?' As she uttered the words, she felt the walls of her professional training crumble around her.

He dropped his hand. 'What's the matter?'

She reached behind her chair and gently lifted her orange handbag. She pulled from its depths the object that had dominated her thoughts all day. She gingerly unwrapped it from its woollen covering and presented it to him, like a child offering a gift. He didn't take it from her. 'Who gave you this?'

'A boy. This morning. He knocked on my door and said that he was a friend of Lena, my sister. Is it loaded?'

They both looked down at the gun. It didn't look like the weapons you saw in the old cowboy films. Those were shiny with snub barrels. This one was long and sleek. Its wooden handle jutted out at a forty-five-degree angle with a long black barrel that resembled more a deadly fountain pen. 'Have you touched it? With your hands, I mean?' Mark's voice was harsh.

'I was scared to. It might be loaded. It fell out of the parcel it came in and then I picked it up with my scarf. I kept the end away from me.'

He was looking at her. His expression unreadable. He moved back and went to the small coffee table separating the two chairs and grabbed a handful of tissues. He then picked up the gun and examined it. 'You needn't have worried anyway. Here.' He was pointing at something at the top of the gun. 'This is the lock. It stops the gun from accidentally firing if you drop it. It's engaged. In any case it wouldn't have mattered. There's no ammunition. Look.' He angled the barrel towards her, and she could see the empty chamber. 'The bullets slot in here.'

Kat let out a big sigh.

He looked at her. Gone was the nervy client she saw on a weekly basis. Instead he looked calm and determined. 'Do you know what gun this is?'

'Of course I don't know. I don't know anything about guns.'

'Is anyone in your family German?'

'German? Of course not. Why do you ask?'

'What about the military? Did any of your family serve in the wars?'

'Not that I'm aware of. Dad was too young to fight Hitler. He was born in 1940. I don't remember talk of either of my grandfathers serving in the First World War. What's this about?'

Mark was examining the gun intently. 'It's a Luger. A German gun. They gave them to the troops. It's a beautiful weapon and pretty collectible. Can your sister shoot?'

Kat repressed the desire to laugh. Because how much did she in fact know about her sister? The woman who had shocked everyone to the core by pleading guilty to the murder of her husband and who was clearly embroiled in a new subterfuge. 'I don't think she can. We never went hunting or anything. We weren't a family into country pursuits. More reading and card games. I don't *think* Lena can shoot.'

Mark wrapped the gun back in its woollen covering. 'But the boy who gave it to you said he knew Lena.'

'Yes. What do you think I should do?'

'Do? You need to give it to the police. Have you any idea what the penalties are for illegal firearm possession in this country? You need to get rid of it as soon as possible.'

'But what shall I say?' She looked up at him, and, for the first time, the relationship shifted. Mark was no longer the man trying to come to terms with his fifteen-year-old self, making a decision to cleave himself from his parent and start afresh. What she saw instead was the person he'd become. Capable and calm.

'You tell them the truth. Andrew Fisher was shot. You really don't want to be found with it.' He picked her bag up from the table and put the gun into it.

She took it from him. 'I'm so sorry about dragging you into this.'

He was looking at her impassively. 'Why did you show it to me?'

A wave of nausea washed over her. 'I couldn't bear it. When I saw it. It seemed so shocking, here in these rooms that I've tried to make a sanctuary for my clients.'

'And?'

'I had no intention of telling you. I was going to wait until I'd finished my sessions for today and then have a think but even when you arrived today, I felt a bit better. I knew you were someone who had at least seen a gun.'

Mark looked grim. 'I've done more than see them. You were right to show me, but now you need to give it to the police. Do you want me to come to the station with you?'

Kat shook her head. 'You'd better not. I've already breached client and therapist codes of conduct. I need to think about our future sessions.'

'But we will still see each other?'

'I need to think what's best for you. I'm so sorry.' She felt near tears again.

He stepped away from her. Surprising her, once more. 'It'll be fine. Everything in my life, I've done on instinct. It's worked for me.' He looked at her. 'I have your mobile number. I'll be in touch.'

22

Connie walked back to the police station along Bampton High Street, keeping a wary eye out for local hoodlums she'd occasionally had to deal with when she was in uniform. She spotted them now and again. Their eyes would lock, and she was never the first to look away. Today the only people out in force were afternoon shoppers taking advantage of the warming spring day to leave their heavy winter coats at home and walk into town.

A figure walked towards her who Connie recognised but struggled at first to place. She was slim, wearing a close-fitting leather jacket in a deep shade of burgundy and dark jeans. Connie looked at the high-heeled ankle boots and shuddered. The last time she had tried heels, she had ended up tripping over the pavement outside her flat. On the way out to a date as well.

She would have carried on walking, but the figure stopped in front of her. 'Hi, Connie. You out on your own?'

It was the voice that switched the light on in Connie's head. Slightly breathy with a hint of a Derbyshire accent. Joanne, Palmer's wife.

'They do let me off the leash occasionally.' It sounded more sarcastic than she'd intended, but, honestly, did Joanne think she had to be accompanied everywhere? However, the frown on the woman opposite suggested that the tone hadn't gone unnoticed.

'Damian at the station?'

It was Connie's turn to frown. What business was it of Joanne's where Palmer was during working hours? Or was she being unfair? Perhaps that's what it was like when you were married. Wanting to know where your spouse was all the time. She made a face. 'Probably.'

There was a short silence. She turned to move on, but Joanne put out her arm. 'Perhaps we could meet for a coffee? Have a nice girly chat. We only ever meet in the pub.'

That was an outright lie. This was their third meeting in total. The previous time had been at Joanne's wedding to Palmer last year. The only interaction had been a kiss on Joanne's cheek in the wedding line-up. She'd shaken Palmer's hand. The time before that had been on one of the team's socials where partners had been allowed but discouraged. It was a time for letting off steam after a difficult case but Joanne had come and had sat there with a frown on her face. She had spotted Connie and Palmer laughing in the corner – only about something innocuous, but he'd been dragged off home. That was the last time, as far as Connie could remember, that he'd been out on a work do.

Connie, for once, was at a loss for words. She had nothing in common with this woman. It was Palmer she liked. Sort of. Why would she want to go for coffee with Joanne? 'Of course. When this case is finished. We'll have more time then.'

Joanne remained impassive, but Connie was sure she saw a flash of fury cross her face. She wondered what went on underneath that polished exterior.

'I've not seen much of him the past few days. He's busy with his job as usual. You're working on that body found at Hale's End?'

So Palmer was the type to bring his work home with him. Well, she could hardly blame him for that, could she? If she'd had a partner she would also have been sorely tempted to tell him about the case she was working on. But that would have been accompanied by a warning for him not to divulge she was discussing the case with him. Joanne, she suspected, was playing games.

'We're all a bit preoccupied. You remember the last murder investigation. It takes over your life.'

Joanne's mouth turned down at the edges. 'I remember. I just thought things might have been different after we were married.'

But why? thought Connie. *Why would getting married make any difference to how much work you have to put in when a killing takes place?*

Perhaps it was better she didn't have a partner in her life continually fretting about what time she was going to arrive home. Her occasional bouts of loneliness could be tempered by the knowledge of the hours she was putting in to further her career. She wondered about saying something reassuring about Palmer. After all, it couldn't be much fun starting off married life with an absent husband.

But Joanne was looking down the high street, beyond the shops to where the road curved out of Bampton. 'Funny that body turning up at Hale's End. When I was growing up, I wouldn't have gone anywhere near the place. It had an awful reputation.'

'It gave me the creeps,' Connie couldn't help herself admitting.

'It wasn't that. It was the local place to go and park your car.

You know, with your boyfriend. A lot of teenage fumbling went on around that building.'

'It's isolated enough but spooky. Why would anyone choose to go there?'

Joanne gave her a look of distaste. 'Best thing about being married. Not having to put up with that sort of thing any more. I'll see you soon then.' She turned away from Connie, who was aware that her bag was buzzing alarmingly.

She dug into it and pulled out her silent mobile. She'd missed a call from Palmer. What now?

23

The Peverill Arms missed cigarette smoke. Many landlords, after the ban came into effect in England forbidding all cigarette-smoking in public spaces, used the opportunity to redecorate their establishments. Yellowing ceilings were surprised with a white slick of paint and the sludge-brown carpets slung in favour of the original wooden floorboards underneath. Not so the Peverill Arms. Its attraction was that it had refused to change. It had even tried to hold out against the smoking ban, but a steep fine after a tip-off to the police had indicated the futility of pitting itself against government regulations. But it still looked like a smokers' pub.

Mark pushed open the door and scanned the room. In the corner, as expected, were two of the men he was looking for. The three half-drunk pints of mild suggested that Brian, the man he particularly wanted to see, was probably in the toilet.

He went to the bar and ordered himself a half of the same brew. He didn't ask the others if they wanted anything because that wasn't their way. Money was tight for all of them, and the niceties of shared rounds were for better times. Like when they had all been in the employ of Her Majesty's armed forces. But that was in the past. Now everyone got his own drink, and it wasn't a problem.

As if on cue, Brian came back from the gents, checking the flies of his trousers. He was a physically imposing man. About six foot three and broad across the shoulders. He was running to fat around his stomach, but over the rest of the body the extra weight was solid enough. He nodded at Mark. 'We don't normally see you in here of a lunchtime.'

'Alcohol in the day sends me to sleep.'

'What you doing here then?'

Mark looked over to the corner. 'Got a problem I need to discuss.'

Brian's features flattened into a neutral expression. 'Get your drink and join us.'

By the time Mark had paid for his beer and joined the gang at the table, there was an expectant hush over the group. Brian had clearly tipped them off. If Mark had any friends in Bampton, these were them. A group of ex-military who had created an informal network to support and help each other. They kept their ears to the ground about job opportunities, benefits they could claim and gossip about others they had known in the forces. The Peverill Arms was their meeting place.

'I don't know how much I can tell you about this. It's not me being shy. It's a friend's problem. I'm helping her out.'

'Her?' Jack, the oldest of the group, grinned a gap-toothed smile at him. 'You're coming to us about a woman's problem?'

Mark drew a face in the froth of his beer. 'Someone sent her a gun.'

The men stiffened. The third, Paul, looked towards Brian. 'A gun?' he repeated, his eyes still on Brian.

'I've told her to go to the police. Which she's doing. At least I'm pretty sure she is, but she wants to know where it came from.'

'How did she get it?'

'It was delivered by hand. From a young boy. Well, a teen-ager.'

It was Jack's turn to look at Brian. 'A young lad,' he echoed again.

'What's this?' Mark frowned, feeling for the pulse behind his temple. 'Everything I say is being repeated.'

Brian pushed away his beer. 'It's been a couple of weeks since you came here. I know, I know. You don't like drinking at lunch. Although we only have the two.'

'But we do bugger all else the rest of the day.' Again the gap-toothed smile from Jack.

'I had a visitor recently.' Brian leant back in his chair. 'A young lad. Tall, a bit underweight. Anyway, he knocked on my door of an evening and asked to speak to me about something.'

'About mid-teens?'

'Something like that. Couldn't see much of the little blighter, to be honest. He had his hoodie pulled down low over his head. Put me on alert for a start.'

'What did you do?'

'I let him into the hall. No further, mind you. Anyway, he come straight out with it. Asks me where he could get hold of a gun.'

'Seriously?'

'I kid you not.'

Mark decided it was time to lay his cards on the table. Well, some of them. 'It's not exactly a coincidence I'm here.' The three men were silent. 'I made a few phone calls just now. You know. To some of the gang. One of them mentioned I should speak to you, Brian. Nothing else. He didn't give anything away. I just rang around and asked about a gun. They told me to speak to you.'

'What's going on, Mark?' Paul was the person he knew the least. There was a spark of suspicion in his eyes. 'Hang on. It's not to do with that guy shot at Hale's End?'

The group fell silent once more. Suspicion was radiating off the three of them.

Mark decided honesty was the best course. 'I can't tell you who it is. I said I'd try to help a friend, that's all.'

Brian was refusing to meet Mark's eyes. 'I've told you what happened. I told the boy to bugger off. I don't know where he got my name from, but I don't get hold of weapons for anyone. Especially young lads like him.'

'I assume you haven't been to the police. I don't blame you.' Mark could feel the tension of the group relax. 'But I want to know where that boy got the gun from. Call it helping someone who's helped me.'

This went down well. Even Paul had adopted a sage expression.

'I don't know where he got a gun from, but it wasn't me,' said Brian. 'Little sod, arriving on my doorstep like that. If he shot that guy, I hope the coppers catch him. Coming to me. Little bastard.'

24

'Let me go over this one more time. You're absolutely positive that you didn't recognise the boy with the hood. You've never seen him before at all.'

The policeman who she'd first met, a Detective Sergeant Palmer, was taking her statement, writing rapidly on a notepad. He was small and compact with greying hair that did nothing to offset his boyish demeanour. He was wearing a wedding ring that he kept fiddling with as she told her story. When she got to the part about the gun, he had recoiled, even though she kept the weapon in her bag.

'Hold on. Just stay there.' He'd sprinted out of the room and returned a few minutes later with two men in uniform with guns strapped across their chests. They'd demanded her handbag and had taken it away.

It had left her feeling exposed. She had no money and no house keys. She hoped she would be getting these back soon.

DI Sadler had come into the room a few minutes later. It was him that she'd originally asked for, but she had been told sharply by the woman at the desk that he was busy. Clearly the revelation that Kat was at the station with a gun in her bag had been deemed more important than whatever he'd been doing.

It was Sadler who was now questioning her. He looked wary. At their first meeting at the house, she could have sworn there had been a spark of empathy between them. That had gone. During the retelling of the story, she had grown self-conscious. 'I didn't get a good look at the boy's face. His hood was pulled down low but I'm pretty sure I'd not seen him before.'

'And this is the best description you can give us. Tall and thin with brown eyes and possibly blond hair.' Palmer didn't look up as he asked the question but continued to write on the notepad.

'I can't swear to the hair colour. It's just the impression I got. That he had blond hair I mean. But I could be mistaken.'

'It matches the description of around half the male teen-agers in Bampton. Are you sure you're telling us everything?'

Kat should have felt outrage, but she couldn't summon up the emotion, not least because she wasn't giving them the whole truth. There was a large part that she'd missed out. About the conversation with Mark and his reassurances that he would help. She told herself that, at least, she could claim client confidentiality, but she felt like a complete hypocrite. 'Hand on heart, I'd never seen him before.'

'And would you be able to identify him again?' This time the sergeant did look up. His gaze, like Sadler's, was assessing.

Kat looked between them both and felt like crying. 'Probably.'

They let her go eventually. Gave her back her handbag and thanked her for her cooperation. As she came onto the street, the warming May day made her feel feverish. She checked her phone. No messages from anyone.

She passed a figure on the steps of the station and recognised DC Connie Childs, the detective who'd questioned Lena about the finding of Andrew Fisher's body at Hale's End. The detective did a double take when she saw her. 'Are you going out or coming in?'

It should have sounded rude, but Kat felt pathetically grateful that someone cared enough to ask. 'I'm leaving. Something happened today. A boy came to my counselling room and gave me a package, saying it was from Lena. It was a gun.'

'A gun?' She looked shocked. 'The one used in Andrew Fisher's killing?'

'I don't know. I've given it to them inside.' Kat inclined her head.

Connie's eyes flickered, and Kat could see something like amusement in her face. 'Which detective did you see?'

'Detective Sergeant Palmer to begin with.'

Kat was surprised to see her snickering. 'I bet he nearly wet his pants when you showed him the gun. I wish I'd been there.'

Tears blurred Kat's eyes. She felt Connie's hand on her arm.

'Oh God, I'm sorry. Don't listen to me. Gallows humour is rife in this job. It must have been a shock getting the weapon. Was it loaded?'

Kat shook her head. 'No.'

'How do you know?'

Kat's mind stopped in shock. How to answer this without mentioning Mark. 'They told me in the station.'

Connie seemed content with the answer. 'Look, I know a good café nearby.'

'I can't, I'm sorry. I need to get back. Feed the cat and see if Lena's home. It's all getting a bit much for me, I'm sorry.'

'Don't worry. But you must look after yourself. Have you thought about getting away, maybe just for a few days?'

'I can't concentrate. I thought the trip to the coast might

help, but even the delights of Whitby yesterday did nothing for me.'

She felt the hand on her arm suddenly tighten. Through her tears she could see Connie's face come close to hers. 'Did you say Whitby?'

25

'Start with the sex,' Llewellyn had said. Well, the sex was in danger of being forgotten with the discovery of what appeared to be the murder weapon.

Sadler didn't like the discovery of the gun. If it was from Lena, packaging it up in wadding and giving it to her sister, admittedly via an intermediary, didn't sound like the act of a guilty party. If Lena had shot her husband and wanted to confess, then surely the natural thing to do would be to present herself to the police, not pass on the murder weapon. No, whatever reason she had for handing over the gun, if indeed it was her who had sent it to her sister, then it must have another message.

The gun had been passed to Forensics with a fair amount of excitement within the team – and rightly so. Guns weren't unheard of in Derbyshire, but they weren't as much a problem as in the neighbouring Manchester police district. Sadler had taken one look at it and didn't think it was the sort of thing to be found on the streets of any city. It was old. He was no expert, but it most certainly wasn't a modern weapon. They would need to wait for someone to pinpoint its exact make and also whether it matched the bullet extracted from the body of Andrew Fisher.

Start with the sex. Well, according to Lena's statement at the time, she had sex with the man before she smothered him.

Despite the fact she had lied about the identity of the person she had killed, Sadler was going to start with the hunch that part of her testimony had been true. That the man in her bed had at least been there voluntarily.

Palmer had prepared a list of men of around Andrew Fisher's age who had gone missing about the time of the murder. It was pulled from the national police database, and Palmer had done a good job of keeping it sensible. His accompanying note listed who he had crossed off – known absconders, those with a history of drug convictions and petty thefts. Palmer had gone with the hunch that the man they were looking for did not belong to the group of people who were normally reported missing.

Sadler wondered about this approach. The man's relations didn't seem to have kicked up much of a fuss. This likely placed the victim outside a secure family unit. However, given that Lena had been in bed with him, if Andrew was anything to go by, her tastes ran to upwardly mobile men.

'Sir.' Palmer stuck his head through his office door without knocking. Unusual for him. 'We've got reports of a woman's body found in the stream by Fearnley Mill. An initial description suggests it might be a match with Lena Gray. *Might*, sir, but I thought you should know.'

Sadler grabbed his coat and followed Palmer out of the station. When they reached the car park, he made towards his car. 'Any idea where Connie is?'

'Interviewing the woman who believes she saw Andrew Fisher in Whitby, I think. She should be back soon. I tried to call her. Want me to give her another ring?'

Sadler started up the car and reversed, tugging at his seat

belt in frustration. 'Let's get there first. We'll probably get nowhere near the body until Forensics have finished. Far better Connie continues with what she's doing.'

The drive to Fearnley Mill was slow. The beginning of the tourist season meant that sightseers were on the roads, driving well under the speed limit, their eyes drawn to the hills rather than concentrating on the traffic.

'Not putting on the siren?' Palmer looked at his watch.

'I was just thinking about it.'

Palmer gave him a conspiratorial glance as Sadler switched it on. The car in front of them braked suddenly, causing Sadler to swear.

'Why do they always do that?' Palmer's voice was amused. 'They hear the siren and slam on the brakes. I'm surprised there aren't more accidents.'

'Bloody idiots.' Sadler was in a hurry to get to the scene. He sped along the main carriageway and watched with a grim sense of satisfaction as cars moved out of his way.

The entrance to Fearnley Mill was taped off. For a while it had been a small complex consisting of a boutique wool shop, a small art gallery and a café. It hadn't survived the recession. There was a car park for about fifty cars. A constable, spotting Sadler, pulled across the tape to let them into the parking area. As they got out of the car, a scene-of-crime officer left a group of crime-scene investigators and made her way over to them. 'It's going to be a while, I'm afraid. There's a lot of work to do first.'

'What can you tell us?' Sadler looked towards the stream, but the now-verdant trees shrouded the spot he wanted to see.

'It's a woman, lying on her front and partially submerged.

Her face and upper part of her body are in the water. The lower half is on the bank.'

'Does she look like she drowned?' Palmer asked.

'There aren't any obvious marks to suggest how she died. Drowning is certainly a possibility.'

'Who found her? I thought this place was closed.' Sadler watched as the group made its way back down the path.

'It is. There are plans, or proposals at least, to open the place up to the public again. The managing agents were showing some potential investors around. They discovered the body – almost immediately on arrival, apparently. The investors were worried about flooding, so they went down to look at the river—'

Sadler didn't recognise the officer, but she sounded competent. Calm and steady. 'Have you turned the body yet?'

'Not yet, sir, and I think it'll be a while.'

'You know we're investigating the disappearance of Lena Gray, don't you? As part of the wider investigation into events in 2004.'

'Yes, of course.'

'And you've seen the body. Do you think it could be her?'

She nodded. 'I remember her from the original case. It's the same body type. She was tall and slim, wasn't she? And the hair's similar. Long and dark as I remember. It's possible it's her. That's all I can tell you at the moment. It could be her.'

26

Kat went with the policewoman even though she just wanted to go home and step into the old cast-iron bath. It might be chipped and stained at the bottom, but it was a reassuring reminder of her childhood. The huge water tank in the bathroom still pumped out boiling-hot water even though she and Lena lived in constant fear of it packing up. How would they ever afford to replace it?

But she wouldn't be going home yet. The policewoman, for all her tartness, had shown her compassion. A different type to that shown by Mark, but still welcome.

The café that Connie took her into didn't immediately look appealing. It was busy, which repelled Kat, whose buzzing head needed peace. After ordering two coffees, Connie pushed her into one of the booths. 'One of my favourites, this place. The coffee's fab.' Kat smiled at the expression. She liked this detective. More than she had at first when she met her at her home. And she was right. The coffee was strong with a dark bitter taste.

'I don't know where the gun came from. The boy said he was a friend of Lena's. But she wouldn't know anything about guns. The whole idea is preposterous.'

The detective wasn't interested in the gun. She shrugged. 'It'll have gone straight to Forensics. We'll get the results in a few days or so. If it's the gun that shot Andrew Fisher, then your sister's got some explaining to do. Mind you, even if it isn't, she still needs to tell us what her connection is to the boy and the gun.'

Kat was shaking her head. 'I just don't think it's going to have anything to do with her.'

Connie leant forward, her elbows on the table. 'What were you doing in Whitby, Kat?'

Kat felt unable to look her in the eye. 'Lena loved Whitby because of the Dracula connection, initially. We used to stay up late in the eighties and watch the old Hammer movies. Our parents let us have a TV each in our bedrooms.'

Connie smiled. 'A TV in the bedroom? I'd have died for that as a teenager.'

'Well, they were actually quite old-fashioned. That's why we had the TVs in our rooms. Dad didn't really want one in the living room so we were allowed our own. Mum and Dad preferred the radio, which they'd listen to in the kitchen.'

'Did you watch the TVs separately?'

'It depended. We were both big movie fans, especially Lena. We loved all the old horror films. I dreaded her going away to university as I'd have to watch them by myself, but she stopped wanting to watch them anyway.'

'And was it? Bad, I mean, when she left home?'

Kat stirred her coffee. 'She never did. She was expected to go to university, of course. That was the plan for both of us. But aged eighteen, she changed her mind. Didn't want to go away, didn't want to leave Bampton.'

Kat saw Connie frown. 'Any reason for this?'

'Difficult to say. She did okay in her exams. She definitely could have gone but, for whatever reason, she decided to stay put.'

'She became a well-respected artist though. Was she self-taught?'

'No. She eventually did an art degree at the college, but that was later. She worked in a florist's first and then started to paint seriously.'

'What did your parents think?'

'Do you know what? That was the funniest part. They didn't say anything. It was quite strange really. They just took everything in their stride. Let her do what she wanted.'

'And Whitby?'

'Well, she went there when she was fifteen or so on a school trip and fell in love with the place. Have you been?'

Connie shook her head.

'It's got a very strange energy about the place. Quite a lot of black-haired goths wandering among American tourists. Anyway, Lena loved it and used to go there a lot. Especially after I left home to go to university. She found a place to stay and spent days there at a time.'

'What for?'

'What for?' echoed Kat. 'Not for anything. To get away from Bampton. You've seen what this place is like. We all need to get away.'

Connie looked unconvinced. 'So when she went missing, you thought she might have gone there.'

'Exactly. It really was the only place I could think of. I had an old address from years ago, and I went there. It was a long shot really. It's still a holiday home, but the good-looking guy next door said that Lena used to visit a lot and then one day stopped. It must have been about the time of her arrest.'

'But you didn't find her. This time, I mean. You didn't find out where she was?'

Kat shook her head. 'Like looking for a needle in a haystack really.'

Connie lifted her cup. 'It was a good hunch. It's what we usually do. Look for a pattern and investigate that in the first instance. You really should have mentioned it to us, you know. You could have called and we would have contacted the local police. There are procedures in place for working with other Forces. Please don't go haring off on investigations again.'

'But why are you so interested in Whitby? Do you think there's a connection?'

'There's a witness who says she saw Andrew in Whitby a few years ago. There's a possibility that's where he was hiding.'

'What?!'

Connie opened her mouth to speak as her phone went in her bag.

Kat watched her answer and saw her face blanch. She felt the deep pull of dread within her. Connie cut the call. 'I'm sorry, Kat. I've got to go.'

'What is it?' She could see her debating how much to say.

Connie reached across and touched Kat on the arm. 'Go back to the house. I need to be able to find you. I don't know if it's news, but please make sure I can contact you. Can I have your mobile number?' Kat watched as Connie tapped in the digits.

'I'm ringing you so you've got mine. Try not to worry. I'll call you when I can.'

27

Kat turned the volume down low and listened for a noise from Lena. Any noise. But it was silent, not a stir from the bedroom below. The credits for the earlier film were coming to an end, and the feature of the night would be starting soon. *The Devil Rides Out*. A particular gore fest that they had watched years earlier to squeals of horrified delight. However, when Kat had invited Lena up earlier that evening, she'd received a look of scorn. Since then, silence.

She turned the volume back up to mask the sound of her footsteps and stepped out onto the landing. It was chilly, and her bare feet stuck to the wooden steps as she made her way down. She crept towards Lena's room and put her ear to the door. At first she could hear nothing. She wondered if her sister had gone out without telling anyone. Without telling her. Then came a scraping sound. Muffled movements. Kat lifted her hand to the door and tapped softly.

'Go away.'

'The film's about to start. It's *The Devil Rides Out*. One of your favourites.'

'You told me at tea. I'm not interested. I'm painting. Leave me alone.'

Kat stood outside the door for a moment. Willing her sister

to open it just a fraction. But it remained in place. All Kat could hear was silence.

She padded down the remainder of the steps and into the kitchen where her mother was reading the *Guardian* while perched on a stool. Her reading glasses, on a chain around her neck, were smudged with ink from the print. She looked up. 'What's the matter?'

'Lena. She's locked herself away. Again.'

Her mother looked back at the paper. 'Best leave her be. It's a difficult time for her at the moment. She's got her A Levels coming up soon.'

'I've exams too. There's no way I'm as moody as she is.'

'Count yourself lucky then.' Kat felt the sting of the words, but her mum looked up and smiled. 'Fancy cheese on toast?'

'Wouldn't mind.'

'Well, put these on first. You'll freeze without them.'

Ten minutes later, Kat walked back up the stairs with freshly laundered socks that had dried on the Aga warming her feet and the smell of melted cheese wafting from the plate she was carrying. As she passed Lena's door, she comforted herself that it was only in her imagination that she could hear the sound of sobbing.

28

Christ. It looked like Lena Gray was dead. Connie was having difficulty digesting the information. From what Kat had said, she would have sworn that Lena's absence had been voluntary. The bed had been made, and plans were evident for an unnoticed exit from the house.

But the body in Fearnley Mill matched Lena's description. She'd probably given away too much to Kat about the discovery. She clearly knew something was up.

The drive to the mill took about half an hour. The misery of the Derbyshire winter was beginning to thaw into a fragile spring and small flashes of colour brightened the grass verges.

Sadler and Palmer were waiting for her in the car park, their two suited figures incongruous in the rural idyll. Connie was struck once more by how different the two men were. Sadler was tall with blond hair. He had a rangy remoteness that Connie had seen was attractive to women. There had been girlfriends, most recently a glamorous Greek, Christina, but by all accounts he was now single. She had allowed herself to go a short way down that road and had then stopped. He was her boss and, as such, had control over her career. She found him attractive but was prepared to leave it at that.

Palmer was her competitor. He may have had a more senior rank, but they were both, hopefully, on the way up. And because they were both ambitious, and perhaps because he was newly married and therefore unavailable, Connie was prepared to admit her attraction to him. He was much more her type. Taller than her, obviously. Everyone was. Around five nine and stocky. His prematurely grey hair, clipped into a crew cut, added to his attractiveness. And he knew it. Palmer fancied himself. This was what amused Connie the most. His vanity was attractive in itself. It added a human dimension.

Sadler and she had attended his wedding to Joanne. In spite of the wobbly Palmer had thrown on the eve of his wedding, pleading with Connie to let him stay in her flat, he now looked content and back to his usual arrogant self. Connie hadn't liked the doubtful version of him. However much his self-assurance might wind her up, she preferred confidence to vulnerability.

It was Palmer who came towards her, looking grim. 'We've got a body that matches the description of Lena Gray. We've not been able to get near it but we're about to be given the green light according to the CSIs. You've arrived at the right time.'

'Drowning?'

Palmer shrugged. 'She's down by the river. Partially submerged. Bill's been and gone and said he'd call through the results once the PM's taken place. He didn't want to commit himself in relation to cause of death when I asked.'

'He's playing it safe, I suspect. We all are.' Connie looked towards Sadler. 'What does the boss say?'

'Not much. I think he's glad the body's out in the open. He seemed a bit freaked out at finding that guy at Hale's End. The great outdoors is more his thing.'

Connie smiled, and their eyes met.

'Where've you been?' he asked her.

'With Kat, Lena's sister. I've found a Whitby connection although I'm not sure what it means. It was Lena's favourite place. Why Andrew Fisher would use it as a place to hide out isn't clear.'

'Well, it doesn't sound like he was running from her. They must have been in it together. The deception, I mean.'

'Possibly.' Connie again looked at Sadler, who was making his way towards them.

He acknowledged her with a nod of the head. 'We've been given the okay to see the body. We need to get a move on. It'll be dark in an hour or so.'

The three of them made their way down the path. The gravelled car park gave way to grass. It was wet underfoot. Recent rainfall had raised the water table, and Connie could feel her boots sink into the soft ground and the moisture reach up to her ankle. Sadler and Palmer were both wearing wellington boots and trudged ahead of her, their heads bent towards the ground.

The path opened out as it reached the river, where a crowd of white-suited personnel were still going about their business. A woman came towards her, and Connie recognised her from a previous case. Her first name, she thought, was Tracy.

'Do you want to take a look before we turn her over?'

Sadler nodded, and Tracy led the way down to the river. The upper half of the torso was face down in the shallow water, the arms thrown above in a hideous imitation of a dive. It looked like she was wearing a khaki bomber jacket which had ballooned with the water and her jeans, which clung to her legs, were also sodden with water. Her submerged body had been knocked about by the swirling eddies before being deposited on the bank.

Tracy pointed to the body. 'There are abrasions on the face, but the pathologist will be able to tell you if they're post mortem or not. Apart from that, there is little sign of injury.'

'Time of death?' asked Connie, her lungs stinging from the rapidly cooling air.

'Within the past twenty-four hours, according to Bill. Are you okay for us to turn her over?'

'Hold on a minute.'

Connie looked in surprise at her boss. She'd have guessed that he would have wanted to get this out of the way as soon as possible. Clearly not. She watched him as he walked up to the woman's body and looked down at her, nodding imperceptibly to himself. Then he straightened up. 'Okay. Turn her over.' He looked back towards Connie, his face devoid of emotion.

She resisted the temptation to ask him if he'd discovered anything. Surely he would have called them over if there was anything of interest.

Two CSIs went to the body and, with a one-two-three, flipped the woman over. The bloat of the face was, as usual, shocking. Bodies that had been submerged in water and fire victims were the worst, in Connie's opinion. She forced her eyes to focus on the face, and, as she did so, she heard Palmer next to her gasp.

'Bloody hell.'

'Yes,' said Sadler. 'Bloody hell indeed.'

29

As she approached Providence Villa, Kat was surprised to see the daffodils, which days earlier had been a sea of weedy stems, had suddenly become a riot of yellow. They were late, of course. All plants in north Derbyshire blossomed way behind the rest of England. The high altitude and late winters meant a hesitant start to spring.

Her mother had planted these daffs years ago. When she and Lena were children. She could still see her on her hands and knees carefully tending the garden. It had been a thing of beauty once but neither Kat nor Lena had inherited their parents' green fingers. The garden got by, but only just.

For an instant, Kat felt a pang of shame. The heads of the plants swayed softly in the cool breeze. It felt like the first proper spring day, and, despite everything, she felt her spirits lift. As she turned into the front garden, she saw, with a start, that someone was sitting on the front step. He had his head down and appeared to be drawing something with his shoe in the gravel in front of the doorstep. He looked up at her approach. Mark.

'What are you doing here? I didn't give you my address.' Her pleasure at seeing him was fighting with her shock at seeing a client outside her home.

He stood up, his calm eyes on her. 'I found it out. It wasn't difficult. Just asked around. I wanted to see if you were okay.'

'You can't come here. You're my client. I need to main-tain—'

He lifted his arm and then dropped it. 'You can't be my therapist any more. Not since you told me about the gun. I need to help you. Not the other way around.'

She pushed past him. 'I don't need help. I've done what you suggested. Given the police the gun and a right palaver it caused too. As for me, I'm just going to carry on as normal. It's all I can do.'

He was behind her but still didn't touch her. 'Kat, I need to talk to you about something. I've asked around, like I prom-ised.'

'That was only today. You can't have found out much since then.'

'I think I've found out some information about who gave you the gun.'

She wheeled around. 'The boy, you mean?'

He nodded. 'Can I come in?'

She looked at the house. 'It's a bit of a state. Inside, I mean.'

'I don't mind.'

Kat heaved herself against the door, and the smell of damp assailed her immediately. She looked at Mark, but he was watching her, not the house. She took him into the kitchen. The living room seemed too large and formal.

Really, the kitchen was the worst room in the house. It had been refitted at some point in the eighties, and the tiles were beyond retro kitsch. But, again, he didn't seem to notice their surroundings. He pulled out a chair from underneath the Formica table and sat down.

'There aren't many people you can ask in Bampton about a

gun. Take that from me. The ones I know are ex-military. There are a couple of us knocking about, and I can ask them for most things.'

It had come up in therapy sessions – Mark's support network from men like him who had been in the armed forces. They had formed an informal group to help each other out.

'And you asked them about the gun?'

'Yes.'

'And did you find out anything?'

'Yes, but they didn't like talking about it. They wanted to know why I was asking the questions and for who. But it was important to push it because someone had approached one of my mates about getting hold of a gun. A boy. Late teens apparently.'

'You think it's the same one who gave me the package?'

Mark shrugged. 'I don't know, but it's got to be a possibility, hasn't it? No one could give me any better description than the one you gave me. Wore his hood pulled up. Just a pair of brown eyes peeking out from underneath.'

'Sounds about right. He asked how to get hold of a gun?'

'Apparently. It didn't go down well with the lads. For lots of reasons.'

'Such as?'

Mark picked up the pen lying next to the crossword and started to doodle. 'For starters, ex-services have a reputation. For being on the edges of society. It's really not like that. We're struggling for normality like everyone else. So we don't appreciate it when a boy looking for something illegal comes knocking on our door.'

'I'm not sure who I would go to, if I were looking for a weapon.'

He looked at her. 'You thought of me when you wanted advice on the gun though, didn't you?'

Kat swallowed her hurt. Was it as simple as that? That he was just someone who was familiar with the thing that had caused so much fear?

'And, anyway, we've also seen the damage caused by guns. You get a few trigger-happy ex-soldiers, but not as many as you might think.'

'So what was he told?'

Mark smiled. '"Bugger off," basically, but the point was he was asking for something.'

Kat rubbed her aching head. 'But why? Let's say this boy had got hold of a weapon for illegal purposes.' She saw his face. 'Okay, to kill someone. There are other ways of doing it. Strangling, poison or whatever. Why draw attention to yourself by the business of acquiring a gun?'

'I'm not sure. Answer that question, and you might be on the way to finding out what's behind all this. If I were the police, though, I'd be wondering where exactly he got that gun from. It was more like an antique.'

'Maybe they should be checking the old people's home.' It was a feeble joke.

Mark didn't laugh. 'Maybe they should.' His eyes were still on her. 'But you're deliberately avoiding the key question.'

'Which is?'

'Come on, Kat. What's all this got to do with your sister? Okay, that boy's got some questions to answer, but your sister is seriously implicated in all this. You ended up with that gun and he specifically stated he knew Lena.'

'But it can't have been an act of guilt,' protested Kat. 'Why not give herself up then too? Why give me the gun through an intermediary?'

'I don't know. Are you sure there's nothing you can think of?'

Kat shook her head.

'Are you sure? What happened in 2004, and Lena's imprisonment? It's all going to be connected. She's lived an extraordinary life. These things don't happen by chance. Everything's connected. One thing leads onto another. We might need to go back to 2004.'

'We?' She found she couldn't look him in the eye.

'You did ask for help, and I'm going to help you. Find your sister and work out what's going on.'

His reassurance removed some of the fear gripping her stomach, but she was still overwhelmed by the weight of guilt as she considered the offer of help from her former client. She could feel his eyes on her. 'Why are you helping me?'

He took a step towards her. 'I'm returning some of the solace you've given me. In the only way I know how. With practical help.'

30

'It's definitely not her,' said Palmer. 'I've just come back from the PM.'

Sadler looked up. 'Sorry?'

'The body found down by Fearnley Mill yesterday isn't Lena Gray.'

'Bill's confirmed it?' He gestured for Palmer to sit down.

'I think we can safely say that. You should see the measures in place now to check the identity. There's this huge chart on the wall with a list of cadavers waiting to be autopsied. Then, next to each name, there's the ID that they've been through. Visual, dental, tissue samples and so on.'

'Doesn't sound very high-tech. There must be computer files for that.'

'Of course there are. This is a home-made thing. Looks like Bill's work. A big whiteboard. It's as much for him as for anyone else. It's hit him hard. The misidentification of Andrew Fisher.'

It's hit us all hard, thought Sadler.

'Anyway, the body we found isn't Lena Gray,' continued Palmer, 'which we could tell as soon as the body was turned over at Fearnley Mill. Also, the dental records don't match. So we've a woman's body, found in Bampton, of approximately the same age and description as Lena Gray.'

'That's two deaths within a week.'

'There's more. It may well be that the deaths aren't connected. Bill is doing toxicology tests, but at the moment he's saying the death doesn't look suspicious. Her pockets were weighted down with stones for a start. Not that it's up to him, of course. We'll have to wait for the Coroner to open the inquest.'

'Any chance at all of it being foul play?'

Palmer shrugged. 'Bill is being very cautious but he is one of us. He doesn't think so and basically told me that.'

'Do you think the two deaths are unconnected?' Sadler leant back in his chair.

'I'm not sure. It does look like a case of suicide. Do you think they are connected?'

'It's too much of a coincidence. Do we have an ID then? If it's not Lena Gray?'

'Not yet, but if it's suicide, hopefully it's only a matter of time. It's fairly early for someone to be reported missing, although a hostel has called in to say one of the residents didn't come home last night.'

'Hostel? Which one?'

'Shallowford. It's a women's home. Offers medium-term accommodation from what I can gather. It's run by a charity. They don't seem overly concerned by the woman's absence, but the policy is to report things immediately.' Palmer looked down at his notes. 'The missing woman's name is Stephanie Alton. I'm going over to check now but I wanted to touch base with you first. So you know that Lena Gray is still officially missing.'

Sadler nodded. 'There's something we're not getting, isn't there? There's something bigger going on here. And we haven't found it yet.'

'What do you think it is?'

Sadler shrugged. 'Llewellyn thinks it's about sex.'

Palmer smirked. 'Isn't everything?'

'Is it?'

His sergeant blushed. 'Well, it was a joke but sex can often be a catalyst, can't it?'

'I suppose so.' Sadler wasn't convinced. Was it really all about sex? 'Go and talk to the hostel. It sounds like Stephanie Alton is a possibility. Give me a call when you've got something. Anything.'

*

Palmer took Connie with him to Shallowford House. She wasn't her usual sparky self. She seemed subdued and appeared to be thinking things over. As usual, it wasn't long before he discovered what was on her mind.

'There's something really off about this case, you know. It's all smoke and mirrors.'

Palmer laughed. 'Sadler thinks it's all about sex.'

She turned around in her seat to look at him. 'He said that? I can't imagine it.'

He glanced down at her. Her eyes were brimming with laughter. 'Well, it was Llewellyn who said it apparently. Sadler's not so sure.'

'I bet.' She looked like she wanted to say something else but had thought better of it. He watched as she folded her arms and settled back into the passenger seat.

'But you think it's about smoke and mirrors?'

He could see her smile out of the corner of his eye. 'We're

being had. We were had in 2004, and someone's still playing with us.'

The car stopped at traffic lights, and he turned fully to her. 'Lena?'

She shrugged and didn't look at him. 'Probably. But not definitely.'

'Kat?'

Again she shrugged, and Palmer turned back to watch the lights in frustration.

She opened her bag and pulled out a metal cylinder. 'Do you mind?'

He glanced down at what was in her hand. 'I do, actually. God knows what's in that stuff. You'd hardly smoke in the car, would you?'

Connie stuffed the e-cigarette back in her bag without comment, but he could feel her eyes on him. 'You okay?'

Irritated, he put his foot on the accelerator. 'Of course I'm okay.'

Shallowford House was a modern building, built probably in the 1960s. It was two storeys of glass and hard plastic lines. A sea of blank windows faced them.

Connie turned to him. 'It's not very welcoming, is it? These are women fleeing abuse and God knows what else. And they come to this.'

He walked up to the entrance. The reception was empty, although a camera stared down at him, its red light blinking. Connie joined him, puffing slightly. 'You need to do some exercise,' he whispered to her and winced in amusement as she jabbed him in the ribs.

Footsteps along the corridor indicated that their arrival

hadn't gone unnoticed. 'Can I help you?' The voice was deep and rich. A tall woman with jet-black short hair with a streak of purple across the fringe came into view. She was casually dressed in black jeans and stretchy black jumper. Palmer reached inside his jacket pocket for his warrant card.

The woman held out her hand for it and scrutinised it for a moment. 'You're here about Stephanie Alton.' It wasn't a question, and her voice had a flat tone.

'You made a report that she has gone missing. We're here to follow it up.'

'Of course. I'm Julia Miles. The manager here.' She handed Palmer's card back to him and motioned them to follow her into the office behind reception. Unlike the brutal façade, the room was a welcoming space. It was warm, perhaps overheated on this spring day, and the walls were adorned with pictures of women, children and an assortment of animals.

She offered them chairs but no refreshments and got straight to the point. 'Although this is a hostel, we have a fairly stable body of residents. It's a medium-term facility. We can take emergency referrals, under the charitable terms of reference, but Shallowford is for residents who need to stay a few months, or even a year if necessary, while they sort out their domestic difficulties. Therefore, we get to know the people who stay here.'

'Is it unusual for Stephanie to go missing?'

'It's never happened before. Steph has addiction problems but has got on top of them over the past year. We are in the process of assessing her for a transfer to a housing-association flat as part of helping her to move on.'

'And how did—' Palmer corrected himself, 'does Stephanie feel about this?'

The woman opposite frowned. 'I would have said she's fine with it. She has family who are unable to stay overnight. A daughter. Mary, I think. And though she's quite settled here, she misses being with her child.'

'And you last saw her . . .?'

'She had lunch yesterday at around midday. Then we noticed she wasn't around for breakfast this morning. We checked her room, and it didn't look like her bed had been slept in. So we checked the swipe records.' She saw Palmer frown. 'You can't wander around this building willy-nilly. You need a swipe card to get inside the building from reception although you can leave without the card.'

'And what did the records say?' Connie leant forward.

'Nothing. The records say nothing. As I said, you don't need to use the card to get out. You just press the release button next to the door. So she must have left the building at some point but didn't come back. She's not here. We've checked everywhere.'

Palmer wasn't so sure about this. Police searches in the past had missed some embarrassing discoveries. He wondered how extensive the search had in fact been. 'The reason we're here is that a body has been discovered in the water at Fearnley Mill. As yet, the identity of the victim is unknown. Do you have a picture of Stephanie?'

Julia Miles blanched. 'I must have something.' She scanned the walls of her office and reached towards a picture of a woman blinking into the sunlight. 'I think this is the best one.'

Palmer took the snap from her, and Connie leant over next

to him. She smelt of hairspray and coffee. The woman in the photograph was a slim woman with long dark hair. He looked to Connie and then at Julia Miles. 'I think you're going to have to accompany us to the mortuary.'

Kat walked into her living room and sensed immediately that someone had recently been there. It was the indescribable feeling you get when you know things aren't as you left them. She sniffed at the air but could only smell the usual fustiness of the house. She walked over to the rear window and looked out into the garden. Was she still feeling Mark's presence from yesterday? But she hadn't brought him into the living room, and it was here that she could feel the trace of someone else.

As children, she and Lena had longed to see a ghost in the house. They had tried everything, impromptu seances, harassing elderly neighbours to tell them if anything tragic had occurred within the building. But they had come up with nothing, much to their disappointment.

Kat wasn't so fanciful as to think that they had a resident spirit in Providence Villa, but someone had definitely been in this room. She could swear it. The question was, had it been Lena?

She stopped and listened. *There's no one here*, she told herself. Not any more. She needed to talk to someone. Mark? She was an idiot and heading in only one direction with him. That would be a catastrophe. She sat on the arm of the sofa and picked up the phone from its cradle.

The number she dialled rang a few times, and then a husky voice answered. 'Patricia Meale.'

'Pat, I'm sorry about this. It's me, Kat.'

'Kat. I'm glad you rang. I've been thinking about you a lot. I did wonder about sending you a message but, well, you know how it is.'

Kat did. 'Can I come and see you? There's stuff I need to talk through.'

She heard the rustling of paper. 'I've got a slot at two. Will that do you?'

*

Kat left the car in the driveway and decided, instead, to walk the half mile to Patricia's house. Rather than stick to the main road, she crossed over to the small kidney-shaped park that their house overlooked and walked along one of its side paths. Two children cycled past ringing their bells at her, and she smiled, stepping out of the way. The weather was warm, and a few people were sitting on park benches, their faces turned to the sun, desperate for the blaze after the long winter. Kat wanted to join them. Wanted to rest her aching head and weary limbs. Instead she carried on with her hands thrust into her pockets.

She could feel someone looking at her, and the hairs on the back of her neck began to rise. She stopped suddenly and looked around. No one was paying any attention as far as she could see. Still the same children cycling and the elderly sunbathers. She carried on down the path and glanced across the green space. On one of the far benches sat a boy with a blue hooded sweater pulled low over his face. Kat stopped again and squinted at the figure. He noticed her scrutiny and stood up. She could see that he was tall. 'Hold on,' she shouted across the grass. A few people looked at her curiously as she broke into a run. The figure was making his escape through one of the side gates.

She made it to where he had been sitting and looked around, helpless. Had he been following her? Keeping watch on the house? She looked towards Providence Villa. The gable on the left-hand side was visible from where he'd been sitting. As was, perhaps more importantly, the front door.

Her eyes dropped to the bench. He had left something there. A supermarket bag. She reached out to touch it. The thin handles were tied together in a knot. She pulled angrily at it, her fingers tearing through the plastic. Inside was a piece of yellow material, thin and silky. For a moment, she thought he must have been stealing women's underwear. From a shop or a clothesline perhaps. As she opened out the material, she saw it was a woman's blouse. A mustard-yellow colour. Kat put the cloth to her nose and inhaled. It smelt old, and the scent brought a pang of fear like a stabbing pain in her chest. Whose was this blouse? Was it Lena's? If so, she didn't recognise it. She wanted to sit down on the grass and cry. Instead, she turned towards Patricia's house and her own place of safety.

*

'You've been through a lot in the past couple of days. Don't rule out the possibility that you might be in shock yourself.'

It often came as a surprise to people to hear that therapists had their own counsellors. Kat found this hard to fathom. Doctors went to other medics for their ailments. Dentists needed their own teeth looked after, so why shouldn't therapists visit their own profession? Of course, she knew what they were thinking. *If you're so damned good at your job, why do you need to visit someone yourself?* But the monthly supervision sessions were her godsend. She'd have gone more often if she could've afforded it. She didn't always want to talk about her clients. She often wanted to talk about herself, but an hour a month gave her precious little time to do so.

Patricia's consulting room was almost a mirror image of hers. She'd had this little oasis of peace in mind when she was setting up her own quarters but she'd never managed to recreate that perfect sense of stillness that she found here. Patricia sat opposite, reassuring as always, her calm brown eyes on Kat, waiting for her to speak.

'I don't know where to start.'

Patricia shrugged. 'Start anywhere.'

'I've crossed a professional boundary with a client.' For a moment, a look of consternation came into Patricia's eyes. It was quickly gone but it had been there and Kat regretted saying anything. 'Nothing sexual.' She told Patricia about the gun and how she had asked Mark to help her.

Patricia listened intently and then shook her head. 'I can understand how it happened. Who's to say how any of us would react in that situation? But the question is, where do you go from here?'

'I've told him I can't be his therapist any more,' said Kat quickly.

'And how did he take it?'

'Calmly, I think. He seemed to accept that the boundaries between us had shifted.'

'So you think he will accept the fact that he can no longer see you?'

No longer see me, thought Kat. *I never said that.* Patricia was right, though. Stopping seeing each other inside the counselling room also meant no contact outside. For a moment, Kat considered the implications of never seeing Mark again. He had offered to help her find the origin of the gun and to give her whatever practical help she needed. But he was also offering her something else. Something that Kat, at this moment in time, didn't feel able to articulate. Call it friendship for now.

She met Patricia's eyes and realised that more than one relationship was shifting. She couldn't tell this woman, who she would have said she trusted with the most intimate of secrets, that Mark was helping her on a personal level. It was too much. She needed help managing her professional life. Her personal one would have to wait for another time.

'What are you thinking about?'

She made for safer ground. 'About something that happened to me on the way here.' No need for obfuscation over this. She reached into her bag and brought out the smaller plastic one. 'The boy who brought me the gun. I saw him again today on the way here. I'm not sure if he was waiting for me. Or following me. Or what. But when he disappeared, he left this.' She shrugged out the blouse. Again she felt the needle of discomfort. Why was this shirt doing this to her?

Patricia leant forward. 'May I?'

'Of course.' She passed the shirt to Patricia, who examined it closely. 'It's silk, I think. Is it Lena's?'

Kat frowned. 'I'm not sure. It's possible, I suppose. I've not seen her wearing it though. It smells mouldy. As if it's been kept in damp drawers.'

She thought of her house. That was damp enough to

produce the smell on the garment, but what was the blouse doing on a park bench opposite?

Patricia handed the shirt back to her. 'You were given, from this boy, first a gun and then a silk shirt. Do you think it's him who is sending you these items, or are they coming from Lena? Or from someone else, possibly?'

'I don't know. If the boy's to be believed, he knows Lena, but what would he want with a silk blouse? It must be from Lena. It's like she . . .'

'Like she's what?' prompted Patricia.

'It's like she's giving me a message.'

32

A rap on his door caused Llewellyn to put down his pen and sigh. He'd deliberately shut the door, giving Margaret strict instructions not to let anyone through. It was his secretary who put her head around the door. 'I'm going out to get a cappuccino from the new place across the road. I'll be five minutes. Brenda's sitting at the desk while I'm gone. Do you want one?'

Llewellyn reached into his trouser pockets. 'How many shots do they put in a large cup?'

'Two I think.'

'Can you get them to stick an extra one in?'

'Need a pick-me-up?'

'I need something to help me get through this, certainly.'

For the first time that Llewellyn could remember, his secretary looked uncertain, like she wanted to say something. 'Come in, Margaret, and shut the door.'

She did as she was told and stood with her back to the closed door.

Llewellyn tapped the report. 'How much do you know?'

'I helped gather the files last year. When it all started. I didn't like it. Going behind people's backs.'

'But the files weren't in this building were they? You'd have gone to the records office.'

'I still had to lie when I was there. I didn't like it.'

'No.' Llewellyn removed the finger that was keeping his

place and inserted a slip of paper to mark the page. 'Did you see the files?'

'Only to check that they were the ones I needed.'

'But you know the substance of them.'

Margaret nodded. She looked like she wanted to escape the room.

'It'll come out soon enough, Margaret. It's better this way.'

'It's not it coming out that I have a problem with. It's that it happened in the first place.'

Llewellyn rubbed his hands over his face. 'I can't do anything about that. I can only deal with the doable.'

'I'm sorry. It's not really any of my business. I really should go and get that coffee. Brenda has other things she should be getting on with.'

Llewellyn nodded. 'Fine. Remember about that extra shot.'

She turned to go.

'And Margaret. It really *is* your business.'

33

Sadler was on the way out of the station when he heard footsteps running behind him. It must be Connie. Only she ran at
him like this. Palmer played it far too cool to come charging at
him. Sure enough, he saw her petite figure round the corner.

'Sir.' She was panting and had to bend double to get back
her breath. 'We've got an ID on the body. A Stephanie Alton
from Shallowford House. Palmer's interviewing the manager at
the moment to get more background info. See if we can link
her in any way to the Andrew Fisher case.'

'What do you think are our chances?'

Connie scuffed her feet on the floor. 'Difficult to say. Something's not right. From what I heard at the hostel, Stephanie
Alton had various problems, but these have been ongoing for
a few years. A bit strange she suddenly decides to top herself
now.'

'Did the manager have any idea what might have prompted
this?'

'Not really. Stephanie had been more subdued recently but
nothing that rang any alarm bells inside Shallowford House.
I'd swear that Julia Miles, that's the manager, is pretty shocked
about what has happened.'

'Does she have any family?'

'There's a daughter. Her name's Mary, and she lives in
Bampton. She's a teenager but old enough to live on her own.

We're trying to track her down.'

Sadler turned to go. 'Keep me updated, would you? I need to leave earlyish today. I've got a family appointment.'

Connie looked at her watch. 'It's gone six. Not exactly early.'

'It is for me.' He left her in the station car park looking slightly disconsolate and had to quell the sense of irritation that he felt.

It took him a quarter of an hour instead of the usual five minutes to drive to his sister Camilla's house. It was market day, and the stalls were gradually packing up and clogging the roads with their vans and four-by-fours. It had been months since Sadler had found the time to visit the place. He relied on the local supermarket, and he briefly wondered what the bland food was doing to his body.

Camilla lived with her family in a large Victorian semi-detached house on the outskirts of Bampton. Superficially, the house was similar to that of the Gray sisters. They would certainly have been built around the same time. They had the same imposing proportions and sense of solidity but Camilla's house was a well-maintained family home. As Sadler drew up, he could hear the screams of his nephews in the front room.

His sister answered the door. 'They're going stir-crazy in there. Roll on the summer when I can throw them outside.' One of the boys, seven-year-old Ben, ran up to Sadler and threw his arms around his waist. The other, Samuel, twelve, was more cautious and hung around in the doorway looking embarrassed.

'Uncle Francis. Do you want to see my new Lego?' Ben grabbed him by the hand and pulled him into the living room, which was strewn with the hard plastic pieces.

'Don't take your shoes off,' warned his sister through the door. 'It'll take your feet weeks to recover.'

Behind the living-room door, a woman was sitting on the sofa, assembling a Lego model. It looked like a spaceship. She looked up and smiled as Sadler entered. 'I don't remember anything as exciting as spaceships when I was younger. Although I think my brother had a petrol station.'

Sadler wondered if it was by chance that this woman was sitting in the living room when he had told his sister earlier that day that he would be coming around. Camilla continually fretted about his single status, and he had rebuffed any matchmaking overtures she had suggested. It was hardly likely to be this woman's fault, though. He smiled at her. 'Hi. I'm Francis.'

'He's Uncle Francis.' Ben danced around the living room.

Samuel looked grave. 'He's a policeman.'

A look of alarm flashed across the woman's face before disappearing. 'In Bampton?'

'Yes. You live there?' He sat down next to her and let Ben climb into his lap. His nephew handed him a model, three wheels stuck together at improbable angles and a wing added to the confusing melee.

'I used to. I live in Manchester now. It's easier for work. I'm a solicitor in a law firm there.'

'Criminal law?'

'No, corporate. Not very exciting, I'm afraid.'

So her job hadn't been the reason for her look of consternation, thought Sadler. 'How do you know Camilla?'

'Through her work with the Early Birth Trust. She was at a fund-raising event in Manchester, and we vaguely recognised each other. She asked if I was originally from Bampton, and

I said I was. You know how insular this place can be. For a decent-sized town there's not much people don't know about each other.'

Sadler wasn't so sure about this. Bampton had grown from its market-town origins to a place of tourism and business. He could go for weeks without recognising anyone in the street. Perhaps it was different for women.

He looked at her more closely. Camilla was involved with the Early Birth Trust because she had lost a baby at twenty-three weeks. A girl. He had gone to see the tiny child in hospital, and, even then, they knew there was little hope of survival. Ellie had lain in this huge incubator like a little sparrow, and he hadn't dared touch her, even though he'd wanted to more than anything else in the world. Even now, with these two rambunctious nephews, he thought often about Ellie and her short life. Her tiny moment in this world had been as blessed as the lives of his nephews. For the first time, Sadler wondered how often Camilla thought of her daughter.

'I'm Anna, by the way.'

Anna had fair hair pulled back from her face into a ponytail and pale skin that wouldn't darken in the sun, only go red. She was dressed casually in blue jeans and a cream cotton shirt. There was a smudge of green down one side. She saw him looking. 'The boys had peas for their lunch. Ben came for a cuddle afterwards.'

'You ratbag.' Sadler tickled his nephew, who squealed with gap-toothed delight.

'I've learnt my lesson. I'll be wearing dark colours next time.'

'You don't have children yourself?' He kept his voice casual.

'No. Although I'd like them, I think. Eventually.' She

sounded relaxed as she stood up. 'I really ought to go. Let you spend time with', she shot him a look, 'the ratbags.'

'I'm not a ratbag,' complained Samuel from the floor. He was cross-legged in front of the TV and flicking randomly.

'Do you need to sit so close, Sam?' Camilla came back into the room. 'Are you going?' she asked Anna.

'I think I ought to. It's an hour back into Manchester. I've probably missed the worst of the traffic though.'

Sadler nodded goodbye to the woman and started to disassemble the Lego contraption his nephew had given him. When he heard the front door shut, he lifted his nephew onto the sofa and walked into the kitchen where his sister was peeling potatoes.

'Mash all right? It's Sam's favourite, and he's been a bit grumpy recently. I think it's pre-adolescence. I've got all that to look forward to. His teenage years, I mean.'

'Anna said she met you at an EBT event.'

'Yes. Her company's been pretty good. We were their chosen charity for last year. They raised over ten grand for us. One of the partners lost a child last year. I think that's why we were chosen.'

Sadler watched her put the potatoes into a saucepan and turn on the heat.

She turned to him. 'What did you think of Anna?'

He shrugged. 'Nice.'

'Just nice?'

'Actually, yes. Just nice.'

Camilla sighed. 'You go for the wrong type, that's your problem. Unavailable women, for a start, like Christina.'

But Sadler didn't want to talk about the married woman

he'd been seeing previously. He adjusted the lid of the saucepan. 'Do you often think of Ellie?' He glanced up and saw that his sister's eyes were filled with tears.

'Think of her? I don't need to think of her. She's with me all the time. What a bloody stupid question, Francis. You men really have no idea.'

And she shoved him out of the kitchen.

34

After leaving Patricia's house, Kat returned to her silent consulting room to wait for her next client. She was early and, as she sat in silence, could feel the heavy weight of misery descend on her. If she'd been the religious type, she'd have offered up a prayer to whatever God there was, asking for help.

She'd been given two 'gifts', if that's what you wanted to call them. The gun was now with the police. Patricia had teased out of her that there might be a message associated with the presents but what could it be? Could Lena be saying, 'Here is the gun that I shot my husband with?' If so, then her sister was a murderer. Possibly twice over.

Then there was the second gift of a blouse. More innocuous but also more perplexing. It had come via the same boy. Of this Kat had no doubt, but why would Lena be giving her the present of a blouse? There was a resonance to the garment, but Kat couldn't put her finger on it.

A noise outside the front door made her jump, and she got up and went to the window. It was just the movement of one of the other businesses shutting up for the day. A short woman with a riot of blonde curls was taking in a sandwich board for her dressmaking business. Kat watched as she heaved the heavy wood through the narrow door and then came back to pick up the rack of silk scarves that she left outside when it wasn't raining. Against the darkening sky, the scarves waved gently in the wind.

The silk reminded her of the blouse in her bag. Kat racked her brains trying to remember the name of the woman across the way. It began with a T. Tana, Tara? They hadn't spoken since the time of the power cut last month.

She went to her front door and opened it, startling the woman. 'Hi. Sorry for making you jump. I just wanted a quick favour. Can I ask you something?'

The woman smiled. 'Of course. Is everything all right?'

'Well, I've got a bit of a mystery. I could do with some help. It's confidential . . . ' Kat let her voice trail off, and the woman nodded understandingly. She clearly thought it was something to do with one of Kat's clients. Kat felt a pang of guilt, which she quickly quelled. In the general scheme of things, this minor lie hardly counted. 'I've got a yellow silk blouse here. No label, I'm afraid. I wondered if you could have a look at it for me? See what it says to you?'

'I'll certainly try.'

Kat suddenly remembered the woman's name. Terri.

Terri took the blouse with a professional air and examined it, first by opening it out fully and then examining the stitching. 'Where did you get this?' she asked, handing it back to Kat.

'I'm sorry about the smell. It's probably been lying in a drawer for a while.'

'A long while,' smiled Terri. 'I used to have one of those myself at the end of the eighties. During my Madonna phase. You remember? Silk shirt, black leggings. I think I even had a black hat to complete the outfit.'

With a jolt, Kat did remember. Both she and Lena had

dressed like that. She remembered an emerald-green silk shirt that she'd worn over leggings with black gym pumps. No hat though. She clearly hadn't been as fashionable as Terri. 'You think it dates from back then? The late eighties?'

'Smells like it does.' The woman smiled. 'It's the sleeves that give it away. The cut of the body could be from any time but look how the sleeves are designed: narrow at the shoulders, puffing out at the elbows and back in at the cuffs. When did you last see a blouse looking like that?'

Now that Kat looked, she could see what Terri meant. There was a dated feel to the garment, but she wouldn't have been able to pinpoint what it was. 'Why's there no label?'

Terri shrugged. 'It's not home-made. The stitching is professional enough. Sold at a market, I'd guess.'

As teenagers, Kat and Lena had often bought their clothes from one of the stalls in the Bampton market. Could this blouse be one of them? It's something she might have worn. In fact, they had swapped clothes during that time. 'You definitely think this is from the eighties?'

'It's eighties style, certainly. It might have been designed retro, but the smell . . . ' She let her voice trail off.

Kat grimaced at the dank odour emanating from the cloth. With a smile of thanks she went back inside to think.

35

Mary Alton looked like her mother. Tall, with long limbs, she was dressed in faded jeans and a floral shirt that hung off her thin frame. Connie looked up at the clock. Eight o'clock. Those with normal jobs would be home, having a glass of wine with their partners. Discussing the day's events and settling into a relaxed evening. Here she was in a dreary interview room with a grieving daughter.

The girl was wearing a lot of make-up that had smudged with recent tears. Perhaps she'd been on her way out when she was informed of her mother's death. Her brown eyes were ringed with thick black eyeliner, and her eyelashes stood to attention in a row of spikes interspersed with glittering tears. The intensity of her gaze on Connie contrasted with her pink frosted lips, which were turned down in a sulky expression.

'You needn't have come here. You could have gone back home to your flat after visiting the mortuary. I'd have happily spoken to you there.'

The family-liaison officer who'd brought Mary into the station and who was sitting in the interview room looked like she wanted to say something. To justify her actions. But Connie had already been brought up to speed by the duty sergeant. The girl had been informed of her mother's death, had insisted on seeing her body and had then refused to go back to her flat. She wanted to be interviewed at the station.

Mary looked at her nails. The varnish appeared recently applied. 'I hate my flat. It's like a prison. It's a shoebox. Mum and I wanted to move in together somewhere. Like the old times. We were waiting to see what the Council could come up with.'

Connie frowned. 'Are you working, Mary?'

The girl shook her head. 'I'm on the social at the moment. There's only part-time stuff around at this time of year. It's not worth my while coming off benefits. I'm waiting for the summer. Last year, I got a job in a gift shop selling tat. They've said they might take me on again come July. When the kids are off school.'

Nineteen years old. In the prime of her life, and it wasn't worth her while coming off government support. Connie shook the thought away. Not her job to judge. 'You were close to your mum?'

Mary looked defiant. 'She'd had a hard life. It's not easy bringing up a child by yourself, and she did a pretty good job.'

Connie massaged her head. The words sounded formulaic, an oft-repeated mantra that had become second nature. 'Didn't you spend some time in care?'

The girl winced but kept eye contact. 'Only now and then. Usually only for a few weeks at a foster place. When she couldn't cope.'

'How long was your mum at Shallowford House?'

'About a year. Things got bad again, and she went there to get help with her problems. I couldn't go. I was too old. So they found me that shoebox to live in.'

'Julia Miles, the manager at Shallowford, says that your mum had been doing better recently.'

Mary Alton once more inspected her nails.

'Mary?'

'It was always like that with Mum. Sometimes she'd be okay. She taught me to drive last year. I passed my test first time. Then other times she got really down. Couldn't be bothered with anything. Angry with everyone, including herself.'

'When did you last see her?'

The girl hesitated. 'About two days ago. We met in town and had a coffee.'

'And how did she seem?'

'Okay. We talked about the usual stuff. Me finding a job and her looking for a flat for us. Nothing out of the ordinary.'

'She didn't seem depressed?'

'No more than usual. Did she kill herself? I've been told she was found in the river.'

Connie looked across to the family-liaison officer. 'We're waiting for a few more tests. I'll let you know the cause of death as soon as it's confirmed. I'm sorry I can't be any more specific than that. Do you think your mother was suicidal?'

'I don't know.'

'There's one thing though. The news is beginning to leak out. It's on Twitter that a body was found down by the mill, and the local press have picked up the story. The more reputable sites won't mention your mother's name until we confirm the identity of the body but we can't control what gets put online. Is there anywhere else you can go? Apart from your flat.'

The girl shook her head. 'Back to the shoebox.'

Connie rapidly typed up the notes of the interview and left copies on Sadler's and Palmer's desks for next week. She didn't mind working late on a Friday night if it got the paperwork out of the way.

The station was quiet. She could hear footsteps at the other end of the corridor, but the CID room was silent.

A voice behind her made her jump. 'I'll be off then.'

Connie swivelled around in her chair. The family-liaison officer was belting up her coat, holding a set of car keys between her teeth.

'How was she? When you dropped her off?'

'She seemed a bit subdued, but that's not surprising. Probable suicide is one of the causes of death that I hate working with. It leaves the relatives completely dumbstruck. They have to live with the "whys" for the rest of their lives.'

Connie picked up her own coat. 'Funny she didn't want us to go to her flat. What was it like?'

The other woman shrugged. 'Small.'

36

Monday morning, Palmer and Sadler sat with Connie's interview notes in front of them. Palmer had also arrived early and
had telephoned Julia Miles for some additional information.
It all tallied with Mary's account. 'Stephanie Alton left school
at sixteen and went to work in a card shop in Bampton town
centre. Her employment record was mainly in retail. A series
of jobs in Bampton's small shops. None held down for a long
period of time.'

'Any reasons given for her leaving her work?' asked Sadler.

'I'd guess a mix of personal circumstance and her addiction
problems. According to Ms Miles, she became pregnant in her
twenties and was given a flat in a housing-association development. After eight years, she fell behind on rent payments and
was eventually evicted. She doesn't seem to have been working
at that time.'

'And a history of substance misuse?'

'Mainly alcohol and codeine, which seems to have been fed
by easy access via the Internet. It was only in the past year that
she had made a serious attempt to clean up. And, according to
Julia Miles, she'd been largely successful.'

Sadler picked up Connie's report. 'The daughter seems to
have had a clear-eyed view of her mother's problems. She hints
at frequent relapses.'

'Ms Miles seems uncertain why Stephanie suddenly started

drinking again. But it's not that unusual. The demon never leaves you, apparently.'

'That it? So, according to Bill, it's a clear case of suicide. No marks to suggest she'd entered the water involuntarily.'

Palmer frowned. 'So not worth us bothering about?'

'I didn't say that. When's Connie coming in?'

Palmer shrugged and repressed the stab of jealousy that he felt when the DC's name was mentioned. He was her superior. So why couldn't Sadler discuss anything important without her being present too? He twisted around and looked through the window into the CID room. 'She's not at her desk.'

Sadler sighed. 'Any connection whatsoever with Andrew Fisher?'

'None that I can see, sir, although she's a similar age to Lena and Kat. As well as Andrew Fisher, come to think of it. They may have bumped into each other socially.'

'It's possible.' Sadler didn't look convinced. 'I'm the same age as the sisters and I certainly hadn't met them before the investigation in 2004. What else did Ms Miles say?'

'She gave us quite a lot of background on Steph. It's a sad story really. The only possible lead is there's a man Stephanie used to talk about a lot. A "Philip Staley". Said he'd ruined her life. Possibly worth looking into? It could be a love affair gone wrong.'

Sadler nodded. 'Her daughter didn't mention him, did she? But if he's her absent father, that's not surprising. Look into it but don't spend too long on this, will you? There's a possibility it's a dead end, a strong possibility, and we don't have time to waste.'

'Of course.'

Palmer left the office and saw Connie breeze in. 'Where've you been?'

She looked up at the clock. 'It's only five past nine. That's normal starting time for most people, you know.'

'Having a lie-in then?'

She picked up a paper cup from a nearby desk and threw it across the room at him. He ducked, but not before drips of water settled on his suit jacket. 'Bloody hell, Connie.'

'Whoops, sorry.' She didn't sound it as she slid behind her desk. 'Any news?'

'I'm doing a final check on Stephanie Alton. It's probably nothing.'

She looked across at him. 'Bit boring that. Surprised the boss didn't give it to me.'

'Well, he did wonder where you were.'

She looked up. 'Really? Shit, Palmer. What did you tell him?'

'I told him I didn't know. Which I didn't.'

'Are you two going to shout across the office at each other all day?' An irritated voice from another detective got them smirking at each other.

Connie got up and walked across to Palmer's desk. She cleared some papers and then sat on it, swinging her legs. 'How's married life?'

'It's okay.'

'Just okay? That's hardly the greatest advert for matrimonial bliss.'

'It's not that much different from being engaged, to be honest.'

'Does Joanne feel the same way?'

'I'm not sure.'

'I saw her the other day. On the street. She stopped to say hello. It looked like she'd been doing some shopping.'

Palmer rolled his eyes.

'She asked where you were.'

'Me?' He looked angry. 'What business is it of hers where I am during working hours?'

'Innocent enough enquiry.'

Palmer tried to swallow his irritation. It was natural enough for Connie to side with another female, but he wanted her on his side. Her robust attitude was what he needed now in contrast to Joanne's neediness. Her eyes were on him, but he couldn't read her expression. 'She wants us to try for a baby.'

'Bloody hell.' Connie slid off the desk. 'That'll be the end of your night's sleep. Is that what you want?'

'What? A baby?'

'Yes, idiot. A baby. Is that what you want?'

She was standing completely still and he felt the sudden need to confess. 'No.'

37

The chill of Providence Villa hit Kat as soon as she pushed open the door. 'Lena?' She'd shouted for her sister every time she entered the house since the day she went missing. Kat was still convinced that her sister's absence was voluntary. Which meant that she could, if she wanted, return home.

But silence was all that met her.

Her first client wasn't due at her rooms until two, which had given her the time to fit in a trip to the local shops to get some provisions. She took them through to the kitchen but couldn't face putting them away immediately. Instead, she made herself a coffee and took it up to Lena's room.

The bedroom was large, bare and neat. The wooden floor-boards, snarled by age and with huge gaps from which balls of fluff constantly appeared, were covered with two blue striped rugs from IKEA. Kat had made a special trip to the store when she'd heard that Lena was coming out of prison. The gesture had gone unremarked. The white walls were unadorned with the exception of a small simple icon above the bed. None of Lena's paintings were in the room. It hadn't changed since she'd entered it that first morning of Lena's disappearance.

Kat went over to the chest of drawers and opened it. The clothes inside, woollen jumpers and plain T-shirts, were neatly folded. Kat sniffed slightly. There was no smell of damp. She pulled open the wardrobe and again breathed in the air. A little fusty, possibly, but nothing to match the rancid smell of that blouse.

Where else could Lena have kept the thing? The cellars were dank and uninhabitable. She and Lena had made the decision earlier that year to close them off and leave them empty. They'd had a clear-out of what detritus was down there, and that had been that. No cloth would have survived those conditions. There was an attic, of sorts, above Kat's bedroom. A largish room that opened out over the west gable. But it had been years since Kat had gone up there.

She heard a rap on the front door and groaned. Surely not the police. She couldn't face them again so soon. She pulled the door shut and made her way down to the hall. When she opened the front door, she saw that it was Mark.

'No news, I'm afraid. I just came around to see how you are.'

He looked like he hadn't slept over the week-end. Dark shadows swept arcs under his eyes, and the scar on his cheek was an angry red.

'Are you okay?'

'Of course. Why do you ask?' He sounded surprised.

'You look, well, tired.'

She let him in but was at a loss what to say or where to take him. 'Coffee?'

He laughed and shook his head. 'When in doubt, offer me coffee. No, thanks. Anyway, I can tell you've just had one. I can smell it on your breath.'

She felt her cheeks burning and turned away in case he spotted her confusion.

'I've got a bit of a mystery for you.' She went to her handbag and showed him the blouse. 'The boy who gave me the gun had another present for me. He left it on the park bench opposite here.'

Mark took it from her and frowned. 'I don't like the idea of him following you. How do you know he's connected to Lena? He might be acting by himself.' His nose wrinkled with distaste. 'What's the smell?'

'I've got a horrible feeling that it comes from this house. I think the blouse might once have been mine. Or perhaps Lena's. When we were teenagers we were forever borrowing each other's clothes. Often without asking. It would cause no end of arguments.'

'For God's sake, Kat. Why would she leave a rancid blouse for you to try and guess its meaning?'

'I don't know, but I do know where to look. Are you scared of the dark?'

He looked at her with amusement. 'No. Of course not.'

'Why "of course"?' she retorted.

'I was in the army for eight years. Have you any idea what training we go through? It takes more than the dark to scare me.'

'Come with me.' She forced herself to resist the temptation to hold his hand. She led him upstairs, as far as her bedroom, but didn't open the door. Instead, she pointed to the hatch in the ceiling of the landing. 'That's the attic. If this blouse has come from anywhere in this house, it'll have been from up there.'

He looked at her in amusement. 'Do you have a ladder? Or are you expecting to give me a leg-up?'

'There's a ladder attached to the hatch. It's ancient and I'm not sure where to find the pole to push up the board to let it down.'

He pulled his arm away from her and looked around. Seeing the door of her bedroom, he pushed it open and came out with the wicker chair she used to throw her clothes over. He stood on the chair and pushed up the board. Then, to Kat's astonishment, he grabbed hold of the two sides of the opening and swung himself up into the void.

'Were you in the circus in a previous life?' she shouted up into the now-empty space.

'Army training,' came a faint voice from above. 'Is there a light up here?'

'Yes, the switch is actually on the floor to the left of the opening. It's not very bright but it will show you something.'

She saw the light come on.

'Good, good. Have you any idea what's up here? Hang on. I'm sending the steps down to you.'

A flash of steel and the ladder descended in front of her.

'It's coming down a lot easier than I expected.' Mark peered at her. 'I'm pretty sure someone's been in this loft recently. You coming up?'

Kat stepped onto the metal gingerly, but the ladder held as she made her way up. The attic had been boarded years earlier, without any great skill, but enough to support the pile of unwanted things that their parents had hoisted up there.

Mark stood in the middle of heaps of cases, cardboard boxes and black bin bags. He had his hands on his hips and was staring around in mock despair. 'What exactly are we looking for?'

Kat crouched down and started rifling through cardboard boxes. 'I'm looking for photographs. Anything to give me a clue why that blouse is so familiar.'

38

'Andrew Fisher was a big fat liar.'

Sadler, on his way through the office, stopped by Connie's desk. 'Why?'

She waved a sheaf of papers at him. 'I've been looking at his CV. A lot of hype and one big, fat stinker of a lie. It says here that he has an MBA from Cranfield University. I've checked, and he has no such thing. He says he got it in 1996. I've gone ten years either way and there's nothing doing. Liar.' She slapped the papers down on the desk.

'Do you think that's significant?'

'I'm not sure, but it tells us what kind of guy he was. You were at school with him. What was he like then?'

'A rugby player. Liked drink. Girls.'

Connie's look was sour. 'Rugby players. You know he was the same build as our first victim. If they knew each other, do you think it might have been through rugby?'

'Possibly. Do you have anything particular against rugby players? They're not necessarily a bunch of louts, you know.'

'I came up against a gang of them when I first joined the force. I was policing one of the matches. They said something about my "knockers".' Connie's look had changed into a martyred air.

Sadler could hear Palmer laughing into his coffee.

Connie was looking down at her chest. 'I don't actually have that much to comment on. I was surprised.'

'Fishing for compliments?' asked Palmer.

Sadler backed away. It was probably best if he left them to it while they were in this mood. They certainly seemed on friendlier terms than they had been in the past few weeks.

*

Llewellyn's secretary was typing rapidly and only looked up for a brief minute. 'You can go straight in. He's waiting for you.'

Llewellyn was reading a report. His glasses were on the tip of his nose, and he was squinting at the print, frowning in concentration. 'Ah, Sadler. I've got the results from Ballistics. I'm reading the fine print and I'd like you to study it too because it makes interesting reading. Ballistics have proved that the 9mm bullets extracted from Andrew Fisher's body were shot from the Luger that was sent to Kat Gray. Is *anyone* German in this case?'

'Not that I'm aware, but I heard once that Lugers are a form of trophy gun. Lots of them were taken off captured and killed German soldiers. In both wars. And then brought back.'

Llewellyn grunted. 'It says the same thing here. They're pretty good guns. Got an excellent reputation.' He put down the report. 'My dad was a copper. Did you know?' Sadler shook his head. 'He never got beyond sergeant. Never wanted to. But he looked like a copper. All right, Sadler, I know I do too. He was a giant of a man. All the boys in the village were scared of him. When he was roused, he'd take the belt off his trousers, ready to strap them. Different times then.' He glanced at Sadler. 'Anyway. He was a man with plenty of stories. He used to keep all his family and friends entertained with them. You know what the countryside's like. There were some strange tales, you know.'

Sadler did know. His own mother had been brought up in the adjacent village to Llewellyn's. She too could tell some interesting tales.

'Well, anyway. I remember him telling me about an incident in the village. It must have happened in the 1960s. A farm labourer holed himself up in one of the cottages with a rifle. Drunk, of course, and had his girlfriend and a baby inside as hostages.'

Sadler shifted in his chair. A story he hadn't heard before.

'So there was a bit of a stand-off, and the official police gun then was the Smith & Wesson, and only a few sergeants had been trained in their use. Which was a bit daft as it wasn't that long after the war. All the coppers knew how to shoot. So, before going to the village, they all went to their homes and came back with the guns they kept in their houses: hunting rifles and an assortment of pistols. It was a sight to be seen apparently. There were Lugers too. My dad said it was a beautiful gun.'

'What happened? I mean, to the hostages?'

Llewellyn shrugged. 'I can't remember. The reason I'm telling you this, Sadler, is that, believe me, there are a lot of old guns knocking around this place if you care to look for them. So you've got your work cut out for you. However, according to this report, this Luger was a First World War model. I won't go into it now. You can read it yourself. Do you think that's why Hale's End was used for the killing?'

Sadler was flicking through the report. 'I don't know. The building was used by the Canadian regiments mainly. I can't see any connection, apart from the war, obviously, but the fact that Kat Gray was sent the gun does have a positive side.'

Llewellyn nodded. 'If the person who used the gun is the person who sent it to her, then that suggests that they have no further use for it.'

'There won't be any more deaths,' said Sadler.

'I should bloody well hope there won't be. How many more bodies do we want in Bampton?'

Sadler raised his hands. 'I'm saying it because it means that it's Andrew Fisher who was meant to be killed. The killer got the right person.'

'Got the right person the second time around, you mean. Have you made any more progress on the first victim?'

Sadler shook his head. 'Not yet. We've got so little to go on and we've been distracted by the body at Fearnley Mill. Although maybe that's the wrong word. She might not be a distraction at all.'

'You think she's connected to all this?'

Sadler thought of the woman he had seen in the river, her resemblance to Lena and Kat, and the manner of her death. 'Yes. I do.'

39

It was Mark who found the photo. He had looked grimly through all the old family shots. His own fractured family life must have been a huge contrast to the shots of Kat and Lena and their parents. At the beach. Having picnics.

It didn't last, she wanted to tell him. We were close, and then we weren't.

He'd been focused in his search. Childhood photos had been quickly passed over in favour of teenage snaps, and these he'd studied with care. It was he who had discovered the one with the mustard blouse. Lena had been wearing it.

They'd taken the box of photos down to the kitchen table and were studying the snap.

'Don't you remember?' he asked. Curious.

She didn't. Some clothes she did remember. The paisley silk shirt with the long tails that she had worn over a black pencil skirt. Perhaps because it had lasted for years, surviving numerous washes. She could still feel the softness of the material against her skin. She'd finally chucked it when the background was more grey than white.

'She looks a lot like you.' Mark was studying the image. 'Except her face is a slightly different shape. You've hardly changed at all, Kat. Is there a painting up there that's ageing while you stay forever young?'

Kat smiled, pleased. He was leaning in close to her, and

she could smell his skin.

'Who's this?' Mark was pointing to a third girl in the photo.

Kat peered at the photo. The three of them were standing inside the hall of Providence Villa, arms wrapped around each other. The picture had probably been taken before they went out. They'd often done that. Spent hours putting on their make-up and teasing their permed hair into the gelled licks that had been fashionable then. They could have been in a pop band, they were so similarly dressed. Lena had a pair of black leggings under the hateful blouse while she was wearing a scarlet top over what looked like a long, stretchy dress. The third girl had on a white blouse and a short pleated skirt. 'It's a friend. There were a few of us that used to go out together.'

'Are you still in touch with her?'

Kat shrugged. 'When I went to university, I lost touch with a lot of friends. Most of them, in fact.'

'Can you remember who this is? She's in this picture of Lena wearing the blouse. It may be her sending you the messages.'

'Of course I remember. Her name was Stephanie. Stephanie Alton. She was a friend of Lena's. Not from school though. From her Saturday job in the florist's. Steph worked in another shop nearby, and that's where she and Lena met.'

'What did you say her name was?' Mark's voice was harsh again, the same tone she'd heard in the counselling room when she showed him the gun.

'Steph. Stephanie Alton. What's the matter?'

'There's a rumour that someone of that name's dead. It's all about town. Didn't you know that a body was found down by Fearnley Mill?

155

'No! It's Steph?' Kat sat down gingerly on a chair. 'Are you sure?'

'I don't think it's been officially confirmed but the lads in the pub last night mentioned a name. Steph Alton. I'm sure that it was.'

'How did she die?'

'I don't know. Have the police contacted you?'

Kat shook her head. 'Thank God it's not Lena.'

'I suppose it's a good thing they haven't been to see you.' Mark was scrutinising the photo. 'They're not connecting the case with you. Yet.'

'You think someone might have killed her?'

'I don't know, but I don't like the fact she's dead just after Lena disappeared. This doesn't look good. You need to pack a bag. This boy knows where you live. I don't want you here by yourself. I'm worried about you.'

'But what about Charlie?'

'Charlie?'

'The cat.'

The look on Mark's face was resigned. 'Then Charlie had better come too, hadn't he?'

40

Philip Staley's mother lived in a dingy terrace in Maccles-field. Because of thick fog, it had taken Connie over an hour to drive over the hill known to locals as the 'Cat and Fiddle' because of the pub perched on top of the moor. It was a dangerous stretch of road at the best of times, but the thick fog had slowed her car to a crawl. Her drive wasn't helped by the idiots trying to overtake her. It was with relief that she finally made her way down the hill into the town centre.

Janice Staley was around eighty, with sharp eyes in a wrinkled brown face. The house smelt of fried food and stale smoke. 'I've got the chip pan on. Eric's due home at five. He likes his tea straight away as he's hungry by then.'

'Eric is ...'

'My son. My other son. He works in the plastics factory up on the industrial estate. He likes it. Regular income and so on. On the phone you were asking about Philip.'

Her face had an impenetrable look that had Connie's in-stincts on high alert. She would need to ask the right questions. By the look of things, here was a mother ready to protect her son. 'His name's come up in an investigation and we just wanted to ask him some questions.'

'What kind of investigation?' Janice demanded.

'A woman's body has been found. Suicide,' Connie hastily

added. 'But we think she might have been friendly with your son.' This was stretching the truth somewhat given that Philip Staley was supposed to have ruined Stephanie's life.

'When did she die?'

'Last week.'

The woman's face relaxed slightly. 'Then it's nothing to do with Philip. He emigrated to Australia.'

'Emigrated?'

'That's right. He was talking about it for a while. Wanted permanent sunshine. He used to spend too long on the sun-beds, he liked having a nice tan.'

'Do you have a picture of him, Mrs Staley?'

The woman frowned. 'Of course I have a picture of him. He's my son.'

Connie bit back the retort on her lips. 'Do you have anything recent? Perhaps a photo?'

She had hit a nerve. Janice's mouth settled into a thin line. 'I've not had sight nor sound from him since he emigrated, the ungrateful little beggar.'

'Ungrateful?'

'I lent him five hundred quid for the ticket. Put the money straight into his bank account. He called me up. Could I lend him the money for the airfare. Five hundred pounds. I'm not rich. It was everything I had.'

'He never said why he was leaving?' The blood was beginning to stir in Connie.

'The last I heard from him was when he called to say he'd received the money and he'd ring again when he got there. Ungrateful little sod. I never heard from him after that. He'll call again some day. Probably when he wants more cash.'

'Is that normal? I mean, not to hear from him for long periods of time?'

'Normal? What's normal for kids these days? The problem with Philip was that he could never settle at anything. Tried all sorts of jobs but he'd leave after six months. Get bored and then he was off. He went all over the place. Nottingham, Swansea, London.'

'So when was it exactly that Philip emigrated?' *Could this be the breakthrough that we need?* thought Connie.

'Quite a few years ago.'

This time Connie couldn't hide the sigh. 'When you say "quite a few years", how many exactly do you mean?'

'I can't remember.' The woman folded her arms.

Time for a change of tack, thought Connie. She leaned forward. 'Mrs Staley. We're worried about the welfare of your son. I'm extremely concerned about the fact that you've not heard from him for a few years. Could you tell me exactly when you last heard from him?'

'August 2004,' said Janice promptly.

Connie exhaled a long breath. *Well, bloody hell*, she thought. *Bloody, bloody hell.*

41

'Why are we here?' Kat was standing in a field in the middle of nowhere. Well, that wasn't completely true. They were about ten minutes from the old Macclesfield road. Ten minutes on foot, that was. After depositing Charlie and her suitcase at his house, Mark had taken her out in the car up onto the Moor. When he had parked up at a lay-by, for a heart-stopping moment, Kat had felt fear. Perhaps her instincts about her client, or, rather, former client, had been wrong.

Then Mark had turned to her and said, 'I want to show you something.' And so they had tramped along no known path to this spot. All Kat had to distinguish the ground from the rest of the bleak landscape was the linear indentations that criss-crossed underneath her feet. 'Where are we? What are we doing here?'

He was looking around him. 'A mate told me about here. He's ex-forces too. Obsessed with the First World War. He knows all about this area. Hale's End too.'

Kat groaned. 'Don't mention Hale's End to me.'

He turned to her. 'Why not mention it? It's where your brother-in-law was found killed.'

'But that's nothing to do with me, is it?'

'But why Hale's End?'

'I don't know. Why have you brought me out here to ask me all this?'

'Because here's somewhere neutral for us. Not my house or yours. And not the consulting room. A neutral place, but relevant. Where do you think we're standing?'

'In the middle of the moors.'

He moved towards her and put his arm around her shoulder. 'Right. But look at your feet. What do you see?'

She peered down. 'There are a load of indentations in the ground. Like lines.'

'Very good. It's where something has been infilled. Look at the shape of the lines? What do they look like? Connected to the war. The First World War?'

Kat stepped away to get a wider view of the ground. Suddenly the fog in her mind cleared. 'They look like trenches.'

He beamed at her. 'Excellent. That's exactly what they are. Former trenches.'

'You're kidding. Why are there trenches in Derbyshire?'

'We're not sure. Experts think that they were maybe used for training exercises. The Coal Board found them in the eighties when they were surveying the land.'

Kat crouched down and touched one of the indented lines with her hands. 'We're a long way from the fields of France here.'

'Geographically, yes. But men who were going off to fight, going off to be killed, they did some kind of training here. Even if it was just to learn how to dig a trench.'

'What's this got to do with me?'

Mark's eyes were on her. 'Think, Kat. I know this is difficult for you, but part of the solution must be something you know. You know your sister better than anyone else, I'm sure. What's the connection to the First World War?'

She looked at him in frustration. 'I swear to you, I have no idea. No one in my family served in that war, as far as I'm aware. Perhaps Hale's End was just a convenient place to put a body.'

'And what about the Luger? That's a German gun and it's old. I reckon easily the same period.'

Kat took a deep breath. 'The only thing I know about that war is what I learnt at school. You know, the poetry and so on. Lena and I weren't into that stuff. It was Dracula and *Top of the Pops* for us.'

Mark drew her to him and put both arms around her. 'Fair enough but I still think the answer lies somewhere in the past.'

Mark dropped her off in Bampton in time for her next client. He seemed reluctant to go to her practice, so she hopped out at the lights and walked the rest of the way. When she put her key into the door she noticed that it was stiff from the recent rain and gave it a kick with her foot to prise it open.

The place smelt damp. The whole of Bampton was clearly going through a fetid phase. She hung her umbrella on a hook and shut the door behind her. When she glanced at the floor, she saw with a jolt the package lying on the inside.

'I don't believe this.' She said it out loud to the empty space. She kicked it gingerly to one side and hurried over to Terri's shop.

Terri was inside, reading a book. 'Have you seen someone go through my door this morning?'

Terri looked confused. 'I haven't seen anyone at all. Is there a problem? Have you had something stolen?'

'Not stolen. It looks like someone dropped something off inside the door. It's just that I've not given my key to anyone.'

'Sorry. I saw nothing.'

Kat made her way back to her rooms. Lena had a key. It was natural to give her sister a key when she came out of prison but she was sure that Lena had put it with the others on the hook in the kitchen. Had she used it to get in? Kat bent down and picked up the package. *Now what do I have to face?*

The package was wrapped in the same way as the gun. While the shirt had been loose in the plastic bag, the one she held in her hand was a thick parcel wrapped up in newspaper. Resisting the temptation to tear at it with her fingers, this time she went to the kitchen to examine it before cutting into it. The newspaper was from the *Observer* – a Sunday paper and Lena's preferred reading choice. Kat squinted at the date. Last week's edition. After Lena had gone missing. This time she got her scissors and cut carefully along the tape.

The object had been wrapped carefully in some kind of thick plastic. Kat carried on cutting. Inside, something glinted. She took it carefully from its casing. It was a gold chain with a small pendant. She laid it out on her palm and saw that it was a dolphin. She took it over to the table where she could examine it in a better light. This time the item was familiar. It had been their mother's.

She remembered the story. When her mother had been training at Guy's Hospital in London in the sixties, she had been a regular visitor to Portobello market. She had spoken sentimentally of those days, before she had met their father and before the daily toll of having their own GP practice had taken the spring from her step. This necklace had been something that she'd cherished. A sign of freedom, the mammal's back arched as it frolicked through water. It wasn't valuable. She'd let the girls play with it, even when they were seven or eight.

But Kat couldn't remember the last time she had seen the necklace, let alone worn it. She weighed the charm in her hand and thought. The gun had no resonance for her. Her rational mind told her that it was connected to the shooting of Andrew and therefore linked to Lena's involvement in the 2004 killing. But it held no deep-seated feeling for her. The shirt too, initially, had held little meaning, but she had been forced to recognise that for Lena it was part of the narrative of their teenage years. Perhaps so too was this dolphin pendant but Kat could only remember wearing it during her childhood. She and Lena had fought over it occasionally. Had Lena, eventually, claimed it as her own?

Possibly.

42

Saturday, 7 April 1990

Kat lounged across one of the large sofas in the living room. Her parents were on week-end call, and they both had been summoned to separate patients. That left her, bored on a dull morning, with the silent Lena. After two terms away at university, she'd hoped that things would have thawed with her sister. Absence makes the heart grow fonder and all that. Fat chance. Lena hadn't even bothered to say hello when she'd come home for the Easter holidays. Kat stuck her headphones in her ears and let the portable CD player whirr as she clicked onto the first track. A movement in the doorway made her start. She pressed pause.

'I'm off.' Lena appeared with an oversized khaki rucksack.

'Where you going?'

'Off to Whitby. I'm not at the shop this weekend, so I thought I'd get away from it all.'

'Lena! I've only just come home. You could spend some time with me.'

Lena said nothing, her features calm. 'You won't miss me. You'll be back at Sheffield next week.'

Kat swallowed to stifle the hurt. 'But I do miss you.'

Lena's features, for an instant, softened. 'I have to get away sometimes, Kat. It's the way things are.'

'But why Whitby?'

'Because it's not Bampton. That's why. Don't ask so many questions. And don't go out all the time. I think Mum and Dad would quite like to see something of you.'

'More than could be said of you,' muttered Kat under her breath as she listened to her sister make her exit.

43

Theresa was back. She'd called to cancel the appointment and then telephoned again to ask if she could come after all. Now Theresa was in the chair opposite her, looking composed. Only a slight flicker underneath her left eye indicated repressed tension.

'You called to cancel this session.' Kat kept her expression neutral.

The flicker in Theresa's eye grew more marked. 'It's not you. I thought after the last meeting that you were really good. Very empathetic. But—'

'If there's any issue with our relationship you want to tell me about, this is a safe and secure environment for you to let me know.'

'It's not you. I just heard about your sister and thought you had enough on your plate without listening to my problems.'

It was inevitable that her clients knew about Lena. It was, however, not surprising that none of them had mentioned it in a session. Kat had become accustomed to the lack of curiosity displayed by the people she saw in her rooms towards her own personal life. Theresa's reference to her sister reminded Kat that here was a patient who had spent years in therapy and who was prepared to push the boundaries slightly.

'I'm able to leave any personal problems I may have outside our sessions.'

'I just thought with the police investigation and everything, you might need a break from work.'

'I don't. But thanks.' Time to move things on. 'Theresa.' Kat leant forward in her chair. 'Have you ever thought of going to the police?'

*

Theresa left looking troubled. Perhaps Kat had pushed it too far, but she had thought it important to mention the possibility of judicial intervention. A crime had been committed, and Theresa might stop blaming herself if she accepted a process that would, in essence, be an independent inquiry into those traumatic events. Kat could also sense resistance from her client, and she hadn't referred to the police again. It was something to be explored, possibly, in a later session.

And now, she herself had the police to deal with. Her client was replaced, three minutes later, by Connie. To be fair to the detective, it seemed that she'd stood in the courtyard outside the rooms waiting for Theresa to leave, judging by how quickly the knock came after her client's departure. Kat appreciated the courtesy, even though she didn't want any police in her professional place of work.

Connie was making her nervous. She was roaming around Kat's rooms, picking up the few items she kept as trinkets. 'I'd have preferred it if you'd come to my home. It's more suitable for a discussion about my sister. This is my workplace. I have to earn a living here.'

Connie put down the wood carving that she'd been examining. 'I went there first. You weren't there, were you though? It's gone six, and I assumed you'd be here. That you'd have evening clients, I mean.'

'It's that urgent?'

The detective looked a little shamefaced, but then her eyes lit on one of Lena's paintings hanging on the wall. 'That's by your sister. It's similar to the ones I saw in your house.'

'It is. Her style is easy to recognise, isn't it?'

'Is that all she paints? Flowers, I mean.'

'Well, why not? She left school to work in a florist's, and you're told to paint what you see around you. That's what she saw every day. Flowers.'

'But they're always blue? I mean, not just the flowers. Even the black background's got a slight blue tinge. Is it her favourite colour?'

Kat's thoughts strayed to the yellow blouse. 'I wouldn't say so but, for her paintings, that's what she uses. It's her motif. Big blue paintings of flowers.' She glanced at Connie and smiled. 'I wouldn't read too much into it. Blue is also one of my favourite colours, and I'm not a depressed person. It's just a colour.'

Connie reached out and touched the canvas. 'It's really beautiful but also sterile. You don't get emotion from the image. It's like a photograph. Perfectly captured but no emotion.'

Kat didn't look at the picture. She'd seen it often enough. She kept her eyes on the young detective. 'You're right. It is sterile. Yet flowers don't have to be like that. Have you heard of the American artist Georgia O'Keeffe?'

Connie shook her head.

'She paints these pictures of petals and stems. They're lush, sensual drawings. Full of sexual imagery. Don't laugh. There can be something sexual about flowers. In shape and form. But not Lena's. You're right.'

'Why? She was married. She presumably wasn't a cold person. I mean, sexually.'

Now Kat did look at the picture, its icy perfection repellent to her. 'I'm not sure I can answer that question. About her sex life.'

'Did she have any boyfriends before Andrew?'

'A few. I didn't live at Providence Villa for about ten years and Lena was a private person. But, yes, I believe there were boyfriends.'

Connie seemed unable to drag her eyes from the canvas. It was almost casually that she asked, 'Do you know someone called Stephanie Alton?'

For a split second, Kat was tempted to lie. She wanted it to be all over. Sick of death, sick of that rackety old house. And, yes, sick of Lena. 'She was a friend of Lena's.'

Connie swung around. 'How? How was she a friend of Lena?'

'They met when Lena had a Saturday job. At the florist's. This was before she left school and worked there full-time. Anyway, she met Steph through her work.'

'And they were close?'

Kat tried to remember. Her sister had still been fun then. She'd enjoyed her Saturday job, and the three of them had gone out to bars. She picked her words with care. 'I didn't know Stephanie well. She was more Lena's pal than mine but we were friendly.' Kat took a deep breath. 'There's a photograph. Of the three of us.' She felt Connie's eyes on her. 'I found it while I was going through the attic looking for something.'

'Do you have it on you?'

Kat reached for her handbag and pulled out the image she and Mark had looked at.

Connie studied it. 'So you knew each other as teenagers? What about more recently?'

'I haven't seen her for about twenty years.'

'And Lena?'

Kat looked angry. 'Lena was in prison until last year. The only person she saw was me.'

'It's important, you know. It's another connection between Stephanie and Lena.'

'Another?'

Connie looked at Kat, assessing her. 'Do you know a man called Philip Staley?'

Kat shook her head. 'I don't think so. In fact, I'm pretty sure I've never heard the name. Who's he?'

'As I mentioned, another possible link between Lena and Steph.'

'I'd heard Steph's death was suicide. Don't look at me like that. This is Bampton, remember. Nothing stays secret around here for long. Everyone's talking about it.'

Connie's cheeks took on patches of red. 'She didn't just die. No one just kills themselves. They do it for a reason. There's a chain of events that are entwined, and I don't know what they are.'

Kat took the photo off Connie. Should she tell the detective about the other clue? She thought of the yellow blouse and shook her head. 'I can't help you, I'm afraid. I have no idea what this is about.'

44

Kat had expected minimalism and perhaps a temporary feel to the accommodation of a man who had, in his therapy sessions, admitted he had a problem settling down with any permanence in any place. But his terraced house had a messy charm to it. Newspapers, books, and cigarette packets vied for space in the small living room. This house, in comparison with Providence Villa, felt like a place of safety.

She shouldn't have been staying there, of course. An hour with her supervisor should have put paid to any thoughts that what she was doing was okay. 'Be careful' had been Patricia's warning. But Kat was no longer kidding herself that she was just relying on Mark for help in finding her sister.

She watched as Mark put newspaper and kindling into the cold grate of the fire and lit it. 'Fire in spring. We must be in Derbyshire.' He smiled up at her, and she felt her heart lurch.

The fire gave the room a welcome warmth, but there was an awkwardness between them that nothing she said could dispel. Kat wasn't on home turf, and he seemed discomfited to have her in the house. Conversation was interspersed with difficult silences. They were sitting in front of the television, both smoking.

She tried again. 'You don't have to help me. Lena's obviously still alive, thank God. There's no way the boy could have known about the blouse. She must have handed it to him to give it to me. I guess that could also be true about the gun.'

He didn't answer her immediately but leaned forward and stubbed out his cigarette. 'Why have you never married, Kat?'

He had surprised her, and she wondered what answer he was expecting. She tried a smile. 'Never met anyone worth the bother.'

He didn't smile back. He was frowning at the fire and still wouldn't look at her. 'Really? Or is that just the flippant answer?'

Kat considered. 'It's true actually. I've had a few boyfriends over the years. I nearly got engaged to one of them in my twenties. God knows why as I hardly think about him now.'

He still had his eyes on the fire. 'But you're attractive. It seems strange.'

'It doesn't work like that. Anyway, this is the twenty-first century. We women don't judge ourselves on whether we've ever made it down the aisle.'

'Was Lena's marriage happy?'

This was more comfortable ground. 'I heard it was so-so. She married Andrew when I'd just got back from living abroad. I didn't know him very well because he was away from home a lot. I wouldn't have said either was blissfully happy but they seemed to exist in a contentment of sorts, side by side.'

He stood up and poked at the fire, which hissed at him but responded to the touch with a belt of heat. 'It's not much is it? I mean, I appreciate I'm not one to talk, but even so I like to think I can recognise a decent enough relationship. It sounds like Lena settled for a fairly tepid marriage. It's not what most people would do. What did you think when she was arrested for murder?'

Kat lay back against the cushions of the sofa and closed her eyes. She'd been convinced it was all a ghastly mistake and that the police would realise it too but that was shown to be a case of serious underestimation of her sister. Because Lena had pleaded guilty during the trial. Kat had been unable to believe it. She had constantly sought out her sister's eyes during the various court hearings. Glances her sister had refused to meet. And there were further secrets that needed to be unravelled. She opened her eyes to find him looking at the length of her body. 'I lost Lena at some point in our teens. The more I think about it, the stranger it seems. We were so close for years, and then, suddenly, she switched off.'

'Perhaps it was puberty. These things happen. There's a wide gulf between being a child and a teenager. You start to explore your own identity.'

Kat shook her head. 'It wasn't that. It was after I was fifteen or sixteen maybe. Lena just withdrew. Changed her mind about everything. She lost interest in school. Didn't want to do her exams, but my dad was adamant. She did okay. Definitely well enough to go to university but she didn't want to go.'

'What about your mum?'

'Well, the funny thing was that Mum was much more sympathetic. Which is surprising really because she'd had a hard time of it getting to university in the first place. She had a very traditional father who didn't believe in educating women. He wanted her to work in an office at sixteen. Which would have been a tragedy as she was incredibly clever. It was only after a teacher at her grammar school came round and talked to him that he changed his mind. She was a wonderful doctor. Very humane. It's difficult to believe that it very nearly didn't happen.'

'If she was a kind woman, then she probably understood about Lena's decision, wanted Lena to do what she wanted to with her life.'

Kat leant forward and took another cigarette from the packet. She made a face. 'Possibly. When I think about it though, it's almost as if those two were in cahoots.'

'Cahoots? That's quite an emotive word.'

Kat lit the cigarette. She needed to stop soon, otherwise she'd have serious problems quitting again. 'All I'm saying is that there seemed to be some kind of understanding between the pair of them. My mother could kick up quite a fuss when she wanted to but she never did with Lena. Funny really.'

'What did she do instead?'

'Lena? She went to work in a florist's but she was always a good artist. She started this thing where she'd draw blue flowers on glass vases. It sounds a bit naff, but they were really wonderful things. Almost ethereal in their beauty. From there she moved on to canvas. She'd dabbled as a teenager, but now she got serious. Painting flowers, I mean. Really beautiful things, but always clinical-looking. Always blue.'

'Have you got any of them?'

'There's a lot around the house. She painted in the back bedroom. Most of the unsold stuff will be there.' She looked across at Mark. 'If you're really interested I can show you.'

'I'm asking, Kat, and I know I've said it before, but something's not right. What you're telling me makes sense because you lived it. It's the norm, as it was your upbringing. But something's not right. Lena goes from being bright academically to refusing to go to university. She's close to you and then she's not. Come on, Kat. There's something not right there.'

Kat felt tears well up in her eyes, but Mark made no move across to the sofa next to her. 'She said something to me. When the police came this time around. I asked her about what had gone on. If she knew the man in her bed wasn't Andrew. She said to me something along the lines of "You of all people should know that everything can't be told." What the hell did she mean by that?'

Mark was still sitting stock still, his eyes on the fire. *Does he feel the same way about me?* she thought. He must have felt her eyes on him because he stood up. 'I'll make us a brew.' He leaned over and kissed her hair.

As he left the room, Kat wondered what he'd meant when he said he wasn't one to talk about relationships.

45

Connie burst into Sadler's office full of repressed excitement. He frowned up at her. 'Some people are scared enough of me to knock first.'

'Well, you'll never believe this, but you know that "weak lead" we had? Philip Staley, who Stephanie Alton complained ruined her life? Well, I've seen his mother and spoken to Kat Gray and I think he's our possible first victim.'

She was waving a photo in front of him which he took off her. It showed a man with a pale orange tan which couldn't have come from Derbyshire sunshine – or any natural light, in fact. He had a mane of curly hair that licked around his neck. In the photo he must have been somewhere in his early thirties.

'You wouldn't trust him with your life's savings, would you? He emigrated to Australia sometime around August 2004 and hasn't been seen since. I hope someone would notice I'd gone missing before twelve years had passed, although I wouldn't guarantee it.'

'I'd send a squad car around to look for you after a week or so.' Sadler was joking, but he could see from her hurt expression that it hadn't gone down well.

'I'd like to know what you want me to do next. It's definitely a goer as far as I'm concerned.'

Sadler tapped a pencil on his desk. 'I agree. Start the usual searches. Look at Philip Staley's bank accounts and see what's happened since 2004. Look for any connections with Lena Gray. Macclesfield's not far. They could well have met each other. You also need to go back and interview the woman at Shallowford House. What was her name?'

'Julia Miles.'

'Find out how Philip Staley was supposed to have ruined Stephanie Alton's life. And I want to know more about her background, family and so on.'

'We're getting there, aren't we? I've just interviewed Kat Gray and I've found out that Lena and Steph were friends as teenagers. There's a photo of them together.'

'Were they still friends?'

'Kat doesn't think so. But Lena's a dark horse and it's another link between the cases.'

Sadler smiled at her. 'I think, Connie, we're beginning to make progress.'

*

Julia Miles looked tired as she took her seat opposite Connie. 'The women here are pretty upset by Steph's death. We're all feeling unsettled at the moment.'

'Do you have much trouble here?'

'There've been incidents over the years. Not as many as you might think. Most major problems happen initially after a woman flees domestic abuse. The men can't believe it, sometimes. That the break's been made. Or perhaps macho pride means that they think they stand a decent chance of getting them back. Promising to mend their ways.' Her tone was bitter.

'It never happens?'

'Not in my professional experience. Yours?'

'It's been a while since I attended a domestic. There were quite a few when I was first starting out. It used to make me really angry and then I lost it.'

'The anger?'

'Yes. There's only so much you can be angry about in this job. You can't keep hold of it all the time. It can eat you up. So you put it to one side. You pretend it can't touch you any more.'

Julia looked concerned. 'And does it? Touch you?'

'It stops being as difficult.'

'But you still care?'

Connie felt a rush of anger. 'Of course I still care.'

'The stories you hear. It can make you doubt your instincts when it comes to men. I'm lucky. I grew up with four brothers. Man-hater I ain't but, God knows, some of the stuff I hear . . .'

'Are you married?'

Julia Miles grinned. 'Living in sin. You?'

'God no. I meet people, have a few dates, and then, well, work happens. When we're on a case I can't focus on anything else.' Unbidden, Connie's thoughts turned to Palmer. She mentally shook the thought away and concentrated on the woman in front of her. 'So Stephanie Alton was the victim of domestic abuse?'

'No. I don't think so.'

'I thought this was a facility for women who were victims of violence.'

'It is. Mainly. But as I mentioned when you first came here, it's run as a charitable trust rather than under the umbrella of the local authority. Our Trust status gives us certain flexibility but also comes with problems. The grounds used to belong to the Shaw family. Heard of them?'

Connie shook her head. Julia got up and walked over to the bookcase. She slid her hand behind it and levered out a large painting. It was a watercolour, badly faded, depicting an elderly woman with grey hair pulled back into a bun. She was wearing half-moon spectacles and a determined expression. 'That's Genevieve Shaw. The last of the family. She bequeathed this land when she died in 1967 to a trust set up to support women fleeing unhappy relationships. That's what the wording actually says. "Unhappy relationships." You'd never get away with that now. I should know, the amount of bureaucracy I have to jump through to keep this place ticking along.'

'Are you short of money?'

'Not especially. There was a fair inheritance, but it's only to be spent on capital stuff. For the fabric of the building, for example. It's revenue funding I need to constantly monitor. The goalposts keep changing. Plus, if I was to be totally honest, the Social Services don't like the fact that this is a charity. They prefer to work with government-funded organisations. They don't like some of our terms of reference. For example, the rather wishy-washy term "unhappy relationships".'

Connie couldn't really care less about bureaucracy. She saw enough of it in her job. What she wanted to know about was Stephanie Alton. 'So what happened to Steph?'

Julia frowned. 'She got pregnant, and it seems to have destroyed her. It was the moment in her life she decided that everything went wrong. A rubbish relationship, an unwanted pregnancy, and it's all over.'

'It seems a bit extreme.'

'Yes, it does, doesn't it? But you see it all the time in this job. Something that one person would put down as a bad experience will destroy another.'

'And Philip Staley was the man responsible for this disastrous relationship?'

'Apparently. I've always connected the two events. She would keep saying, "Philip Staley ruined my life."'

'Any idea how long they were together?'

'I can't give you any more information as I don't have any. Steph came here because she was still considered to be vulnerable in her previous residence, but she was well enough to manage by herself. Given the long-term impact of the breakdown following her pregnancy, she appeared to satisfy our charitable terms.'

Connie's eyes were on the badly faded watercolour. 'It's a bit strange though, isn't it? It's not as if Stephanie was a teenager when she got pregnant. She was a grown woman. She's not the first person to be unhappy with her choice of father for her child.'

Julia shrugged. 'I'm beginning to lose the concept of what's normal.'

'And how was her relationship with her daughter?'

'You've met Mary? Well, she was initially brought up by her mum until she came to the attention of Social Services when Steph hit the bottle. There were a couple of periods in foster care.'

'And recently?'

'She visited occasionally. I don't think she liked it here. We try to avoid Shallowford feeling like an institution, but it's not easy. It may well have reminded Mary of children's homes she was placed in. It was one of the reasons Steph wanted to leave.

She fancied getting a place with her daughter if that was possible.'

'And was it?'

'It's not straightforward. A mother and adult daughter. The local housing association was looking into it. Can I ask you a question?'

'Okay.'

'Why are you so interested in what happened to Steph? I've heard there were stones in her pockets. Like Virginia Woolf.'

'Virginia Woolf?'

'She weighted herself down with stones and threw herself in the river. That's what happened with Steph, isn't it?'

'Probably.'

'So why the interest?'

Connie leaned forward. 'Because even though we both agree that we've lost what our sense of normal is, we're sitting here dancing around each other well aware that something's not right with Stephanie's story. There's something we're not getting.'

'You think there's more to it than a woman gets pregnant and has an unwanted child.'

Connie folded her arms. 'That's half the story. And I'm going to find out the rest.'

46

'Anna asked about you.'

Sadler rolled his eyes at his sister. 'I've told you not to bother trying to set me up with anyone. I'm capable of finding my own girlfriend.'

'Are you, Francis? I'm not so sure about that. You seem to like the married types.'

'That was only one girlfriend.'

'One is enough. Try to find someone who's at least single this time.'

'Like Anna.'

'Like Anna,' echoed his sister. 'Didn't you like her even a little bit?'

Sadler stretched his feet out in front of him and kicked off his shoes. 'She didn't like the fact that I was a policeman.'

'You're kidding. She's a solicitor, for God's sake. I'm sure that's your imagination.'

'You think I can't read people's reactions to my job? Anna is a very nice girl, who, when she heard what I did for a living, for a moment looked alarmed.'

Camilla bent down, picked up his shoes and moved them to the side of the room. 'Sorry. Force of habit, clearing up after two little boys.' She plopped herself down next to him. 'Funny that. Maybe I should mention it in future. I have a very attractive brother. Single, but he's a policeman. Does that put you off?'

Sadler put his arm around his sister. 'Probably a good idea. Put off the potential criminals.'

His sister looked up at him. 'You don't mean Anna?'

'Probably not. She might have had a bad experience with the police. Not everyone is as nice as me.'

Camilla smiled. 'You are nice and you're always welcome here. You don't need an invitation.'

'I know. It's just, once a case starts . . .'

'. . . you become the local celebrity. I do know. Finding the body of a long-dead man at Hale's End.'

Sadler made a face. 'It gave me the creeps, to be honest.'

'I'm not surprised. Horrible place.'

'I know. What's worse, I used to go there as a teenager. Larking about.'

'Me too.'

Sadler turned to her in surprise. She smirked. 'Different type of larking, I suspect. My then boyfriend, Graham, used to drive me down there. You really don't want to know any more.'

'You're right. I don't.'

He thought back to the dark copse. 'I don't think it's used for that kind of stuff any more. You couldn't get a car near the place. The old track is pretty overgrown.'

Camilla glanced up at the clock. 'The kids will be back from Scouts in a minute. Thank God those days are over. Best thing about being married, take it from me. No more snogging in cars.'

'You don't miss it?'

She grimaced. 'I suspect it's different for men.'

*

'How's the case going?' Joanne had to raise her voice to be heard over the music that was playing a fraction too loud for normal conversation. They were waiting in the restaurant for their friends to arrive, a couple who were habitually late for any evening out. Palmer had once made the mistake of showing his irritation at their tardiness, and he was now convinced that they did it on purpose. He looked at his watch. 'It's going okay, I suppose.'

'Not solved it yet, then?' She smirked at him across the table.

'Come on, Joanne. You know it's not that straightforward.' He signalled to the waiter. 'I'm ordering some wine. God knows when those two will turn up.'

'Not for me. I'll have sparkling water.'

'Come on, Jo. You're not pregnant yet.' It was the wrong thing to say. At the sight of her face, he reached across the table. 'Sorry. But stop worrying. A glass of wine will do you good. I'll order a Chablis. Your favourite.'

As the waiter opened the bottle of wine, Palmer noticed him giving Joanne a sidelong glance. She was wearing a black Grecian-style dress with flat sandals, even though she'd complained in the car that her feet were freezing. The draping fabric emphasised her body's curves, and he was amused to see that she was enjoying the waiter's attention.

After the man departed, he commented, 'You've got an admirer.'

'Not my type. I prefer handsome policemen.'

'Got anyone in mind?'

She ignored the wine and picked up her water glass. 'Anyway, I'm not the only one with an admirer.' She gave him a knowing glance.

'Who? Me?'

'When I saw your colleague Connie in the street the other day, she was very cagey about your movements. Very protective towards you.'

'Connie? Don't start this again. Anyway, if I was working, why should she say where I was?'

Joanne put her glass down with a bang causing the water to slop over the sides. 'Don't get uppity. I'm just saying, I think you've got an admirer too.'

Palmer rolled his eyes and picked up the menu. 'Connie? I really don't think so.'

47

Sadler walked back on foot from his sister's house. The nights still had the hint of winter on them. Ridiculous in May, but there you were. Derbyshire Peak District danced to its own tune. To ward off the chill, he increased his pace through the Bampton gloom and began to enjoy the spurt of adrenalin. At first, all he could hear were his footsteps tapping on the pavement.

A woman, high-heeled shoes in her hand and limping slightly, looked in alarm as he approached. He crossed over to the other side of the street to reassure her and looked at his watch. Just gone eleven. Which meant kicking-out time at Bampton's pubs, most of which still kept to the old opening times.

Sure enough, as he approached the town centre, sounds of laughter and shouts of exuberance pierced the air. There weren't many of them huddled together, fifteen in total he thought, but enough to make him quicken his pace and keep his head down. A patrol car was parked in one of the delivery bays outside a wine shop. Sadler squinted but didn't recognise the figures inside. They took no notice of him, intent on watching the group for a sudden eruption of violence.

As he left the central square, the town fell silent again, and there was no one to disturb Sadler's reverie. At the end of the road, he had two choices. Turn right, and he would pass

Connie's flat in the converted mill and walk along the canal path towards his small terraced house. If he took the road on the left, this would lead him directly past Providence Villa, where Kat Gray lived. Neither route appealed. On balance though, he thought Connie would show more displeasure if she happened to bump into him. He turned left.

The streetlights were already off by the time he made his way down Waverley Road, and the only light there was leaked out of the windows of the houses he passed. Peering up, Sadler could see that some of the larger properties had been turned into flats. Small kitchens filled what had once been box rooms, making a strange juxtaposition of living arrangements. The final house in the row, Providence Villa, was in complete darkness. It was around half eleven. Kat Gray must have gone to bed.

To the right of him was Heanor Park, a kidney-shaped recreation ground that still had a touch of Victorian grandeur to it. It might have been because of the small bandstand sitting proudly in one corner. He'd never seen it used. The park was locked at night, which deprived him of a short cut to his house. A wave of weariness washed over him. He was now in a hurry to get home. A small movement made him stop. He turned around but could see nothing in the street behind him except a cat sniffing a wall.

He instinctively looked towards Kat's house. Nothing untoward but he couldn't get rid of the impression that he was being watched. He turned towards the park. All looked well. He carried on walking, and the clouds moved so that moonlight was thrown down onto the street. Sitting on one of the benches was a hunched figure. Staring straight at him.

Sadler stopped. 'Who's there?' he asked through the railings.

The figure unfolded itself, and, for a moment, Sadler felt the thud of fear but the person was anxious to get away. He started into a sprint, shouting over his shoulder, 'She's not there.' Sadler stared after the boy in astonishment, then looked up at the empty house.

48

Kat woke up in Mark's uncomfortable spare bedroom. After their conversation about Lena, Kat had pleaded a headache and had gone upstairs to bed. Charlie followed her and settled on her blankets. The cat had made himself comfortable in Mark's house, and she could hear him purring contentedly as she stirred awake.

If Mark had made an effort with the rest of the house, he hadn't bothered here. The walls were bare. Thin, cheaply made curtains hardly blocked out any light. But it was warm, probably from the water tank in the airing cupboard. Kat stretched out her legs and reached into her bag for the novel she was reading. It wasn't there. She must have left it in the living room. She checked the time on her phone. Half eight and, unless she was imagining it, she'd slept straight through the night. She pulled on her woollen jumper over her pyjamas and headed downstairs.

From the living room she could hear men's voices, muted, and then a chuckle of laughter that wasn't Mark's. She turned on the kettle and watched it boil, wondering whether to alert them to her presence. How would Mark explain the fact that she was in his house?

A man came into the kitchen, a mug in his hand, and started when he saw her. Then smiled. 'You're Kat? I'm Brian.' He held out his hand, a curiously old-fashioned gesture. She took it. His palms were calloused. He saw her looking. 'I was a mechanic. In the army. Tanks are harder on the skin than cars.'

'That's how you know—'

'Mark. Yes.'

The unspoken question hung between them. 'He told me about the gun. It must have been a shock. It's better you're staying here. He can keep an eye on you.'

'It was a shock.' She didn't know what else to say. She marvelled at the wider world's acceptance of her presence in Mark's house.

Brian walked over to the sink, rinsed the mug and tipped it upside down onto the draining board. Mark came into the kitchen, and she slid past him. 'I'd best get dressed. I didn't realise you had visitors.'

He smiled after her. 'There's someone I want you to meet. We'll wait for you in the front room.'

Kat hadn't brought enough clothes and searched through her bag for the last pair of trousers. She'd need to go back to Providence Villa to pick up some clean stuff. The thought of doing her dirty laundry in front of Mark didn't appeal. She dressed hurriedly and went back downstairs.

In the living room sat a man so resembling Father Christmas that Kat did a double take. He was in his sixties with cropped white hair and a long beard. He was rifling through what looked like a set of black-and-white photographs.

Mark did the introductions. 'This is James Plower. I wanted you to meet him. He's from the university in Manchester, but he lives in Bampton and is a friend of Brian's. There's a couple of things I want him to talk to you about.'

James didn't stand up but gave her a welcoming nod. 'I've

brought some pictures of the old place. Taken two years ago, admittedly, but the building hasn't changed much.'

Kat joined him on the sofa and took the first image out of his hand. It was a well-produced shot. The black earth and white sky were dominated by a huge chunk of grey slab. 'Where's this?'

'It's Hale's End. The old mortuary. Where your brother-in-law was found dead.'

Mark was on the chair opposite, assessing her. 'You don't recognise it at all?'

Kat took the rest of the photos from the bearded man and looked through them. The place was incredible. Frightening and yet majestic in its beauty. The love and care that must have gone into building it. She shook her head. 'I've never seen this place before in my life. I knew about it. It's common knowledge around here. But why the hell would I want to visit an old morgue stuck out in the middle of nowhere? It has absolutely no interest for me whatsoever.'

'That's a shame.' James didn't appear too offended but took the photographs back from her. 'Mark thought you might want to see me, nevertheless. Not just about Hale's End.'

She looked across at Mark.

'Brian's the one who told me, in the pub, about the boy,' said Mark. 'He lives in the same street as James and they got talking about Hale's End and the murder there. In the course of the conversation something interesting emerged. So Brian rang me this morning to ask who I was trying to help. He thought it important that you hear this.'

At the thought of the teenager, Kat swallowed.

'Are you sure you want me to tell you about the place?'

asked James. 'If you're not interested in its history?' There was a wry glint in his eye.

'I didn't mean to be rude. Andrew was murdered there. That's literally all I know about it.'

'I know, and I'm sorry, but from a historian's point of view it does add an extra layer to an already fascinating story.'

'Glad to add extra drama.'

James touched her lightly on the arm. 'I think you should hear the story. I can do my five-minute spiel, no problem. So this place, as you probably already know, was built when the Canadian regiment was stationed in Bampton. There was a main hospital off Bampton High Street which was demolished in the sixties. Then there was a subsidiary infirmary about two hundred metres from here. Records suggest it was for the more severe cases, including contagious diseases.'

'And the mortuary was built for those who didn't make it.'

'Well, quite. It stayed open until 1919 and then was abandoned. That it hasn't fallen into more disrepair is largely, I think, due to its isolated location. It's been forgotten about.'

'Until a few weeks ago. When Andrew turns up dead there.'

Mark was shaking his head. 'I don't think so, Kat. We've already spoken about this. Are you sure that Lena never mentioned this place? Or perhaps your parents?'

'My parents? Good God. My mother and father were busy GPs. We hardly saw them when we were growing up. They had no time to come out hunting for old buildings. There's nothing that connects us to the First World War.'

'You must have had a relative that served in the war,' said Mark. 'Most of us have. It was tales of my great-grandfather's exploits that made me want to join the army.'

Kat shook her head. 'Not in my family. Or, if there was, no one ever talked about it.'

'I knew your father, you know.' James was putting the photos back into a brown envelope.

'Dad? How did you know him?'

'He was my GP when I first came to Bampton. I remember both your parents well. Especially your mother. But I saw your father a few times too. They were GPs of the old kind. They physically examined you. I went to my doctor recently complaining about a sore chest and he never even got out of his chair.'

'Do you know what? I haven't thought about him in weeks. It's Mum I've been thinking about. With everything that's happened with Lena. What she might have said. She had such a strong personality. Dad . . . well, he was just there.'

'As well as being a good doctor, he was also a very interesting man. We would swap stories and one of them, in particular, I think will interest you.'

'Story? What story?'

James hesitated.

Mark motioned for him to carry on. 'Tell her.'

49

Saturday, 17 October 1987

Lena sat in front of her father, whose face was flushed from the exertion of shutting the sash window in his surgery. It was a warm day, and the room felt stuffy. He was wearing his tweed jacket, one of the two he'd alternated since her childhood. She'd never seen him wear anything else over the checked shirts he bought from Dunne's, the men's outfitters on Bampton High Street.

'This can't go on.'

'Are you speaking as my father or doctor?'

He sighed. 'Of course I'm not speaking as your doctor. I'm not your GP for goodness' sake.' He saw Lena look around the room. 'I'm talking to you here because I don't want Kat to overhear us at home. She's suspicious enough as it is and rightly so.'

Lena looked at the floor. Her father relented. 'I've got something I want you to have.'

He reached into a drawer, pulled out a cloth parcel and unwrapped it. He picked up the gun and seemed to hesitate. 'I don't approve of guns. You know this. But I did learn to shoot when I was doing my National Service.'

'Are you going to show me?'

'No! This is an antique. I have no idea if it works or not. I'm letting you have it because your mum thinks it'll give you reassurance. I trust you not to go waving it about in Bampton.'

'If you're not going to show me how to use it, what's the point of giving it to me?'

'Because guns are scary things and I think it'll make you feel safer. Sleeping with it. And don't go looking for ammunition.'

Lena looked down and weighed the gun in her hand.

50

'Remind me again why we're focusing on Stephanie Alton's suicide when we've got the murderer of two dead men to find?'

'Is that a serious question or have you got the hump about something?' Connie frowned across the room at Palmer, who was looking intently into the computer.

Palmer smirked into the screen. 'You've established that Lena Gray and Stephanie knew each other as teenagers. So what? Sadler knew Andrew Fisher. It's the way things are in small towns. Remember? Everyone knows each other. It's why you and I can go out and enjoy ourselves in the evenings. We didn't grow up here.'

'I grew up in Matlock.'

'But not Bampton. It's not the same thing, is it?'

'So you think it's coincidence that the real Andrew Fisher is shot, Lena disappears, and her teenage friend kills herself?'

He smiled across the room at her. 'Coincidence. Very occasionally happens in real life, you know.'

Connie stood up and walked across to his desk. 'It does and I am bearing it in mind. But don't you think it's strange? That Stephanie kills herself now? I've been through her past history with Julia Miles at Shallowford House. It's grim but nothing compared to some of the stuff we've heard. Something's not right. Not only with her past, but with the fact she decided to kill herself. I mean, why now?' Palmer wasn't listening. 'Hello. Am I talking to myself?'

Palmer was squinting at the screen. 'I think I've got something, Con.'

She frowned at the shortened use of her name. It was his fault that she was known as Connie rather than by her last name, which was the norm around here. Other female detectives didn't have a problem getting men to refer to them by their last names. The problem was that when she had first arrived in CID, Palmer had spotted a rival and had promptly called her Connie. Probably to put her in her place. And the team had picked up on it. At least it was better than her full name, Constance, an old-fashioned moniker which she couldn't bring herself to dislike because it was also the name of her beloved grandmother. Now Palmer was trying to call her Con. She'd have ignored him if she could. She looked over his shoulder.

'Philip Staley is coming up on the computer. He's not got a record, but he was arrested for assault. We nearly missed it because some idiot typed in his first name with two "l"s. So he's in here as a *Phillip* Staley.'

'Don't we check dates of birth and stuff like that?'

Palmer looked smug. 'It's because I'm checking the date of birth that I've noticed it. Anyway, he was arrested for assault in June 1998.'

'Does it say what kind of assault? Maybe Julia Miles was wrong when she said Stephanie Alton hadn't been battered by Staley.'

'There's mention of a nightclub but the charges were dropped. I would guess by the accuser. It's common enough. You know that as well as me. I've got the alleged victim's name.

A Rebecca Hardy. She's probably traceable, even though it was a long time ago.' He looked down at the keyboard. 'We'll need to do this together.'

*

Rebecca Hardy was easy to find, but when Connie called her she hadn't wanted to meet them in her home. Nothing particularly suspicious about that, although it was slightly unusual. Women often preferred the comfort of home territory when dealing with the police.

Palmer had suggested a local coffee shop. Not Café Aroma, their preferred refuge for a decent cup of coffee. He instinctively realised that the hard plastic seating and abrupt service might not be congenial for a woman who had made a report of abuse. Instead, they were in one of the tourist cafés with wooden tables and a laminated menu. Palmer took one sip of his coffee and pushed it to one side.

Rebecca Hardy was about late thirties with pale, naturally blonde hair pulled back with a silver clip. Her freckled face was make-up free but she didn't need it, thought Palmer. She was attractive. He looked down and saw she was wearing a wedding ring, a simple band next to an engagement ring with a pip of a diamond in it.

He let Connie take the lead. The woman barely glanced at him. He clearly made her uncomfortable. Perhaps he shouldn't have come.

Connie was checking her notes. 'As I mentioned on the phone, we wanted to ask you a few questions about a complaint you made against Philip Staley in 1998. You said that he assaulted you at a nightclub?'

Rebecca spread her hands out over the table. 'It was a Saturday night. A group of us girls used to go out to a pub, Ups 'n' Downs. It would stay open until about two in the morning. After midnight there would be a DJ, a bit of dancing. Nothing special but the only thing going on here.'

'I can imagine.' Connie smiled. 'I grew up near here. Not much more there either.'

Rebecca smiled back. 'It was a regular thing. A group of us who'd gone to school together. Well, occasionally one of us would meet a guy. To be honest, it wasn't really the reason we were clubbing. We were just letting our hair down on a Saturday night. We were young, single. You know how it is.'

'Of course. You met this Philip Staley there?'

Palmer frowned. That wasn't good. Connie should let the witness bring up the accused man. He glanced at her, but she was ignoring his look.

'Yes. I met him there. He was medium height, with curly hair. Good-looking, I suppose. We got chatting. Danced a bit. You know.' She looked at Connie for reassurance, who nodded. 'Well, the thing is, towards the end of the evening, when it was getting late, my friends came to find me to say they were taking a taxi home. That's how it worked. We looked after each other, even if we'd met someone in the course of the evening. None of us would leave until we'd checked the others were okay.'

Connie nodded again. Palmer could feel weariness washing over him. He could see where this was going.

'Anyway, Philip said he'd get me a taxi if I wanted to stay on a bit with him. The club wasn't due to shut for an hour or so. So I agreed. It'd happened before. Not very often, but oc-

200

casionally.' She shot Palmer a glance. Seeing if he was judging her. He kept his face neutral. She took a deep breath. 'Anyway. At the end, we went outside. Occasionally there would be a taxi waiting there but this evening, nothing. Philip said he had a car.'

'He told you his name was Philip.' Connie's voice was gentle.

Rebecca nodded. 'Yes. I didn't find out his last name until after I went to the police. I didn't think he would have given his real name. I mean, given what he did to me. But he had. I just knew his name was Philip, and police told me later his last name was Staley.'

'Okay. I was just checking. Sorry I interrupted you. Carry on.'

'Well, I went with him in his car. Stupid now when I think of it. I have two daughters. The thought of them doing what I did gives me the shivers. But I was nineteen.'

'And what happened?'

Palmer sat still. He really shouldn't have come. He might as well not be here.

'He drove for a bit. Then pulled into a lay-by. Just outside Bampton, I think, but I was a bit disorientated. I couldn't really work out where I was. Then, well, he raped me.'

Palmer pulled back his coffee and took a gulp of the cold foul brew.

'I couldn't believe it was happening to me. It seemed completely unreal. I remember lying there, thinking, *He's raping me. I'm being raped.* There was absolutely nothing I could do about it.'

'You survived.' Connie was leaning forward towards the

woman. 'There was something you could do about it. You survived, reported the attack and got on with your life. That's a lot of things that you did.'

'It never went to court though, did it? And that was my fault. I withdrew the allegation.'

'Why? It must have taken a lot of courage to report the assault to begin with. What happened?'

'After the attack, I was on autopilot. He drove me to the top of my street. Didn't even look at me. I got out and went home. I was still living with Mum and Dad at the time. Then the next morning I was in shock but really angry. I walked out of the house without telling anyone what had happened and went to Bampton police station. I reported the attack.'

'How was it?'

The woman's face took on a closed expression. 'It was okay.'

'Okay?' asked Palmer.

She didn't look at him. 'I mean, it was obvious that I'd had sex. He hadn't used a condom or anything and afterwards I got thinking, how could I prove it wasn't consensual? I mean, it was his word against mine.'

'It's not like that with rape cases,' said Connie.

Rebecca was shaking her head. 'I basically got cold feet. I rang the station and said I was withdrawing my allegation. And that was that.'

Connie risked a glance at Palmer. Victims' withdrawals of accusations of sexual assault were a huge problem in sexual assault cases.

'It's so long ago. I was really shocked when you rang and said you wanted to speak to me. I'd almost forgotten about it. I know it sounds improbable, but it's the truth. I really had nearly erased that whole period from my memory.'

'Did you ever see him again? In Bampton? It's a small place,' asked Palmer.

Rebecca shook her head. 'No. Although I never went back to the club. I stopped going out completely for a while. When I would go out, I'd drive everywhere. Then I met my husband and had a family. I've no time for the pub now. Why are you asking? Has he done it again?'

Connie looked again at Palmer. He shook his head. 'His name has come up in an ongoing investigation. There was a record of your allegation on file. That's all.'

Had he done it again? Well, that was a very good question. If it was Philip Staley who had ended up in Lena's bed, then perhaps the sex hadn't been voluntary.

'There's something else that I need to tell you. It will be on the file. I told the original policewoman. He took a picture.'

Connie's head shot up. 'You mean a photo?'

'Yes. With a camera. It was awful. At the end, he just reached into his pocket and pulled out a camera. Then he took a photo.' The unasked question hovered in the air. 'Just of my face but that was bad enough. Worse even, perhaps. Because I'm recognisable. From my face. Bastard.'

'Yes,' said Connie. 'Bastard.'

Palmer sighed. *Connie*, he thought. Time to bring the interview to a conclusion.

51

Llewellyn's phone rang, making him jump. He ignored it, and the call went through to his secretary. He could hear her murmured voice, and a second later she put her head through the door. 'It's the Assistant Chief Constable.'

He picked up the receiver and listened to the voice. At the end, he said, 'I'll sort it. Thanks for bringing it to my attention.' More anxious words. 'It's not a problem. I'll speak to those concerned.' He put the receiver gently back down to rest and resisted the temptation to pick up the phone and fling it out of the window.

How did we get to this? he wondered. He'd joined the force in the late seventies, straight from school. He'd never wanted to do another job because he'd seen how much his dad enjoyed being a copper, and he had lapped up the stories about policing in rural Derbyshire. It had been a different world then, although it had felt like an exciting new world was on their doorstep. The training courses to discover new forensic advances. Widening the recruitment pool to make the force more representative of society. But he had forgotten how many of these changes had been in response to crises. Complaints about the quality of policing. Miscarriages of justice that had led to scrutiny of investigative practices. And now ignominy was on his patch, and the question was, how much was he to blame?

He made another call.

'Sadler here.'

'It's me. Just thought I've been swamped with paperwork this past week or so. I've been neglecting you. It'd be a good idea if I got a quick update on the case.'

There was a moment's hesitation. 'Do you want me to come down and see you?' asked Sadler.

It was his turn to hesitate. 'Are Palmer and Connie with you?'

'They're both out, I believe. I can give you an update myself though.'

'It's fine. Tell you what, Sadler, wait for those two to come back and then bring yourselves down here. I'm in all afternoon.' His voice had a note of forced jollity to it. He wondered if Sadler had noticed. But he merely said, 'Of course, sir.'

Llewellyn got up and parted the slats of his window blinds. In the two minutes he stood staring unseeingly out of the window, he had concocted a suitable narrative in his head.

52

'So Lena's a killer.'

They were sitting in Mark's car. After James Plower and Brian had left, he'd offered to drive her home to sort out more clothes. The engine was running, but he made no move to drive off. Although the heaters were turned on full blast, Kat still couldn't stop shivering. She pulled the hood of her coat up over her head and immediately thought of the boy who had given her the gun.

Mark sighed. 'You know, for a therapist, you're incredibly judgemental. Just because we know your family had a Luger, it doesn't mean Lena pulled the trigger. There's a long way to go yet until we discover what really happened.'

'Only the other day you were telling me that she was implicated in this and now you're defending her.'

'I'm not defending her. Believe me. Based on what James told us, your father definitely had a Luger in his possession. So she's a strong suspect but you're the one who's made the full leap into believing that she's a killer.'

She turned fully towards him in her seat. 'Well, she went to prison for it once, didn't she? And how come I don't know about the gun? Lena appears to have known, and even a complete stranger, James, knows that Dad had acquired a Luger. Why the hell don't I know this?'

'For God's sake, Kat, don't ask me about how families work.

I'm the last person you should be asking.'

James Plower's story was innocuous enough. Once, during a home visit, in the days when doctors did home visits, Kat's father had asked what he did for a living. At the time, James was finishing his PhD into the facial disfigurements that afflicted soldiers returning from the Great War. Her father remembered a patient who came to the practice, an elderly man with a portion of his face missing. When this patient had died, he had passed on to his doctor a Luger he'd picked up during a battle. A simple story, and yet the ramifications were huge.

The question was, what next? 'Do you think I should tell the police?'

Mark was silent for a moment. 'Have they asked you again about the gun?'

'Not since my initial statement. I told them I'd never seen the gun before, which is the truth. Do you think I should tell them about this connection?'

'I don't know, Kat. It's your decision, and she's your sister.'

Hurt, Kat turned away. 'Don't you care?'

'Of course I care!' He was shouting. 'Have you any idea how hard this is for me? I'm trying to help find out what happened.'

Kat opened the door. 'It's not just practical help that I want.'

'Kat.' He reached over to her. 'Don't go. I'm worried about you.'

She couldn't tell him now. About how she was feeling. The tumult of her emotions towards him mixed with the concern for her sister. So she did what she always advised her clients against doing. She retreated. Left him sitting in the car and stalked off towards the centre of Bampton.

There was plenty of time to think as she walked. It was a

good three miles to her house and it would take her at least an hour to reach it. She didn't expect Mark to follow her, and she was right. At least, amid all this, she hadn't completely lost the ability to read people correctly. She walked quickly, facing the oncoming rush-hour traffic, which was still streaming into the town centre. It gave her a sense of going in the opposite direction to where everyone else was heading. There was an allegory there somewhere.

Each step brought her closer to Providence Villa, and a sense of longing began to wash over her. Because all she really wanted was to be there. Her and Lena's house. Something was connected to that building and the years they had spent there. Lena might have absented herself voluntarily, but she was reaching out to Kat with the gifts. It was the time to start making connections.

Soon Kat was sick of walking and regretted leaving Mark so hastily. She could feel large blisters forming on the soles of her feet and wondered how strange she would look if she took off her shoes. But as she neared the house, the familiar roads she was tramping down brought a renewed sense of purpose. Finally arriving at Providence Villa, she swung open the old iron gate and halted.

She could see the ceiling lights in the living room were on. The dirty glass pendant was missing a few bulbs, but the yellow glow was unmistakable. *Right*, she thought. She had no time to feel fear. In a fury she pulled her keys out of her pocket, put the right one in the lock and charged into the living room.

A tall man turned around. Kat saw who it was and paled. 'What the hell are you doing in my house?'

53

Sadler was waiting for them when they returned. He was flicking through a file Connie had left on her desk. She had to hide the surge of irritation she felt when she saw him leaning over her work.

It was just as well they hadn't gone for the drink that Palmer had suggested on the way back. He'd seemed subdued by Rebecca Hardy's testimony. Well, that was hardly a surprise. No matter how much training you had in dealing with victims of sexual violence, there was always the element of subjectivity when it came to listening to individual testimonies. And Rebecca Hardy's story didn't exactly show men in a good light.

'What have you two been up to?'

Connie looked to Palmer. 'We've been interviewing a potential victim of Philip Staley.'

'You didn't think about telling me where you were going?'

Connie looked at Palmer again. Two red patches had appeared in his cheeks. 'We were about to come and update you. We didn't know what we had until we'd interviewed the witness.'

Sadler relaxed a fraction. 'You have two minutes to update me. Then we're going straight to Superintendent Llewellyn to repeat that update.'

Connie frowned. Sadler seemed riled. 'Is everything okay?'

Sadler's expression didn't change. 'We'll soon find out.'

They sat in Llewellyn's office like schoolchildren seeing the headmaster. It was only the second time that Connie had been inside the room. The first had been an earlier case, the previous year. A child who'd gone missing in the seventies. During that time she had seen Llewellyn's emotions exposed in a way she hadn't thought possible. This time he looked serious.

He started without preamble. 'I've called the three of you here because I want to talk to you about what Rebecca Hardy told you. Yes, I know who you've been to see. When you requested the full file off the computer system, DS Palmer, it raised a flag that was referred to me.'

There hadn't been much time to update Sadler on the meeting with Rebecca, and he kept his face deadpan. Connie wondered what he was thinking.

'I thought I'd call you in to give you a bit of background information on the Rebecca Hardy case. This is mainly for you,' he nodded at Connie and Palmer. 'Only you, Sadler, were a copper in 1998, so I'm not principally talking to you. But you two: don't underestimate the changes that have taken place since then.'

Connie frowned. What the hell was this all about? There had been various initiatives to improve the treatment of women who reported rapes. Part of it was the result of keeping up with the times, some of it was in response to some truly awful instances of victims being treated badly following their allegations. She knew that, and so would Palmer. She glanced at him. His face was still red.

'So the thing is,' continued Llewellyn, 'this case has got

"sensitive" written all over it. You're being shielded from all the flak I'm getting about the misidentification of Andrew Fisher. That's deliberate. I want you concentrating on the current investigation, not on any mistakes that may have been made in the past.'

'Which is what we are doing.' Sadler's voice was neutral, but, in contrast, his complexion had paled to marble.

'But now the fact that the first victim, if that's what you've concluded,' continued Llewellyn, 'the *original* victim, also had a rape charge made against him that was subsequently dropped, adds to the mire in which we find ourselves. We can call it', he grimaced, 'the fourth cock-up.'

Connie risked a glance at Sadler. His eyes flickered, but he said nothing.

'We're certain it was Philip Staley?' asked Llewellyn.

Palmer was on firm ground, and it was he who spoke. 'From Bill's, I mean Dr Shields', original report, it seems that the body found in Lena Gray's bed had a scar on his forearm about the size of a ten-pence piece. The uniform shape suggested a medical excision rather than an accident. Philip Staley had a suspicious mole removed when he was thirty. Medical records stated that Staley was a habitual user of tanning machines. The medical notes about the mole removal match the location of the excision as far as we're able to ascertain. I mean, given that we have no body.'

Llewellyn looked to Sadler, who nodded. 'Philip Staley was last heard of in August 2004, when he telephoned his mother asking for a loan of five hundred pounds to enable him to buy a ticket to Australia as he wanted to emigrate there. It appears that his mother was more annoyed than worried about the fact that he never called from his destination. She hasn't heard from him since.'

'So we're pretty sure he's our man, are we? I mean, even the excision isn't conclusive.'

'In the absence of the original body, there's no way we're going to be one hundred per cent sure,' said Sadler. 'We're going to have to talk in terms of probables. Given the physical evidence, plus the timing of his disappearance, I think we've got a good basis to suspect that he's our man.'

'We've looked into his bank accounts.' Palmer leant forward in his chair, keen to impress. 'There have been no deposits or withdrawals since September 2004. The last was from a cash machine, in Bampton, on the fourth of September of that year. It puts him in Bampton around the time that the man was found in Lena Gray's bed.'

'Philip Staley.' Llewellyn drummed his pen on his desk. 'What's his background? Was he originally from Bampton?'

'He grew up in Macclesfield. Left school at sixteen. Then had a series of jobs, mainly the office type. He was clearly clever but also couldn't settle at anything. His last known job was working as a clerk in a bank.'

'What about outside work? Hobbies and so forth,' asked Llewellyn.

'He enjoyed playing sport,' continued Connie. 'I called his mother for more details about his life. She naturally wanted to skirt over his employment history but she told me he liked sports and rugby in particular.'

Sadler looked at her. 'You didn't mention that before. I told you Andrew Fisher was a rugby player. Did Staley play for a team?'

'Yes.' Palmer didn't need to look through his notes. 'One of the local ones.'

'He and Andrew Fisher could easily have known each other through rugby games. The local clubs are always playing each other. We need to check it out. Palmer, can you do that?'

Thank God for that, thought Connie. The idea of interviewing a bunch of rugger buggers didn't appeal at all. Mind you, Palmer wasn't looking best pleased either. That was a point in his favour.

'That's it then,' said Llewellyn, shutting a notebook on his desk. 'Keep me updated, will you? I don't like the sound of this Philip Staley. Nasty business, a rape allegation, whatever eventually happened to the man.'

Connie looked at the other members of the team in surprise. Was that it? What was this all about? Even Sadler was looking surprised. A twenty-minute meeting with the Superintendent just to chat about the personality of Philip Staley? That wasn't normal.

Sadler stood up without catching anyone's eye. 'We'll keep you fully informed, sir. Of course.'

Llewellyn nodded and turned to his computer screen. They were dismissed.

They walked down the corridor towards the main CID offices. Still not looking at them, Sadler said, 'Go in and grab your coats. I'm taking you for a drink. The first one's on me.'

54

'You're a long way from Whitby.' After the initial fright, Kat's heartbeat had settled into a more regular rhythm.

The man didn't move but lifted his hands in a gesture of resignation. She had last seen him outside his own home next to Lena's bolt-hole in that windy seaside town. There, his clipped beard and bare feet had given him a hippyish look. Now, in his thick jacket and hiking boots, he looked more threatening but his manner seemed more anxious to appease than intimidate.

'I'm looking for Lena.'

Kat snorted. 'We're all looking for Lena. Join the club. How did you get into my house?'

He looked confused. 'Your house? I thought it was Lena's. She left a key with me once. Years ago. She said she lived by herself and wanted someone else to have a key. When she got married, I offered to give it back to her, but she told me to keep it.'

'The house belongs to both of us. We were left it between us when my mother died. Lena's never wanted to move and I stayed here while she was in prison.'

The man winced.

'You know about her conviction, then. You said in Whitby that she just disappeared. Stopped coming. You knew she'd gone to jail.'

The man looked unhappy. 'Lena and I got to know each

other over the years. She first came to the town as a teenager, although I didn't know her then. When she was working, she started renting the cottage next to me. She was a pale wraith of a thing. I used to just knock to see if she was okay. This was before she was married.'

'Did you have a relationship with her . . . um . . . do you have a name?'

'I'm Daniel. Daniel Frears. And no. I didn't have a relationship with Lena.' Something in his voice struck a sour note.

'You sure?'

He shook his head. 'Not for lack of trying on my part, I have to say. In the early days, I mean. She just wasn't bothered and I didn't push it. I got used to us being friends.'

'And after she got married?'

'Nothing really changed. She still came to Whitby just as regularly and I'd still see her. We'd have a glass of wine at mine.'

'What did she do? In Whitby, I mean?'

It was the man's turn to look at her in astonishment. 'She painted, of course.'

Kat snorted. 'Not many flowers in Whitby.'

He looked confused. 'Flowers?'

'The flowers that she painted. Not many of them in Whitby.'

'But she didn't paint flowers. Not the canvases I saw.'

Kat stared at him. 'That's all she bloody does paint. Come upstairs and have a look if you don't believe me.'

She led him up to Lena's studio and pulled out some of the large canvases leaning face to the wall. Against the white background were the usual blue daubs, frozen and stark.

Kat watched him examine them.

'These are completely different to what I saw her paint in Whitby. She painted figures. I mean people. Men and women embracing. She painted passion. And pain. She was better at it there. These are okay but not as good as the Whitby ones.'

Kat's head was reeling. Lena had always painted flowers. It was her thing. The thought that her sister had another side was bewildering. 'Are you sure?'

'Of course I'm sure. There aren't many of them. She was a really slow painter but what she produced was good. It all stopped when she went to prison, of course.'

Kat scrabbled to clear her mind. 'So what are you doing here?'

'I told you. I'm looking for Lena. I haven't heard from her, and I'm worried.'

'You know she's missing. I told you when I saw you. She's disappeared.'

'I know. I thought she'd come to Whitby. It's always been her escape. Somewhere to go when she felt down. I waited, but she never came.'

'When did you last see her?'

He put one of the canvases back down. 'I can't answer that. I'm sorry, Kat, but some things can't be told.'

Wasn't that what Lena had said to her? When the police had come to question her about finding the real Andrew Fisher? *Not everything can be told.*

Kat could feel the fury rising again. 'There's one question you can answer me. According to a very nice police detective working on this case, Andrew Fisher was seen in Whitby about four years ago. Given that you clearly know more about my family than I do, I'd like you to tell me what he was doing there.'

55

Sadler had chosen the White Swan because it was quiet. It played no music and had no quiz nights. It was given over to the consumption of drink, and the preference for real ales over bottled beer meant that the clientele was largely past the age of forty.

Each of the three gathered around the circular table was, for different reasons, slightly out of place in the pub. Palmer had clearly never been there before. In Sadler's opinion, he was more likely to frequent one of the bars on Bampton High Street. His well-cut clothes looked too smart for the basic bar. Connie, on the other hand, had made herself comfortable. She was sitting with her short thin legs stretched out in front of her and her arms behind her head. Her confidence and mischievous look had attracted a few glances from some of the men sitting at the bar, who clearly weren't used to women taking such enjoyment in the masculine space. Sadler was known to the landlord, who gave him a brief nod when he entered, but he never felt comfortable in pubs and could never think what to drink. He had settled for a glass of red wine. Palmer and Connie were drinking beer.

'What was that all about?' demanded Connie, as usual skipping the preamble.

Sadler tasted the wine and frowned. 'I honestly don't know.' And he didn't. He was as perplexed as the others as to why

Llewellyn had called them into the office. 'I could have briefed him myself on our progress regarding Philip Staley. Once you'd updated me, of course.'

Palmer looked like he might sulk, but curiosity got the better of him. 'It was strange though. He seemed to be pumping us for information. What was he talking about when he talked about the "fourth cock-up"?'

'It's not the term I would have used. There have been four mistakes, or, if not mistakes, then problems in this case. Llewellyn, in his usual fashion, has called them "cock-ups".'

'Let me guess,' said Connie. 'The misidentification of Philip Staley in the original investigation; the killing of the real Andrew Fisher; the disappearance of Lena Gray; and, finally, the dropping of rape allegations against Staley.' She beamed at them both, her hands still behind her head. 'A quartet of cock-ups.'

Sadler was amused but made an effort not to show it. He could feel his mood lifting. 'Don't remind me. I was around for all four of those mistakes.'

Connie dropped her hands and leant forward. 'They're not your fault, and two of them I wouldn't even describe as mistakes. Okay. This misidentification of Philip Staley. That is a massive fu—' Connie caught Sadler's eye and changed her mind, 'mistake. However, the killing of Andrew Fisher? That's murder and not our error. Letting Lena Gray give us the slip? Well, that's a mistake, but as much mine as yours. I interviewed her. I should have spotted she was giving us the runaround.'

'And as for the rape accusation,' Palmer said, after taking a sip of his pint. 'Is that a blunder? If the victim withdraws her accusation, even now, there's not much we can do.'

'But measures are in place now to ensure that it is less likely to occur. And quite right.' Connie drained the rest of her beer.

The group fell silent, and Sadler could feel two pairs of eyes on him. Connie, as usual, articulated his thoughts. 'There's something fishy going on.'

Sadler picked up his wine glass and took a large gulp of the musty liquid. 'Yes. It would appear so.'

56

Daniel sat in the kitchen with his head in his hands. In front of him was the empty can of cold beer that he'd finished in three swift gulps. 'It's actually been hard keeping it all in. I live by myself now in Whitby. I've had girlfriends, lots of them, but Lena's always exerted this fascination over me. Over the years, coming and going from my life. If she'd been a regular girlfriend it might have fizzled out long ago, but it was the enchantment of the unobtainable. Can you understand that?'

Kat had calmed down, and her professional curiosity kicked in. 'Of course I can understand that.' *But has it helped you?* she thought. *Is your life better for it?*

'For a long time she was quite distant from me. She'd come in for a drink, but I never found out anything about her. That never really changed but we did get closer. Despite the distance, if you see what I mean.'

'So you knew her for, what, ten or so years?'

'Twelve or thirteen. Right up until she went to prison.'

'Did you visit her there?'

Daniel stood and went to the fridge. 'Do you mind if I have another?' He reached inside and took out another can. 'I would have visited her but times were limited. She wanted to see you during those times.'

Kat frowned. 'I didn't get that impression over the years I was going there. We never talked about anything of any consequence. She didn't even seem particularly pleased to see me.'

'I'm not sure if this helps, me saying this, but she was always very protective of you. She wouldn't talk about you at all.'

'But you knew about me?'

'Of course. I knew Lena had a sister. She seemed proud of what you had done with your life but she never really wanted to talk about you.'

'Not interested.' Kat's tone was bitter.

'I really don't think it's that.'

'So what changed? You implied, just now, that you and Lena did get closer.'

Daniel fiddled with his can. 'In 2004, Lena came to me for help. I got a phone call in the middle of the night. Just after midnight I think it was. Or maybe a bit later. I'm not a night owl. She woke me up when she rang.'

'September 2004?'

'Yes. She rang me to say she'd just killed a man.'

'Just like that?'

'Yes. Just like that. She still had her wits about her, you know. She'd driven to a phone box across town to call me. So nothing would come up on her mobile or house phone records. It was the first time I'd heard her like that.'

'Like what?'

'Completely focused on what she wanted doing.'

'Which was?'

'When she called, I thought she'd want me to help get rid of the body. Which, you know, I probably would have done. Probably.'

'But she didn't want that.' Kat could see where this was going. 'She wanted you to hide Andrew Fisher.'

'So you know.'

'Well, I've guessed. The police have a lead that Andrew Fisher was holed up in Whitby, at least for a while.'

Daniel stared at the can of beer. 'She had a plan. A pretty good one, actually. She said that if she pretended the next morning that she'd woken up next to her dead husband, it would take them a day or so to work out that a murder had actually been committed. Which would give us a chance to get Andrew up to Whitby and any other affairs sorted out before she was arrested.'

'What about the deception? Didn't she think that the police would work out that they had the wrong man?'

'I think she did, but that never happened. It surprised us both. I hid Andrew Fisher for the first few months. Until the spring of 2005. He stayed in my house. Didn't go out unless he was wrapped up in a hat, scarf and so on. It was winter, so it was pretty easy to do.'

'And after that?'

'He moved into a house the other side of the river. Where the tourists don't venture. I sort of kept an eye on him. Only for Lena's sake. He was pretty self-sufficient.'

'And then what happened?'

'I don't know. For ten years or so I never bothered. Lena wouldn't see me in prison and Andrew'd made a life for himself in Whitby, I think. I'd occasionally see him in a pub. Or walking about the town. We tended to ignore each other. Too much history.'

'But why? Why did you help her?'

Daniel reached forward and took a sip of his beer. 'I've told you the answer to that. Because I'd have done anything for

Lena. Don't ask me how he ended up dead in Bampton. I last saw him at the beginning of April. He was alive and well then.'

Kat said nothing. She allowed the silence to settle around her. Daniel was watching her. He was a huge bear of a man. Long limbs, a solid torso. It was no surprise that Lena had chosen him to depend on.

'You haven't asked me the key question.'

Kat sighed. 'That's because I'm not sure I want to know the answer. Okay. I'll ask it. Why? Why did Lena kill someone in her bed, pretend it was her husband and then send him up to Whitby to hide?'

Daniel's smile was grim. 'I have absolutely no idea.'

57

Sadler left them at ten. He had looked at his watch and made his excuses. Connie looked after him with a sardonic eye. 'It's not even as if he's got far to go. He only lives around the corner.'

'As, in fact, do you.'

'Opposite direction though.' She wondered how Palmer knew where she lived. 'Funny case this is turning out to be.'

He turned to her. 'I don't want to talk about the inquiry. It's one bloody thing after another with this investigation. What happened to those simple cases that you see on TV? You know, the ones you can solve in two hours?'

'Oh, those.' Connie had moved on to brandy and Coke, and she took a long gulp from her glass. 'You want an easy life? You can always go back into uniform. Climb the greasy pole. Go for an inspector post.'

'Now you sound like Joanne.' His voice was sulky.

Here we go, thought Connie. *I'm going to get his marital woes. Again.* At least she never got this with Sadler. But it was Palmer's weaknesses that held the key to her attraction to him. It made him more human. 'Problems still?'

He picked up his glass. 'I should never have got married. It was all right when we were engaged. At least I had some say in decisions we made. Now she just tells me what's going to happen. Like she's decided to come off the pill.'

'If you don't want a baby yet, you've got to tell her. You

know what this job is like. It's her that's going to bear the brunt of bringing up the child. She needs to know that.'

'Do you think I've not tried?' he hissed. 'She's decided to have a baby. And I don't get any say in it.'

Connie smiled into her glass. Poor bugger. She wondered how he'd be when his expensive suits began to be marked with baby sick. The thought made her snigger. He saw it, and his eyes narrowed. 'You were right, you know. When you suggested I call off the wedding. I was just too pig-headed to see it.'

'You're too conventional, Palmer. You never would have backed out. Just as you're going to let Joanne have her own way about the baby.'

'Well, if she wants to get pregnant, we'll have to have sex.'

She leant towards him. 'You not getting it at all?'

'Nothing. Not. At. All.'

Connie snorted into her glass. 'Join the club, but at least I'm single. How's that come about?'

'She's too tired in the evenings. Actually, so am I.'

'It's different for men.'

'Well, as I said, if she wants a baby, it's not going to happen by itself.'

Connie, for the first time, noticed a coldness in his voice. 'Don't you love her?'

'Probably, but it's not how I expected it to be.'

Only probably. She really was better off single if that was the best it got.

'Remember before the wedding, when I asked if I could stay at yours?'

Here we go. 'Yes. I do. I remember saying no.'

'I meant it only platonically. I just wanted to stay with a

mate. You know, from work. Who understood what I did all day. It's not changed anything, has it?'

Connie smiled. 'Not for me it hasn't. You're still the same irritating bugger you were before you had your pre-wedding wobble.'

To her surprise, he grabbed her hand. 'As long as things are still the same. I wouldn't want anything to change between you and me.'

She tipped her glass to her mouth to see what was left. Not much, just ice cubes. She poked them with her finger. 'Nothing's changed,' she said, without looking at him.

'Do you think I should have married someone in the business? You know, another copper?'

Connie grimaced. There were a few married couples in the station, but she wasn't clear if or how they ever saw each other. From what she could see, once the kids came, it was the women who resigned while the men carried on with their jobs as normal. Not for her.

'Did you have anyone in mind?' It came out more flirtatious than she'd intended, and she saw Palmer's eyes widen.

He leaned in towards her. 'You said no last time.'

She turned in her seat to face him. 'It was the week you were getting married.'

'Weren't you a bit sorry, though? I mean, that it never happened?'

Connie looked down into her glass. 'More than a bit.'

58

Kat put Daniel in the spare room downstairs. There was a ratty old sofa that was just about big enough to accommodate his long limbs. She heaved a large quilt from the airing cupboard, and he heaped cushions from the various chairs for pillows.

'Will you sleep?' she asked.

He looked dog-tired. 'Probably. You?'

'Probably not.'

He smiled at her. 'You look like your sister, you know.'

'So everyone used to tell us. Less so now. We're rarely seen together.'

'Are you with someone? Boyfriend, I mean?'

Kat thought of Mark. 'There's someone I like. A lot. But it's complicated.'

'Oh, I know all about those relationships. Does he make you happy?'

'Yes, he does, but the timing is terrible. I need to concentrate on finding Lena and finding out what's going on.'

At the mention of her sister, he turned away. 'Lena is a keeper of secrets. Hers and others'. If you really want to know what happened in 2004, you need to unlock the past.'

As she left him settling into the sofa, she picked up her phone to check for messages and wondered if Mark was thinking of her too.

What the hell am I doing? thought Palmer. Connie's back was against the converted mill where she lived, and he was pressed against her. He slid a hand up the front of her jumper and under her bra.

'I think we should stop.' Her voice was muffled against his shoulder.

'Do you want to?'

'Of course not but we're not having sex in the street. That'd be the talk of the station if we got caught.'

'Can I come up then?' It was the second time he'd asked. She'd said 'no' last time. He could see her mind assessing it.

'It's just sex though, right?'

He laughed into her hair. 'Definitely just sex.'

She slid her arm inside his jacket and fumbled to find his skin. 'That's all right then.'

59

Sadler had slept badly. Two hours of fitful sleep and the rest of the night had been spent lying in the dark thinking about the case. Llewellyn's behaviour had unsettled him more than he'd let on to the team. His superintendent was a local, a man rooted in the Derbyshire landscape, and he had been a presence at this station since Sadler had joined the force. Llewellyn was respected. He'd climbed the ranks, studying for extra qualifications at night school, and was still seen by ordinary coppers as 'one of us'. So why did Sadler have the horrible feeling that Llewellyn was involved in something lacking the transparency he so advocated to his teams?

When he arrived at the station, Palmer was already at work, typing information into the computer with expert fingers.

'Where's Connie?'

Palmer looked around the room. 'I haven't seen her this morning.'

'Was it a late one last night?'

Palmer focused his eyes on the screen in front of him. 'Not particularly.'

As if on cue, Connie came through the door, balancing three cups of coffee in her hands. She put all three down on Palmer's desk. Sadler picked up one. Palmer continued to look at the screen.

'Today, can you both focus on pulling together everything

we know about Philip Staley? There's a potential rugby link between him and Andrew Fisher. If it exists, then we need to find it. Focus on all the material we have. Look for any particular links with Lena Gray. She worked in a florist's and then as an artist. That's more of a long shot but try it anyway.'

'What about the fact that he's a rapist?' asked Connie.

Now Palmer did look up. 'He's not been convicted.'

Connie's face reddened. 'But we do believe Rebecca Hardy, don't we? You were there, Palmer. Did it look like she was lying?'

Palmer swung around in his chair. 'I don't think she was lying, no, but he wasn't convicted of any crime. I'm simply stating a fact. You can't go around calling him a rapist.'

Connie put her hands on her hips. 'Look. It's the act that makes him a rapist, not the conviction.'

Sadler looked at the two of them. They were bickering as usual although there appeared to be an edge to their disagreement. Time to intervene. 'Connie, come with me. I'm going to interview Andrew Fisher's mother. I'd like you with me. Bring the coffee.'

Connie's eyes were on Palmer as she nodded, and she followed Sadler out of the station. They both blinked as they stepped outside the front door and encountered sunshine, and not the weak watery kind that had graced Bampton since early April. There was warmth in the air.

'I think spring has finally hit us.'

'About time. Isn't May supposed to be the last month before summer? Bet it doesn't last though.' Connie walked around to the passenger door and flung herself in.

'Is everything okay?'

'Everything is fine,' she said, pulling the seat belt across her body.

The drive to Andrew Fisher's childhood home was brief, but even in that short time Connie's mood appeared to brighten. She stopped looking out of the side window and instead turned towards Sadler. 'Have you ever been here before? I mean, you knew him from school.'

'We weren't in the same circles. He was in the rugby crowd, I preferred cricket and I never drank like he did.'

Out of the corner of his eye he could see Connie thinking it over. 'You know, if you drink like that when you're a teenager, I bet you like a good few when you're older. I wonder how much of a drinker he was as an adult.'

'Did Philip Staley's mother say how much he liked a drink?'

Connie humphed in her seat. 'She didn't tell me that much. She was anxious to protect her son. Except when the bit about the money came out. Then he wasn't such a golden boy.'

'Five hundred pounds is a lot of money for someone in her position to lose. It was probably all her savings.'

'It's not been touched. If we can prove conclusively it was Philip Staley who was killed in 2004 she could probably get it back somehow.'

'True. But the bank account isn't a priority. Don't worry about that for the moment.'

As they drew up outside Andrew Fisher's childhood home, a shadow in the window indicated that they were being watched.

'I rang ahead to say we were coming.'

Connie looked up at the house. 'One thing worth remembering. When I interviewed Jane Reynolds about seeing

Andrew Fisher in Whitby, she poured scorn on our assumption about Pamela Fisher not knowing her son was still alive.'

'It was Llewellyn who told me she had seemed shocked. I have him down as a good judge of character.'

'I'm just passing on what Mrs Reynolds told me. She was a canny old bird in her own way too.'

The front door opened to them as they walked up the path. Pamela Fisher didn't even bother to pretend that she hadn't been awaiting their arrival. She led them into the hall, which was stultifyingly hot. The heating needed turning down on this warm day. The woman was wearing a short-sleeved dress. *Why doesn't she save money by putting on a cardigan and turning down the heating?* thought Sadler irritably.

They followed her into an equally warm living room full of furniture. Connie squeezed past two sofas and sat in the only armchair, leaving Sadler to sit on one of the low sofas.

'Would you like tea?' Pamela Fisher had a clear voice with no trace of a Derbyshire accent.

'We've just had coffee in the car, thanks,' replied Connie. The woman frowned.

'How are you?' asked Sadler.

Pamela Fisher sat slowly down into the sofa, old bones making her movements stiff. 'I'm all right. It's been an awful time, but it was kind of the Superintendent to come around to explain things and see if I was okay.'

'It was a shock?'

The woman smoothed her skirt with her hands. 'I've never had a problem with my heart. Arthritis is my affliction. And low blood sugar. But when I heard what happened, I thought my heart had stopped. The woman who'd broken the news had to get me a sweet cup of tea. There was too much sugar in it.'

'So in 2004, when your son was found dead, you had no idea that it wasn't really him.'

The woman screwed up her face in disgust. 'No idea whatsoever.'

'And what did you think when his wife, Lena, was charged with his murder?'

Pamela's face took on a mottled hue, a complexion that Sadler associated with repressed anger. 'I liked Lena when I first met her. She was a bit airy-fairy, if you get my meaning, but better for him than his first wife, Gail. *She* never gave him any rest. Always wanted to know where he was. Lena gave him more space. Andrew did have to go and live in that big draughty house, although they seemed happy enough. That's all anyone wants for their children.'

'You said you liked her when you first met her . . .'

Pamela looked down at her lap. 'She was cold. It wasn't shyness. It was her personality. You couldn't get near her, emotionally. I used to wonder what was going on underneath that cool exterior.'

'So you didn't visit Lena in prison?' asked Connie.

'Why on earth would I want to do that? She murdered my son. She didn't even make any effort to deny it. I couldn't believe it. She was evil. There was no way I was going to visit her there.'

'And you had no idea about motive?' Sadler glanced over to Connie, who was looking around the room.

'None whatsoever.'

Connie had stood up and was looking at some photographs grouped together on the far wall.

She pointed at a portrait showing a boy in a school uniform. 'Is this Andrew as a teenager?'

Sadler and Pamela turned towards the image and said 'Yes' in unison.

Pamela Fisher looked at Sadler in alarm. 'You knew Andrew? You never said.'

'We were in a couple of the same classes at Bampton High.'

'Did you know him well?'

'Not really. We had different groups of friends.' She relaxed a fraction.

Connie looked at the two of them, frowning.

Five minutes later, walking back to the car, she said, 'She didn't like the thought of you knowing Fisher as a teenager. What was that all about?'

Sadler looked back at the house. 'I have no idea.'

60

Francesca couldn't sit still. She continually crossed and un-crossed her legs. Shuffled from one side of the chair to the other. Fiddled with her bra straps and the buttons on her cardigan. She lived in the High Oaks area of Bampton, and her well-cut clothes, blonde highlighted hair and well-applied make-up shouted money and time to spend on looking this good. Her husband was having an affair with a work colleague. She'd found text messages on a phone that he hadn't even tried that hard to hide. 'He keeps reassuring me it's all over. He wanted me to find out. The spark had gone. He wanted to tell me that he still loved me, and the affair was a way of doing that.'

You've got to be joking, thought Kat. *Demonstrate your love for someone by having sex with a colleague?* 'Do you think he did that? Proved that he loved you.'

Francesca shifted in her seat again. 'No.'

Well, no. That was the whole point of affairs. If anything, you're only proving to yourself what you think you don't have. Your youth, your sexuality, your outward attractiveness to the opposite sex.

But when push came to shove, Francesca's husband hadn't wanted to end their marriage and didn't want to leave the marital home.

'Francesca.' Kat had been wanting to broach the subject for some time, but, after eight sessions, the last few of which had been going nowhere, it was time to move things on. 'What do you want? You've told me a lot about how you've been feeling. You're very open about that. But I don't get any sense of what you want from life.'

Kat watched as her client sat still for a moment. She looked shocked, as if she was being asked a question that she'd never thought about before, but she answered without hesitation. 'I want to be by myself.'

After Francesca left, Kat made herself a cup of mint tea and sat on a stool in her tiny kitchen. So Francesca wanted to be alone. What was incredible was how many people were afraid of the solitude that they so craved. Francesca, shackled to a man she didn't love, and who she probably despised, put up with the relationship not because of money, although that was probably a factor. No, she was afraid of being alone. The thing she most wanted.

Solitude had never been a problem for Kat. In fact, she was desperate for it at times. She and Lena shared that need and it sounded like Daniel had learnt to be by himself, despite his yearning for Lena. She had left him in the house, making himself some coffee.

And what about Mark? Kat once read an article in her counselling journal about therapists who had affairs with their clients. It made grim reading. In the likelihood of you falling for one of your patients, you needed to stop the sessions as soon as was appropriate. That went for former patients too. Two years was the absolute minimum before you were even supposed to meet an ex-client outside the therapy room. Of course, Kat knew of exceptions. Like teachers who fell in love with their students and prison officers who had affairs with their charges, there were therapists who found themselves desiring their clients. But she had never considered the possibility that she might, one day, be in this position. She was unlikely to be prosecuted, but her professional life would be in tatters.

A noise outside in the courtyard interrupted her reverie. There was a click and a muffled sound. She shot out of the kitchen, and her heart nearly failed her. In the narrow hall stood the boy, with a carving knife in his hand.

61

Palmer had his head in his hands when Connie got back to the station. *I'm not having this,* she thought. She went up to him and leant over him. 'Look, all we did was have sex last night. Let's not make a big deal of it, right?'

He looked up and grinned. 'Right.'

She looked at him in surprise. 'I thought you were having an existentialist crisis. You're sat there with your head in your hands like it's the end of the world.'

He put his hand on her arm. 'We can't do it again, Con. Not just because I'm married but because of our jobs here. There's no way Sadler would put up with an affair in his team and I've no intention of screwing up my career.'

'Me neither.'

'That's all right then.' He gave her arm a squeeze and let it go. 'I was actually just concentrating. I can't prove that Andrew Fisher and Philip Staley knew each other but I'd say there was a pretty good chance. They both played rugby for a start. I managed to speak to a massive rugby fan, and he's given me the fixtures for over twenty years ago. Andrew Fisher played for Bampton's team. Philip Staley for Macclesfield Blues. If you look at this list, where I've highlighted is when the two teams played each other.'

Connie picked up the sheet with the highlights. He saw her frowning. 'What's the matter?'

'The thing is, this is good. I mean, they may have known each other twenty years ago. Fair enough. However, Philip Staley died in 2004 when he was thirty-six. And the thing is, how many men do you know who still play rugby in their mid-thirties?'

Palmer winced. 'I wouldn't fancy playing it now.'

'Exactly. It's a young man's game. Most start playing it at school. We know Andrew Fisher did. He and Staley were the same age.'

'But didn't go to the same school.'

'No, but I bet the schools also took part in tournaments.' She thought back to the photos of Andrew Fisher on his mother's wall and her discomfiture at the fact that Sadler knew him as a teenager.

'I think we need to concentrate on the teenage Andrew Fisher. The answer lies there.'

'This a hunch, Con?'

'Listen,' she hissed. 'Will you bloody well stop calling me Con. Before, it was cheek; now, it sounds intimate. Do you want the whole team to know we had sex last night?'

He looked up at her, laughter in his eyes, and shook his head.

'Then stop calling me Con.'

'Ms Childs?'

She snorted with laughter. 'Then they'll definitely know. Just keep with Connie.' She could smell his aftershave and the heat of his skin. After he'd left her flat, she'd taken a shower straight away, waiting for the shame to arrive. It hadn't. Standing next to him, she wanted to reach out and touch him. It wouldn't be him leaving the team at this rate. It'd be her.

He seemed not to notice her presence. He was looking at the fixtures sheet again. 'Concentrate on the teenage Fisher. Maybe. I'll have a look. But it wasn't the teenage Fisher who wound up dead, was it?'

Connie took a step backwards. 'No, but some secrets cast a long shadow. I think you, me and the boss are going to be taking a trip back to the past again.'

62

'I'm not going to use it.'

Kat couldn't take her eyes off the knife. It looked like a meat cleaver, the shiny metal gleaming in the light coming through the window. Its thick blade could do untold damage. Damage to her. She could also smell fear coming off the boy. Teenage sweat and a stale bready unwashed stink that made her want to heave.

'I need to speak to you.' He motioned with the knife, and they went together through to the counselling room, she leading the way and aware of the knife in his hand. Once there, the boy hesitated. The chairs were placed so that they faced each other. A small table in between contained only a box of tissues and a cactus plant. 'Sit down.'

Kat took refuge in her usual chair. The boy picked up the other chair and put it down next to hers. He sat in it and, clearly uncomfortable, stood up and kicked it out of the way. Instead he dragged the little table and sat on it facing her. Kat kept her eyes on the knife, conscious of the menace emanating from it. 'I've a message from Lena.'

'What? Is she okay?'

'Oh, she's all right.' The boy's hood fell slightly away from his eyes, and she could see dark-brown irises set in red-rimmed eyes. He looked like he'd been crying.

'How do you know her? Lena?'

'She's my friend.' The boy seemed proud.

Friend? Kat felt that familiar pang of jealousy. How could Lena be friends with this boy?

'You get my things?'

'You mean the items you've been leaving for me? Of course I got them. You made sure of that. Did Lena give them to you?'

'Maybe.' The boy refused to look her in the eye. 'They're clues. Haven't you guessed yet?'

'Guessed what?'

'Guessed what it's all about.'

Anger coursed through Kat. 'What what's all about?'

But he didn't seem to know. Or wasn't going to tell her. He lifted up the knife and brandished it in triumph. 'I've cleaned it, just as Granddad taught me to.'

Kat's stomach contracted in fear. She kept her eyes on the blade. 'Your granddad?'

'Yeah. His dad had shown him how to clean a bayonet. You use vinegar. Not the stuff you put on your chips, but the clear stuff. You wipe the blade like this.' The boy pulled out a piece of material from his pocket and started to rub it up and down the blade with a leery look on his face. The sexual innuendo was unmistakable.

Kat suddenly caught sight of a purple pattern on the cloth. 'What's that?'

The boy's expression changed from mock lust to fear. 'Lena gave it to me.'

'Lena? It's got nothing to do with her.' Kat reached forward and grabbed the cloth from the boy's hand. He stood in consternation, holding the knife uncertainly in front of him.

Kat made a bolt for the front door, pulling it open. 'You tell my sister that this scarf has nothing to do with her. I'm sick of the sight of you and your presents. Tell her to come and see me herself or just leave me alone. Do you hear? Now get of out of my room.'

He left without looking at her. Kat inspected the scarf. This she did recognise. It was hers. From a long time ago. The eighties? Definitely not that old but maybe from twenty or so years ago. It had been a favourite then. By that time the fracture between her and Lena had been complete. There was nothing this scarf symbolised that could be described as a shared experience.

63

Sadler watched through the window as Palmer and Connie walked across the lawn outside the station. Palmer took off his dark-blue jacket and laid it carefully on the grass before sitting gingerly on it. Connie plopped herself down next to him, making herself comfortable, before lying down with her hands behind her head. Palmer ignored her, untwisted a paper bag, took out what looked like a sandwich and started to eat it. Sadler felt the urge to join them.

The phone on his desk rang, an unwelcome distraction. 'DI Sadler? I've got Julia Miles from Shallowford House in reception. She's looking for DC Childs or DS Palmer but I'm not getting any response from either of their phones.'

Sadler looked back out through the window. The two were laughing together, and Palmer looked like he was trying to stuff part of his sandwich into Connie's mouth. 'I'll come down and get her.'

Julia Miles looked composed when he came towards her. She also looked familiar. Perhaps their paths had crossed at some point in the past. It wouldn't have been surprising. He saw a gleam of recognition in her eyes too.

'You don't remember me?'

In these instances, the truth was usually preferable to obfuscation. 'You look familiar. It's just I'm struggling . . .'

She smiled and looked away. 'You nearly arrested me once.

When they were pulling down the old swimming baths to make way for the housing development. Do you remember? About ten years ago? I chained myself to a drainpipe. The constable was going to arrest me for trespass along with the others there. You stopped your car and intervened.'

Sadler did remember. The building had been beautiful. Made from Derbyshire stone, it had been a solid square building with a small pool. Too small by modern standards and with tiles that were chipped and stained with age. And no heritage listing, which meant that developers had been free to do whatever with it when they acquired the land. Four executive homes with postage-stamp-sized gardens had been squeezed onto the tiny plot.

Sadler had sympathised with the protesters, but they were breaking the law. He'd stopped the car because he spotted a red-faced young constable getting increasingly out of his depth. 'Any other near-brushes with the law?'

She smiled at him. 'I rely on you lot these days. In my job, I mean. It was a one-off, that protest. I swam in that pool as a child.'

'Didn't we all? You wanted to see one of my detectives? They're out at the moment.' He didn't mention the fact that they were sprawled on the lawn the other side of the building having lunch.

Julia Miles' face creased into a frown. 'I'm worried. About Mary Alton. Steph's daughter. DC Childs mentioned that she'd interviewed Mary. Was she okay then?'

Sadler rubbed his face. 'I don't think there was anything significant. What's the problem?'

Julia continued to frown, looking at the floor. 'It's probably nothing. It's just I've been around to Mary's flat a couple of times to check that she's okay, and I'm not getting any answer.'

'You think there might be a problem? Is she a vulnerable teenager?'

'I'd say so, although she's technically off the radar of Social Services now she's nineteen. Given her age, I guess it's probably none of your business either.'

'If you think something might have happened to her, then she definitely should be on my radar.' He took a step back. 'Why don't you take a seat? This shouldn't take long.'

It would have been quicker to go out the front door and walk around to the back of the station. But Sadler, keen to maintain an air of professionalism, both for himself and for his colleagues, instead traced the route Palmer and Connie must have taken after their visit to the canteen. He passed through the warren-like corridors of the station and finally made it to the lawned area.

They were still on the grass. Connie looked like she was having a snooze. Palmer was checking his phone. He looked up, shocked, as Sadler approached. 'We were just having a spot of late lunch or afternoon tea, given the time.'

Connie opened her eyes and looked unabashed, but she was the first to stand up. 'Is everything okay?'

'I've got Julia Miles in reception. She's concerned about Mary Alton. When you interviewed Mary after her mother's death, how did the girl take it?'

Connie frowned. 'She was upset from what I can remember. She looked like she'd been crying. But she was lucid. Told me that her mother had ups and downs. She seemed keen to defend Stephanie but not suspiciously so. Is there a problem?'

'Ms Miles can't get in touch with Mary. She's concerned about her.'

'She seemed okay when I spoke to her. Ask the family-liaison officer who brought her here. She sat in on the interview.'

'What happened afterwards?'

'Afterwards? Nothing happened after. She was given a lift home, that's all. Given that we're treating her mother's death as suicide, there wasn't much else I could do. We're not Social Services.' The sentence was a step too far. Even Connie seemed to have recognised it, and a flush of colour spread across her cheeks.

'Fine. However, there's a possibility that Mary Alton may also now be missing. I don't like what's happening to the women of Bampton. Can one of you try to track her down?'

He noticed Palmer looking at his watch. 'Perhaps I can leave that to you, Damian.'

Back at his desk, Sadler's mobile rang. He was about to switch it off. Nearing the end of the day, he had a number of admin tasks that wouldn't wait until the morning. Looking at the name on the screen, he changed his mind and pressed the answer button. 'Is everything all right?' Camilla never rang him during the day. She treated his job as sacrosanct. In fact, she rarely called him on his mobile, preferring late-night calls when she knew he would be relaxing at home.

'Everything's fine with me. It's just there's something I wanted to talk to you about.'

'To do with the kids?'

'The kids?' She sounded surprised. 'No, of course not the children. They're also fine. It's to do with . . . Look, I don't want to do this over the phone. Can you meet me?'

'Will later do? Or is it urgent?'

Camilla sighed down the line. 'Not urgent but it's to do with work. Should I come in and see you?'

'For God's sake, Cam. There's no need to do that. I'm coming around now. You've got me worried stiff. Stay where you are.'

'Can we meet at Hale's End?'

'Hale's End?'

There was a brief silence at the other end of the phone. 'I think it might help.'

He disconnected the call and looked out through his window into the incident room. Palmer and Connie were back in the office, still laughing together. Something about their stance put a niggle of doubt in his mind. He frowned, but grabbed his coat and walked across to them. 'I'll be back in an hour or so. Call me on my mobile if anything comes up.'

The evening was approaching, that time between daylight finishing and the encroaching night. The gloaming, his mother used to call it. An old-fashioned word, seldom used any more. But for Sadler it encapsulated the mystery of the early evening. There was a nip in the air, and he felt a reluctance to visit Hale's End. Perhaps because of its past history. It had always been a place of the dead. A place of sorrow. In the twenty-first century it had remained so, although he had seen precious little distress in response to the death of Andrew Fisher.

At the entrance to the path to Hale's End he saw his sister's white Nissan parked haphazardly on the grass verge. If he'd had the keys he would have at least straightened it. As it was, its back jutted awkwardly out into the road. Camilla was nowhere to be seen. She clearly didn't share his apprehensions about approaching Hale's End at dusk.

He walked quickly towards the old building, and, as he turned the corner, he saw a blurry shape that coalesced into two tall figures. His sister he recognised straight away. She had his leanness and, although she had put on some weight after having the children, she was still slender. The other he thought at first was Kat Gray. She had the same shape as his sister, but it was only as he got closer that he saw, with a start, it was the Manchester solicitor, Anna, who his sister was so keen for him to know.

Sadler wasn't so crass as to think that this was a contrivance to set him up on a date. One glance at Camilla's face would have put paid to that anyhow. He finally made it to them and acknowledged Anna with a nod.

'Thanks for coming, Francis. You remember Anna.'

'Of course.'

Anna was trying to smile at him but not succeeding. She did manage to look him in the eye. 'Maybe I should explain why we're here.'

'Are you sure you're all right? We don't have to stay here – I know this place well enough' said Sadler.

'So do I, unfortunately,' said Anna. 'But it's better that we're here. This place is important for what I want to tell you.'

Some of the warmth from earlier in the day had held. It didn't entirely dispel the gloom of the place, but it was trying.

'Anna came around today for lunch. We got to talking about Hale's End. I hope I didn't betray any confidences. It was general stuff about what we talked about when we were last together. About you coming here to lark about and about my ex bringing me here for a bit of teenage fumbling.'

'I remember.'

'Well, Anna has her own story about this place. I think you should hear it.'

He looked across to Anna, who was pale but determined. 'Okay but I'll say it again. It doesn't have to be here.'

Anna shook her head. 'It doesn't matter. Let's call it expelling old ghosts. Although I hardly know where to start.'

Sadler was on firmer territory. 'Let's move into the clearing there. We can look at the building while you tell me what you want to say.'

They moved across, slightly out of the trees.

'I'm a bit younger than you both. This place has become overgrown, but how you describe it, that you used to be able to get a car down the track, that's how I remember it too. I can remember when you used to be able to come down here in a car.'

Sadler said nothing. Just nodded.

'I had a boyfriend. When I was in my mid-teens. It was a big secret really. He was older than me. Seventeen. And he had a car. Well, it wasn't his. He used to borrow his mother's, and we used to go driving. I was too young to get into a pub. Although I was tall, I looked my age. So the local pubs were out. Instead, Adam would go to an off-licence and buy a bottle of cider or some beer, and we'd park up here and have a drink.'

'Where did your parents think you were?'

'I had a friend, Paula, who also had a boyfriend. We basically used to cover for each other. I'd say I was going out with her, and vice versa. Of course, my parents weren't daft. They could smell the alcohol when I got home. They just thought I was drinking with Paula.'

'And how old exactly were you, Anna?'

'Fifteen.'

'Go on.'

'Well, one day things got a bit out of hand. Further than I wanted. You know . . . It was stupid. But when I suddenly said that was it, I didn't want to go any further, he just didn't listen to me. Carried on.' Camilla moved a step forward towards her friend. 'The thing was, it wasn't really *that* bad. I mean, I didn't want to have sex with him, but it seemed easier just to, well, let him do it. That's what happened.'

'Here?'

'Yes. Wherever the track ended. There was a small turning circle, wasn't there? Sometimes we had to go elsewhere because there was a car already here, but often we just had the place to ourselves.'

'So you associate this place with where your assault took place.'

Anna flinched. 'Yes, it was an assault, wasn't it? I can see now. It took me a long time to accept that. But my parents, they knew it for what it was straight away.'

'You told your parents?'

'Well, my mum, initially. I was an emotional wreck. I needed support.'

'And did she help?'

'She was absolutely fantastic. I went to the doctor, and she told my mum that we should go to the police. She seemed really angry. She was the old-school type. The mother of that woman who went to prison for her husband's murder.'

'Lena Gray?'

'That's her. Her mother was a fantastic doctor. She was

angry when I told her what had happened. She told me to go to the police.'

'And did you?'

'Yes.'

'And?'

'It was the biggest mistake of my life.'

64

The boy had gone. Her empty consulting rooms, a refuge for so many of her clients, felt soiled. Her shock at seeing the scarf, an item that she recognised as belonging to her, had blinded her to the fact that he had deposited something else on the table when he left. A large brown envelope, thin and neatly gummed shut. For an instant, Kat had an idea of tearing it up into tiny shreds without even looking at the contents. Wasn't that part of taking control of your life? She didn't actually have to open the packages, to play the game that her sister was drawing her into.

She slid her finger under the gummed flap and reached inside for the contents. It was a glossy photograph of a pub. Kat frowned. There was a dated feel to the image, reinforced by the car that was passing when the photo was taken. The shot had to be at least ten years old. She squinted at the building. In large letters were the words, 'Ups 'n' Downs'. A terrible name for a gruesome pub.

She wafted the photograph at her hot face. She remembered the place, of course. It was where she and Lena used to go in the days when they were still socialising together. She could have sworn that the bar was now derelict. In fact, she was pretty much sure of it. It was up by the canal. Not the nice bit with the warehouse that had been converted into flats, but the other end of town. A place that had never managed to be regenerated. It had been a slightly dodgy area when she and Lena had gone there, but safe enough if there was a gang of you. She hadn't been there for years though. Surely the pub couldn't still be open?

Still slightly shaky on her feet, she pulled on her jacket. She didn't feel up to driving, and the distance was just about walkable. The fresh air helped alleviate the anxiety she could feel insinuating itself around her body.

She found Mark's number on her phone and called first his mobile, then his home. No answer from either of them. *Men*, she thought, *are just useless*. You had to rely on your own resources.

When she reached the canal, it was as she'd expected. The pub that had once been Ups 'n' Downs was derelict. The windows and doors were boarded up, and there was just a small slot in the front entrance to post whatever junk mail the postman was inclined to deliver. Even the name had been removed. Just a red strip across the building indicated that there had once been a sign present.

The pub brought back no significant memories for Kat. It had been a place to go out for a sly drink in the days before she'd really been allowed to go to bars, but that was just about it.

She pulled out the photograph from her pocket and compared the image to the present state of the building. Definitely the same place, but that was all that could be said really. A pub she had once frequented. What the hell was Lena up to?

She could hear footsteps coming up behind her and turned sharply. Lena stood opposite her. 'You always were slow on the uptake.'

That stung. Her sister always had the capacity to hurt her, and nothing had changed.

'Where have you been?'

Lena was like a spectre from one of those films they'd watched together long ago. The grey in her hair seemed to have multiplied. Her shoulders were hunched over her thin frame. She didn't answer Kat directly but turned to look at the derelict building. 'Don't you remember this place? What it was like?'

'Of course I remember it. Bloody awful place it was. So what? This is Bampton. You want somewhere decent for a night out when you're eighteen, go to Manchester.'

'We weren't eighteen though, were we? You were fifteen, me sixteen.'

'So? We weren't the first teenagers to go out drinking when we shouldn't have. Mum and Dad weren't bothered. They were happy to turn a blind eye.'

At the mention of their parents, Lena's eyes filled with tears. Kat stared at her unmoved. 'They weren't just your parents, you know? They were mine too.'

Lena moved forward, and Kat got a familiar whiff of sweat. She recoiled. 'You smell like that boy. The one who's been leaving me all those presents from you. Are you sleeping with him?'

Lena moved back away from her. 'He's been helping me. I needed it.'

'Helping you? You've implicated someone barely out of childhood in your schemes. Who the hell is he? Are you going to ruin someone else's life as well as your own?'

'His life has already taken a certain course and it's not something any of us can do anything about.'

'What course? What are you talking about? And why are

you getting him to leave me gifts? I don't understand what they mean.'

'I'm trying to explain. The reason for all this. Haven't you guessed yet?'

'Guessed? What the hell am I supposed to have guessed? All I know is that you're on the run from the police who think you shot Andrew. Remember him? The man you married?'

Lena stared at her. 'The police still think I shot him?'

'What are they supposed to think? Your husband turns up dead. The one you went to prison twelve years earlier for killing. Then you disappear. What are they supposed to think?'

'But I had to leave.'

'Had to? You've always done what you wanted to do. You did exactly the same this time. Disappeared because you felt like it.'

'But Kat,' her sister reached out and clutched at her arm. It was the first touch Kat could remember since they were teen-agers. 'Andrew was killed. How do I know I won't be next?'

65

I've made a right cock-up of things, thought Palmer. *I'm even going to borrow an expression from Llewellyn to describe it.* Connie hadn't made a fuss this morning. She was a good one. There had been no awkward silences or pleading glances. She treated him as she always did. Yet, despite his carefree manner, it was he who was struggling. It wasn't because he felt guilty. The problem was that he didn't feel any guilt at all. Surely that's what he should be feeling. Joanne was at home with her fertility kits. Thank God it was the wrong time of the month. He doubted he could have managed it this morning but there would be no excuses if the time were right.

Connie was jigging her legs to one side of him. He wanted to put his hand out to still them. She annoyed and attracted him in equal measure. What a complete and utter lunatic he was. It was time to go home. The problem was that he was happier here than where he needed to be that evening. He couldn't disentangle his feelings enough to understand if it was the pull of Connie that was keeping him here or the thought of going home to Joanne that was repelling him.

Sadler walked across to them with a face like thunder. 'Come into my office.' Palmer looked at Connie, and she shrugged. They followed their boss into his room. 'Shut the door.'

Sadler didn't seem to notice Connie's frown. *Well, hardly surprising*, thought Palmer. They usually conducted their meetings with the door shut anyway. What was the problem?

Sadler sat down heavily in his chair. 'The trouble with being a local is that sometimes it goes against you. If I hadn't been from this area, I might have paid more attention to the history of Hale's End.'

'The history,' asked Connie. 'You mean the First World War?'

'Forget about the war. I mean its more recent history. Because I spent the odd evening larking about in Hale's End when I was a teenager, that's what I associated it with. Messing about. Somewhere you could go when you wanted to frighten yourself stupid.'

'I think it's still a bit spooky now,' said Connie.

'The problem is that a witness has come forward today to say that Hale's End also used to have a reputation for being a place to go and have sex.'

'What, in the building?' asked Connie.

It's all going to be about sex today, thought Palmer.

'Not inside the morgue, thank God. However, you could once get a car along the path.'

'Like dogging?' asked Connie. 'You know, where people drive and watch other people have sex in cars?'

Sadler's face was sour. 'I can see a hint of amusement in your face, Connie. Get rid of it. I'm not talking about voyeurism. I'm saying that it was a place, literally off the beaten track, where you could go to have sex.'

'Llewellyn said it was all about sex,' said Palmer.

'Yes, he did, didn't he? Well, I dare say most of it was young teenage couples with nowhere else to go. Although there may have been the odd spot of adultery going on too.'

Fuck, thought Palmer. He didn't dare look at Connie.

'You think this is about adultery?' Her voice sounded hoarse to Palmer's ears.

'No, I think it's about non-consensual sex.'

'What?' Connie's voice had returned to its normal pitch. 'You mean rape?'

Sadler tapped his pencil on his desk. 'I've had, from a reliable witness, an account of her being taken to Hale's End, voluntarily at first, and then assaulted during the course of the evening.'

The room fell silent. Both were digesting the information.

Connie, of course, was the first to speak. 'But it's Philip Staley that we're linking with sexual assault. Through the testimony of Rebecca Hardy. It's Andrew Fisher's body that we found at Hale's End. We've not found any connection between the two yet.'

'Well, this might be it. It might not have been Philip Staley who was killed at Hale's End, but he's connected to this case. Now there's a possible link to the location where the murder took place.'

'Who's this witness?' asked Palmer.

Sadler looked down at his desk. 'I'd rather not say at the moment. We'll take a statement in due course. I think we'll have to. But I want to see if we can come up with something more substantial to ensure it's relevant to the case.'

Palmer frowned. This wasn't right. If this woman was a potential witness, then they needed to take a formal statement from her. Any delay might jeopardise a future trial if they cut corners regarding witness statements.

'Is the victim traumatised?' asked Connie. 'If you like, I can take along a victim-support officer. Two women. It might help.'

Palmer saw Sadler hesitate. 'Not for the moment.'

'She doesn't want to speak to anyone?'

Sadler didn't respond, and, in the moment's silence, Palmer felt the need to fill the void. 'Did she report the attack?'

'Yes, but she says she was treated badly during the questioning.'

'Badly?' echoed Palmer. This didn't sound good.

'I don't at this stage want to go into any details. Except to say that she felt one of the officers took a prurient interest in the minutiae of the attack. There doesn't appear to have been an investigation of any substance. She thinks the case was eventually classified as "no crime".'

'Fucking hell.' Connie stood up.

Palmer put his head in his hands. 'No crime' was a police classification for when, following an initial report of a crime, subsequent investigations came to the conclusion that no offence had actually been committed. There were a myriad of reasons why this happened. Some were legitimate, for example when there were few witnesses or little chance of securing a conviction. But for sexual assault, the historic 'no criming' of cases had been because of a lack of willingness to investigate claims further. This wasn't just the case in Derbyshire. It had happened everywhere. A disgrace and often the result of an excessive workload.

Palmer risked a look at his boss. Sadler's expression was calm.

'Sit down, Connie. This is important. We need to keep our emotions out of this. It wasn't Philip Staley who was her attacker. Or Andrew Fisher.'

'So why is her story important?' Palmer caught sight of Sadler's face. 'I mean in relation to this case. Except that she was taken to Hale's End. That's a tenuous link.'

'It's a link all the same though, isn't it?' Connie's voice was subdued. 'I think the boss is right. This is sounding right. There's been something missing, and this could be it.'

Sadler tapped his pen on his desk. 'I want you to do some digging into that club where Rebecca Hardy says she was assaulted by Philip Staley. What was its name?'

'Ups 'n' Downs. It's not open any more though,' said Palmer.

'Well, you're going to have to use your initiative. I want you to go and talk to some of the girls who used to go to that club when it was open. They're going to be in their late thirties and early forties now. Try some women's organisations. Even the Women's Institute. Put out some feelers. I want to know about Hale's End too. What went on inside the club and if the girls ever went to Hale's End. Voluntarily or not.'

'Why don't we go through the files?' suggested Palmer. 'We could see what we can dig up in relation to both locations.'

'Leave the files alone.' Sadler's voice was cold. 'And don't, for the moment, discuss this with anyone.'

He doesn't want Llewellyn finding out about this, thought Palmer. *What the hell's going on?*

66

Lena's life in danger? Kat took a closer look at her sister. She was wearing pale-blue jeans and a threadbare white jumper with a hole in the sleeve. A cigarette dangled from her left hand, burning uselessly. Lena didn't seem inclined to smoke it, but neither did she stub it out.

'You don't believe me.'

It wasn't a question. Kat struggled to form the necessary words. 'I don't know what to believe any more. I haven't known what to say to you for years.'

Lena finally took a puff of her cigarette. 'Well, my life is in danger. It doesn't really matter whether you believe me or not.'

'But why? Why is your life in danger?'

Lena looked at the floor. 'I don't know.'

'Did you kill Andrew?'

Lena remained looking at the pavement. She shook her head.

'But you know who did, right?' Kat was thinking of the boy.

Lena didn't answer. Kat took a deep breath. 'Who was it in your bed in 2004?'

'I can't talk to you about that.' Now she did look up, and Kat nearly recoiled from the look of misery in her eyes. For the first time that she could remember she felt a human stirring in response to whatever mess Lena had found herself in. Even if it was one of her own creation.

'Why have you got that boy to leave me things? I know you always liked to be mysterious, but what do the clues mean?'

'Don't you remember them?'

'I remember wearing the necklace. As a kid. The blouse? It took an old photograph to work out that it had even belonged to you.'

'But you remember the scarf?'

'The scarf? I remember wearing it in the early nineties, I think. So what? What are you trying to tell me?'

Lena looked deflated. 'I'm trying to tell you a story. About what happened back then.'

'Story? So you can taunt me with relics from that time?'

'I'm not taunting you. I'm trying to explain.'

'Explain? Explain what?'

'Why I've done what I've done.'

'You mean killing someone who you pretended was your husband?'

'Yes.'

Kat stood still. 'And? Well, I'm listening. Tell me.'

'Kat. You don't seriously think I'm the only one? The only woman he attacked? It's not only my story. It's the story of others too. Including you.'

67

Thursday, 16 July 1987

The man pressed her against the wall, one hand pushing at her chest to hold her steady. With the other hand he lifted her skirt. *No*, thought Lena. *I don't want this*. She wasn't even drunk. The cider that she'd half drunk had left her feeling nothing more than relaxed while she had watched Kat dancing. Relaxed enough to feel the thrill of pleasure when the man had slid his arm around her and whispered in her ear. For five minutes they had stayed like that, swaying to the sound of the music coming through the walls.

'Fancy a cigarette?'

Lena's smile had been genuine. She'd picked up the habit over the summer holidays last year. While her parents worked, she and Kat had lounged around and read *Cosmopolitan* magazines, giving their own slant on the advice in the problem pages.

She had followed him out the back entrance, past a couple pressed up against a wall, their mouths devouring each other. After the rancid smell of the club, the outside smelt sharp and fresh. He lit cigarettes for them both and watched her as she smoked. 'How old are you?'

'Eighteen.'

He smirked at her. 'Right.'

Emboldened by the sense of adulthood the cigarette gave her, she asked, 'How old are you?'

He took a long drag of the cigarette and blew lustily into the air. 'Twenty.'

For the first time, Lena felt the stab of fear. He was old. Not at school. What was she doing out here with him? She threw the half-smoked cigarette onto the ground. 'I'd better be going in.'

He stubbed out his cigarette on the wall behind her and pushed her back against it. She felt his face descend onto hers and his tongue in her mouth. Repelled, she tried to push him away, but instead she felt his strength.

68

Connie was exhausted. It was gone seven, and, given the precious little sleep she'd had the previous night, she felt a lethargy that made her want to rest her head on the desk for an hour to summon what energy she could muster. But the investigation suddenly had gathered momentum, and, despite Sadler's reticence, she could feel the energy pouring from him too. Palmer was ignoring her on the other side of the room. He seemed subdued by their boss's exhortation not to look at the files. It would go against every conformist instinct he had.

She rang Rebecca Hardy, who clearly wasn't happy being disturbed at home. Connie looked at her watch. She'd probably interrupted her putting the children to bed. All Rebecca could remember was that she had been taken to a lay-by for the assault. Connie couldn't prompt her any more than this. There were strict rules about putting ideas into potential witnesses' testimonies. Which meant she would need to find out more information through hard graft. Which was all right by her. She needed the distraction.

First of all, she wasn't going to get in contact with the Women's Institute. The vast majority of its members weren't teenagers in the eighties, that was for sure. Most forty-somethings were bringing up kids who were nearly teenagers themselves. She saw them going in and out of the fitness centre in the converted mill on the way home from work. That was where she needed to speak to them. Not among the cakes and jams. 'I'm off to the gym,' she shouted at Palmer, who frowned across the office at her.

*

The building was quiet when Connie entered, but the illusion of inactivity was false. It was early evening, the busiest time for a gym, and the subdued noises coming from the various exercise rooms suggested unseen physical strain.

The boy at reception couldn't seem to grasp what she wanted, couldn't see beyond the ID she'd shown him. Connie wondered if he had a record. In the end, she asked for the manager and was directed to an office behind the reception desk.

The manager was around her age, with tattooed forearms that bulged out of his polo-shirt sleeves. He had a well-educated accent. 'Can I help?'

She showed him her ID.

'No trouble here, I hope.' He had an easy manner. Confident.

'I've got a problem I need to pick your brains about.' She told him about needing to track down women in their mid-forties who drank in the Ups 'n' Downs pub in the eighties.

'That place was legendary. I had my first underage drink there too. About 1992 or 1993. It had closed by the late nineties though. I think it lost its licence.'

'What was it like then?'

'Awful. Full of young girls and boys. Gelled hair, acne and overpowering aftershave. I used to nick my dad's. I must have smelt like a perfume factory.'

'What brand was it?'

He grinned at her. 'Davidoff.'

'Not Brut 33 then?'

He looked her up and down. 'That's more your generation.'

Cheeky bugger, she thought.

His face took on a serious expression as he picked up a sheet of paper. 'We've a full evening of classes, as usual. Mid-forties, you say. You might want to try the spinning class.'

'Spinning? Isn't that a bit extreme for the over-forties? Aren't you doing yoga by then?'

He grinned again at her. 'Burns off a lot of fat but it is exhausting. You need to speak to the class before they start, not after. It's Jill taking it today in about twenty minutes. I'll give her the heads-up that you want to have a word first.'

'You okay about me doing this?'

He shrugged. 'I don't see why not.'

A sea of faces looked at Connie as she entered the room. There was a mix of ages, from mid-twenties up to fifty-something, she estimated. However, at least ten to fifteen looked the age she was looking for. She took a deep breath. *Here goes.*

'I'm sorry to interrupt your workout schedule. I'll literally be five minutes unless someone can help me, and then I might need to take more of your time.' She had their attention. 'We're investigating a crime that may have links to the late eighties, and, in particular, a pub, or nightclub you might have known it as, called Ups 'n' Downs that was open then.'

There was a snort at the back of the room. 'Meat market.'

'I'm sorry?' asked Connie, who had heard well enough.

'It was a pick-up place. You went there to have a snog with

someone who was as drunk as you. Dance around your hand-bag. That sort of thing.'

The woman folded her arms on her handlebars. They were clearly days she thought better finished.

'Anyone else remember it?'

A woman near the front put up her hand. 'I went a couple of times. It was a dire place. I could never decide what to drink. I used to settle for Malibu and pineapple. Now the smell of coconut makes me heave.'

Connie nodded. 'Anyone else?'

A third woman shrugged. 'I knew it existed, but I wasn't al-lowed out late. So I never went.'

Okay. She pointed at the first two women. 'Can I have a word with you both outside? I'm sorry to interrupt your exer-cise class, but it's important.'

Both women went willingly. Given the forty minutes of spinning that they were about to endure, it wasn't really sur-prising. She took them to the manager's office, which he left as soon as she arrived.

'As I said, Ups 'n' Downs has come up in the course of an in-vestigation, and I'm trying not only to get a sense of what the place was like, but also to see if any other crimes were commit-ted of which we're not currently aware.'

'What other crimes?' one of the women asked. She intro-duced herself as Karen. A tall, robust woman with solid muscles.

Connie shook her head. 'I can't tell you that. I need you to tell me about what you remember. First of all, I believe Ups 'n' Downs had a reputation for allowing underage teenagers in-side.'

Karen laughed. 'I don't think there was anyone over age. If you had valid ID, why would you go to a place like that?'

'I'm not sure that's right, you know.' The second woman, Lizzie, looked doubtful. 'I can remember older boys there too. And maybe girls. But certainly boys who were older than me.'

'How old?' asked Connie.

'Late teens, I guess.'

'Okay.' Connie did some rapid thinking. 'Karen, in the gym room just now, you told me that Ups 'n' Downs was a "meat market". Can you tell me a bit more about that?'

'Well, it was a place you went to get picked up by boys. You know, a quick chat, have a snog and then tell all your mates about it the next day.'

'Right. Just a snog?'

The women looked at each other. 'We were young. Fifteen, sixteen. That's all there was to it,' said Lizzie.

Connie had to pick her words with care. 'Did you ever hear anything about non-consensual relationships? I'm not talking about kissing either. Were there any rumours of incidents where something got out of hand?'

Karen was shaking her head. 'I never heard of anything bad happening.'

'I'm not so sure of that.' The other woman picked at her gym trousers. 'There was quite a predatory atmosphere in that place. Sometimes I'd keep my head down and hope that I didn't catch anyone's eye. Because once you did they'd be over to you like a shot.'

'Predatory atmosphere. I can understand that. Do you have any specific details?'

Lizzie shook her head. 'Nothing specific, but I'm glad that

the licensing laws have got stricter. My daughter's fourteen – she can't get near a pub these days.'

'Okay. I'm going to ask you outright. Do you think it's possible that individual women could have been targeted for sexual assaults at that time?'

The women stared at her aghast. 'Sexual assaults?'

'Well, that's what it is, isn't it? If someone goes to a club with a specific intention of picking up a woman for sex, it's targeted. It becomes sexual assault when it's contrary to the wishes of the woman.'

Lizzie grimaced. 'I never heard of anything, but, in that place, anything was possible.'

69

Joanne set the dinner in front of him and perched on the chair opposite. He looked at her in surprise. 'Aren't you eating anything?'

She shrugged. 'I'm not really hungry.'

He put down his fork. 'I can't sit here eating while you watch. Did you have something earlier?'

'A little bit, I suppose. I couldn't really eat.'

'Why not?'

'I'm worried about us.'

Palmer sighed and put the fork down again. 'Let's not have this conversation again. There's nothing wrong. You know what I'm like in the middle of a case.'

He looked across the table at his wife of less than a year. She looked exactly the same as when they had met four years earlier. Long dark hair and almond-shaped brown eyes. But she looked like she'd lost weight. He reached across to hold her hand. 'You're not still worried about this baby business, are you? We haven't been trying that long. You know what the doctor told you. We only need to come back if nothing happens after a year. It's only been five months.'

'Are you sure you want a baby?'

Oh God, he thought. 'We've talked about this. I want you to be happy. I'll do anything for your happiness.'

Her eyes were on his plate. 'My period's late.'

'How late?'

'A week.'

'A week?' He gaped at her. 'You've waited a week to tell me this? Haven't you wanted to do a pregnancy test in that time?'

Her eyes were blank. 'Oh, I did a test the first day my period didn't come.'

'And?'

'It was positive. I'm having a baby. We're having one.'

Palmer felt a warmth suffuse him, and he stood up, walked around to his wife and put his arms around her.

70

'How was I supposed to know?' Kat's professionalism was fighting with the familial sense of outrage.

'Mum guessed straight away. I was absolutely awful the next day. You won't remember. You always had your head in the clouds. But I was so angry that I threw my bowl of cornflakes across the kitchen. Mum didn't go to work that day. She pulled me aside and asked me what was wrong. So I told her.'

Kat felt sick. So their mother had known. No wonder she had been so acquiescent about Lena's subsequent decisions. It was she who knew the reasons behind them. 'What about Dad? Did he know too?'

Lena finally stubbed out her cigarette. 'It was he who gave me the Luger. He'd got it from an old patient. Mum was wonderful when I told her. I asked her not to tell either you or Dad.'

'But you said he gave you the gun.'

'That was after.'

'After what?'

'After we called the police.'

'You reported the attack?'

'We tried to but the pair who came around . . . They were these two huge red-faced uniformed men. They were so dismissive. Mum was outraged, and they wanted to take me away to the police station in the car. It was awful. I was crying, and Mum got angrier and angrier.'

'You're joking?'

'I'm not. It was terrible. So I shouted that I wasn't going with them, and they left the house. Just like that.'

'I don't believe it.'

'Mum drove me to the surgery and told Dad what happened. You remember what Dad was like.'

'He would have been mortified.'

'He went into his desk and gave me this gun. Wouldn't show me how to use it or anything. I'm not sure he even knew himself. But, funnily enough, it did offer me some reassurance. I kept it upstairs afterwards. It's why my door was always locked. Partly for safety but also because he told me not to show it to you.'

'But why? Why keep it secret from me?'

Lena looked over at her with eyes shrouded with secrets. 'We were trying to protect you. From the realities of what life was like out there. That man was an absolute bastard. He took from me what I valued most. My dignity. By trying to protect you, I know that I drove a wedge between us. I could never articulate what I was trying to say. So I just stopped trying. I just gave up, I suppose.'

Kat's head spun with the hundreds of questions that were bubbling away. 'But I can still help. It's not too late.'

'But it is too late, isn't it? Me keeping silent didn't stop what happened to you.'

Kat stared at her sister. 'What happened to me? Lena! Nothing happened to me.'

71

Friday, 8 February 1991

Kat stumbled into the hall, anxious to get upstairs before she encountered either of her parents. The light was on in the living room, which meant that one of them was still up. Lena would be in her room as usual. She pulled off her scarf and used it to wipe the tears from her eyes and cheeks. The act of self-kindness rekindled the sobs that she had managed to quell in the street outside the house. She quickly mounted the stairs and, turning the corner, ran past Lena's room, colliding with her sister as she came out of the bathroom.

'Sorry.' Lena made to push past her. The careless act elicited another sob from Kat, and she ran up the remaining stairs to her bedroom and threw herself on the bed.

The bastard. She'd wasted four months flirting and doing an elaborate fan dance around Peter. She thought they were taking it easy. Gradually easing into each other. But he'd just been messing around, and tonight, there he was, in the pub with his arm around another girl. Thinner than her and blonde. Men were just so predictable.

She heard a noise behind her and twisted her head in surprise. Lena was in the doorway, half shadowed from the still-dark landing. 'What's the matter?'

'What do you care?' shouted Kat. 'Leave me alone.'

Her sister didn't move. Kat looked down at her purple pat-terned scarf crumpled into a ball in her hands. She used it to blow her nose noisily. 'Men are bastards,' said Kat.

Her sister came into the room. 'What do you mean?'

'They're just shits, aren't they? They take what they want and we're left to pick up the pieces. I'm never going back to that pub again.'

'What's happened?'

'Oh, leave me alone, Lena. What do you care?'

Her sister stared down at her for a moment, and a shadow passed between them. Kat shivered. Someone walking over her grave perhaps. In an instant it was gone. Along with her sister.

72

'What do you mean nothing happened to you?'

Kat could feel the fragile connection that she'd made with her sister begin to dissolve. Lena took a step backwards.

'Your assault, from what you've told me, was absolutely horrific. But you seem to think something happened to me and nothing did. Okay, admittedly I've had my fair share of idiots, but nothing like you describe.'

'You weren't attacked? Here?' Lena inclined her head towards the disused pub with its maelstrom of memories and its forbidding air.

'No. That place was full of men on the prowl. I remember that. But nothing ever happened to me.'

He sister took another step back, away from the pale yellow light of the street lamp and back into the shadows. 'Then it's all been for nothing.'

73

Sadler had endured another night of bad dreams, this time walking through thick mud. He'd been trying to wade through the sticky viscous substance, but with every step he had sunk lower and lower into the ground. By the time he woke up, he had a sheen of sweat covering his body. In his dream he'd been waist-deep in the filthy mire.

Although a shower removed the physical traces of the night, his mind felt disjointed. As he walked into the communal office, he noticed that Palmer and Connie had only just got in themselves. Connie was yawning, without any attempt to put her hand over her mouth. Palmer had just taken off his jacket and was folding it up neatly to put in his desk drawer.

He gave them a nod and went over to his office and shut the door. He picked up the phone and dialled Llewellyn's number. Margaret answered. 'Is he in?'

'Yes, but he's asked not to be disturbed.'

'It's urgent.'

'Hold on.'

'He's got a conference call in five minutes. It'll last about half an hour. If you hold tight, I'll call you when it's over. You can see him for about five minutes then.'

'That's fine. I'll wait.'

Sadler opened the door to his office and called over to Palmer and Connie. They came quickly. 'Shut the door behind you.'

Connie complied with her foot.

'I want us to go through the narrative of events as far as we've got with this investigation.' Connie and Palmer looked at each other. 'I know we've discussed this before but humour me. Let's start with 2004. Philip Staley is killed by Lena Gray. We've established, as far as we can, that it is Staley.'

'His medical records match the description of the body, in particular the excision of a melanoma in 1998,' confirmed Palmer.

'Plus he received a sum of money from his mother in August 2004 to buy a plane ticket to Australia. This money hasn't been touched except for a small withdrawal.' Connie was leaning forward in her seat.

'Fine. So we're proceeding on the assumption that it was Philip Staley in Lena Gray's bed. What was he doing there?'

'They must have been seeing each other,' said Connie. 'There's nothing to suggest the sex wasn't voluntary.'

'Okay. Let's move on. She pretends it's her husband, Andrew Fisher. Any idea why she might do that?'

Palmer and Connie looked at each other. 'It's our biggest stumbling block, actually. We don't know why she'd do that.'

'Okay. Let's leave that for the moment. Have you found a connection between Philip Staley and Andrew Fisher?'

'We've found a possible connection,' said Palmer. 'I'd put money on the fact they knew each other from playing rugby. It's all there. But we need to find some hard evidence, to go digging to establish that.'

'Well keep on at it. Because, like you, I think there's a rugby connection. Okay, so Andrew Fisher is told by his wife that she's just murdered his friend. He then, voluntarily – let's stick with that for the moment – agrees to hide out in Whitby, pretending to everyone, including his mother, that he's dead.'

'I think his mother knew he was alive,' said Connie robustly.

'I'm not so sure. But the question is why.'

'Why what?' Palmer rubbed his head. 'Why did Lena kill Philip Staley, or why did she persuade or force her husband to hide out in Whitby?'

Sadler looked at them both. 'The two are connected, aren't they? Answer one and then the other.'

'And what about Andrew Fisher's subsequent killing?' asked Connie. 'If he's perfectly happy in Whitby, for whatever reason, why did he come back to be killed?'

'Come back to be killed,' echoed Sadler. 'That's actually not a bad turn of phrase.'

'Come on, boss. It doesn't work like this. If you know something, you're supposed to tell us. Not keep us hanging on like Hercule Poirot.'

'The trouble is, Connie, that I don't know anything. I'm as much in the dark as you are but I think there's a reason for that. What do we know about Philip Staley?'

Palmer got in first. 'That he was a rugger bugger, he overdid the sunbed use, and he didn't ask for permission before he had sex with a woman he picked up for the night.'

Connie was looking at him in shock. 'Permission? I think that's putting it mildly. He raped Rebecca Hardy and then took a photograph of her. That puts it in the definition of aggravated rape these days.'

Palmer turned round to retort, but Sadler silenced him with a look. 'There are two things you've just said that I want you to think about. The first is your mention of "these days". We're all pretty clued up on how we deal with reports of rape now. I want you to think about what Rebecca Hardy told you in the interview.'

'She didn't say anything bad about how she was treated here,' pointed out Palmer. 'She dropped the accusations because she was worried she wouldn't be believed.'

'I just want you to bear that in mind. The second thing that Connie said was that what happened to Rebecca constituted *aggravated* rape. What does that mean?'

'It means', Palmer's tone was subdued, 'that in addition to being raped, the victim is subject to additional trauma. Taking photographs is definitely on the list of serious aggravating features. I remember learning it for my sergeant exams.'

'Can you remember what else was on this list?'

Palmer looked to Connie. 'Not all of them from memory. Infecting the victim was one.'

The phone rang shrilly on the desk. Sadler picked it up. Llewellyn's secretary came on the line. 'The call finished early. He's free now if you want to pop down.'

'Thanks, I'm on my way.' He looked across to his two colleagues. 'Look at that list and tell me what comes to mind.'

'Do you want me to look up some other rape cases from the time?' asked Connie. 'Lena Gray had a clean record before her arrest. There were no allegations made by her in relation to a prior assault.'

Sadler thought to his forthcoming meeting. 'I think this might go further than you think, Connie. Stick to Philip Staley and see what you come up with.'

'What's this all about?' asked Connie. 'What's going on?'

Sadler stood up. 'That's what I'm about to find out.'

74

Kat woke up and had no idea where she was. Not Providence Villa. The floral odour of the bedroom couldn't have come from that musty house. And not Mark's spare bedroom either. That had a flat, synthetic smell, probably emanating from the cheap carpet.

She hadn't heard from him since their argument, and yet surely he must still be thinking of her. Poor Charlie must have been wondering where she'd got to. Perhaps this was his way of punishing her for walking out on him. Absolute silence.

Then she remembered Lena. After Kat had put right her sister's assumptions about the events of twenty-five years ago, that she hadn't been the victim of an attack, her sister had just turned away and walked off down the steps next to the canal bridge. Kat hadn't run after her. Because Lena was still full of her secrets, and Kat was sick of trying to guess them.

Exhausted with despair and worry, she had rung Patricia and asked if she could come and stay the night. When she arrived, Patricia took one look at her and directed her towards the bathroom with the white modern fittings and deep pile towels, so different from the spartan furnishings of Providence Villa. After a long soak, she had gone straight to bed and had slept for eight hours. Not long for some, perhaps, but virtually unheard of for her.

She fumbled around for her mobile and realised, with a

shock, she had five missed calls from a mobile number she didn't recognise. She checked her voicemail. No messages. Could Mark be calling from a different number?

The doorbell rang downstairs, and Kat heard someone being let into the hall. Patricia must have a client. She needed to get dressed and slip out. She heard footsteps on the stairs and a knock on the door. 'Hold on.' She got up and pulled on the jumper and trousers she had been wearing the day before. Patricia was waiting outside the door, and behind her stood Lena. Kat looked at her in astonishment. 'How did you know I was here?'

'I followed you.'

'Followed me? You can't have, I saw you walk off.'

'You saw me go down the steps by the railway bridge. Then you turned and went in the opposite direction and made a call. I doubled back and followed you.'

Kat's confused brain tried to remember the sequence of events. 'Why? Why did you follow me?'

'I was so angry that I'd got it wrong about you, I stalked off. But then I thought how utterly stupid this was and how much I needed to talk to you about everything.'

'Everything?'

Lena looked at Patricia. 'Maybe it would help if someone else was here when I told you this.'

Patricia backed away. 'I'm Kat's supervisor. If you want me to act in a professional capacity, I have to tell you the provisos. Kat knows them too.'

'Provisos?'

'If I hear something that leads me to believe that someone is in danger, and that includes yourself, then I am duty-bound to inform the police.'

'It's true,' Kat confirmed. 'It's probably better that Patricia doesn't hear this. It'll be all right.' She opened the door wider and pulled Lena into the room.

Lena looked around her. 'God, I've forgotten how normal people live.'

'I know. I woke up this morning and thought exactly the same. How did we get to this state?' Kat sat down on the bed, and Lena joined her. For Kat, it was the closest she could remember being to Lena in over twenty years.

'The man I killed in 2004 was called Philip Staley.'

'Philip Staley? I've never heard of him. What was he doing in your bed?'

'I was having an affair with him.'

'An affair? But I never thought—'

'That I was that type of person? Well, no one likes to think of themselves as an adulterer until they're unfaithful to their partner. I met Philip one day and started an affair with him.'

'So why did you kill him?' Silence. Lena's face took on an expression so familiar to Kat. Stubborn and blank. 'Lena. You need to tell me. Why did you kill him?'

'I killed him because he must have been the same man who raped me in 1987.'

'What? If he was the man who raped you as a teenager, what the hell was he doing in your bed?'

Lena looked at her in consternation. 'I didn't recognise him.' Kat stared at her. 'Honest to God. I didn't recognise him from the first time. Think about it. Think of someone you slept with in your early twenties. Did you have one-night stands when you were younger?'

'Well, all right, yes,' admitted Kat. 'A couple of times, but I never enjoyed it. It wasn't really me.'

'Okay. Think about one of those people you slept with. Suppose he waltzed back into your life today. Would you recognise him?'

A pleading note had entered Lena's voice. Kat leant back against the wall and thought. She remembered a man she'd met at a restaurant when she was living in Italy and struggled to find his name. *Jacob*, she thought. *Something biblical from the Old Testament. Or maybe Joseph*. He had blond hair. She could remember that much but that was about it. A possible name and hair colouring. That was all she could remember. She looked at her sister. Despite, or perhaps because of, everything, she deserved the truth. 'No. I wouldn't recognise him again. I could sleep with him tomorrow, and I wouldn't remember him from last time around. But your attacker. Surely after being—'

'Raped? You think that makes you more likely to remember someone? I can tell you, from bitter experience, that it doesn't. I had no idea who that man was until . . .'

'Until what?'

Lena looked stricken. 'Until he was in bed. He was a bastard anyway. It was just about sex. Even if it was good. Andrew and I had stopped. We were sick of the sight of each other. This man, Philip, was a friend of his. They were rugby drinking buddies apparently. I was never part of that crowd, but I did used to go to their annual Christmas dinners. Although I always hated it. The whole thing: dressing up and so on.'

'I remember.'

'Well, I met Philip there. It would be a lie to say we hit it off. We had nothing in common really but we did fancy each other.

He took my number at the end of the evening and called me the next day.'

'So that was Christmas—'

'Christmas 2003, and for the first six months or so it was great. I didn't even feel guilty about deceiving Andrew. I'm pretty sure he'd had some one-night stands along the way. I never paid him a single thought.'

'And that night?'

Lena sighed and reached in her pocket for her cigarettes. 'He had this phone. He was always on it. It was in the early days of smartphones, and he was obsessed. Always calling his mates, checking his texts. I got a bit obsessed about it myself. Wondering who he was texting and so on. I should have listened to my instincts. From his behaviour it was clear that he wasn't to be trusted.'

Kat had heard these stories so many times. Women checking the phones of their husbands. It was something she always cautioned against. Better to challenge your spouse direct than live in a perpetual state of suspicion.

'The funny thing was that he had another phone. One I didn't even know about. That night in September, after he'd gone to sleep, I found it. When I looked at it, I couldn't believe what was on it. Pictures of women. Six of them. I looked at them and knew straight away what they were.'

'What?'

'Kat, the bastard would photograph us. Afterwards, I mean.'

'After what?'

'After he attacked us.'

'He photographed women after raping them?' Kat couldn't believe it. But Lena's ashen expression couldn't have been from anything other than the sickness that comes from a deep humiliation. 'Did he photograph you? After you were attacked?'

Lena looked sick. 'Yes. He pulled a camera out of his pocket afterwards and took a picture.'

'Were they recent? The ones you saw on the phone? I mean, they weren't from the time when you were raped, were they?'

'Of course not. That's the thing. I mean, you can't always date an image just by looking at it now but this was twelve years ago. Phones had only just got cameras then, and these had definitely been taken with the phone. They weren't photos of photos, if you see what I mean.'

'Did you recognise any of the faces?'

'Yes and no. I didn't recognise any of the girls, but I looked at the photos, and I knew. Recognised those pictures for what they were and what those women were feeling. Repulsion and shame and fear.'

'So you killed him?'

'Yes. I didn't even think about it. I put a pillow over his face and pushed. And then he was dead.'

Kat felt sick. She also felt, shockingly, a slight thrill of fear. It both excited and repulsed her. She resisted the temptation to shuffle along the bed away from her sister. There were still questions that needed to be answered. 'But they thought it was Andrew.'

'I know.'

'But why pretend it was Andrew? Why not explain to the police what had happened? People would have understood. You could have got a decent lawyer.'

Lena bent over and traced with her finger a flower that decorated the duvet cover. She looked up through the hair that had spread across her face. 'I sat there panicking about what I'd just done but I was also thinking hard. If it came out that I'd killed Philip Staley and refused to say why, then they'd have started investigating him. And they would have checked his phone and private life and it all might have come out then. I might have been able to cope if it was just about me. But it wasn't, was it? What about those other girls?'

75

'I haven't been entirely straight with you.'

Sadler sat opposite Llewellyn, and, for the first time in his life, his superior was refusing to look him in the eye. It was the cue, of course, for Sadler to say something non-committal. Along the lines of 'I understand' or perhaps, 'I'm sure you didn't have any other choice.' But Sadler was sick at heart with his boss and that was a first for him too. 'You haven't been straight with any of us.'

This did make Llewellyn look at him. It was glance of fury. His pale freckled face reddened, and his large hands shook as he picked up his coffee cup. 'You know how it is in this job, Sadler. Don't pretend you don't. There's a chain of command, and not everyone necessarily knows everything about what's going on. It's always been this way. Do you tell your team everything?'

'I tell them enough.'

Llewellyn winced. 'I'm not particularly proud of myself but I had orders from up high not to reveal anything about what happened. There were reasons for this too. I can tell you, reading some of those files, I'm not surprised they're trying to do things properly this time. There are reasons why procedures are put in place in this kind of job. I didn't like the skulduggery of keeping quiet about the internal investigation, but I'm one hundred per cent sure about the need for an inquiry.'

'Are you able to tell me now?' Sadler turned his head and looked towards the window. Through the slatted blinds, he could see pale sunlight. The room nevertheless felt stuffy, and he resisted the urge to loosen his shirt collar.

'You're not that young, Sadler. You know things were different then.'

'It's not *that* I have a problem with. I know how things were then.' *It's the past that once more comes back to haunt us.* 'The problem is keeping me in the dark about what is happening with the old cases. It's impacting on my current investigation.'

'I know and I'm sorry about that more than anything. I'd never deliberately hinder an investigation. You have to believe me on this.'

Now it was Sadler who found it difficult to look his boss in the eye. 'When did you realise the two aspects collided? What went on in the past and Andrew Fisher's death?'

'This week. After you met Rebecca Hardy. Good God, do you think I would have told you to look at the sexual aspect of this case if I thought it was to do with these cases?'

'This has nothing to do with sex. It's about power and humiliation.'

'Don't lecture me. I know exactly what it's about. I've read those files. It's about a bunch of bloody incompetents masquerading as police officers.'

Sadler stared at his boss. 'Incompetents? We're not talking about an institutional failing here.'

Llewellyn stood up. 'I'm older than you. It was just after I started my policing that changes were made to how we dealt with rape cases and accusations of sexual assault. There were guidelines in place, and we didn't follow them.'

'Why not?'

Sadler's tone seemed to infuriate his boss. 'Because this station was being policed by a bunch of lazy-arsed sods,' he shouted and sat back down in his chair.

Sadler heard a movement outside the door. Margaret knocked softly on the door and opened it. 'Your visitor is here.'

Llewellyn acknowledged her with a nod.

'How many women in total have we let down?' asked Sadler.

Llewellyn didn't make any attempt to contradict him. Or to obfuscate. That, Sadler was willing to credit him for.

'At least ten. I'd say nearer fifteen for definite. And, given the total disgrace of some of the people who had the temerity to call themselves police officers, the number of victims could easily be more than that.'

I can name two, thought Sadler. *Rebecca Hardy and Anna. What a complete bloody mess. And I'm too young to retire. I'd resign, but there's nothing else I want to do.*

Llewellyn said nothing, but his eyes were on Sadler. 'There's someone I want you to meet.'

76

Palmer was silent on the drive out to Bampton rugby ground. Connie let him be. His earlier joshing had been replaced by awkward pauses and introspection. In the space of a few hours. God knows what was going on in his head. Men were a complete mystery to her, and she'd decided long ago not to bother trying to fathom them out. She let him concentrate on the driving while she stared out of the window. 'Good God.'

'What?'

'There's a man out there wearing a pair of shorts. It's not warm at all today.'

Palmer made a face but didn't look in her direction. 'Probably a tourist.'

Connie humphed. 'The first sign of spring, and they think they can get their legs out. It wasn't too bad last week, but it's freezing today.'

A large green sign told them they had arrived at the rugby ground. Palmer pulled the car into a space, and they sat, for a moment, in silence.

'Do you know anything about rugby?' Connie asked.

'Absolutely nothing. You?'

'Me? You've got to be kidding.'

'Great. You can lead the questioning then.'

He was being awkward. She hated it when men were like this. All fun one minute and difficult the next. She opened the car door. The weather was even colder than she thought. The man in the shorts must be seriously regretting his choice of clothes.

They walked into the long oblong building. The only person about was someone wiping glasses behind the bar. He seemed to be expecting them. 'Over to the left.' He nodded towards a door.

As they entered what looked like a boardroom, a man stood up, casually dressed in a long-sleeved polo shirt and shiny tracksuit bottoms. 'Geoff Bradley.' He introduced himself with a handshake, and they all sat around one end of the long table. 'I can offer you coffee. It's not that nice here though, I will warn you.'

Palmer made a face, and Connie shook her head. 'No thanks.'

'You mentioned over the phone about Andrew Fisher.'

'You knew him personally?' asked Palmer.

'I've known him since he was a young lad. He played here from the age of about eight or nine. That was before my time, admittedly, but I definitely remember him from twelve or so onwards.'

'What was he like?'

Geoff shrugged. 'Nice guy.' Silence.

'What about someone called Philip Staley?' asked Connie.

'Philip? I know him vaguely. That's a blast from the past. He hasn't been around here for years. He was very friendly with Andrew though. I heard he'd emigrated to Australia.'

'What was he like?'

'Nice guy.'

Connie, her hackles rising, leant forward. 'Listen, Mr Bradley. We're investigating murder, possible rape, and conspiracy to pervert the course of justice. If I hear you describe one of the suspects as a nice guy one more time, I'm going to haul you down to the local nick. Do you get me?'

Geoff Bradley swallowed. 'Suspects? Surely Andrew's a victim. His wife killed him. Well, she killed someone and now he's been found dead—'

'When I said suspect, I know exactly what I meant. So let's move away from the "nice guy, what goes on tour stays on tour" bullshit and get down to what those two were actually like.'

Geoff Bradley swallowed again. 'Andrew Fisher was a decent guy. I'd swear on it. Philip was a bit of a player. If you know what I mean.'

'I think you need to define "player" for us, Mr Bradley,' Palmer told him.

Here we go, thought Connie. *Good cop, bad cop. And, once more, I'm the baddie.*

'He slept around. A different woman a night, given a chance.'

That gives a lot of possible victims, thought Connie sourly.

'Did any of these women ever make a complaint against Philip Staley?'

Geoff looked shocked. 'Not that I'm aware of. I think he was quite attractive to women. He didn't force himself on them if that's what you mean.'

'Oh really?'

'And what about Andrew Fisher?' continued Palmer.

'In his younger days he had an eye for the women too. In fact, as a teenager, he was worse than Philip.'

Connie froze.

'Definitely a woman a night. He used to disappear outside

with them and then he'd be back inside picking up another.'

'Here?' barked Connie.

'Not here. This would be for after-match drinks and events. The lads liked to go on the razz in Bampton on Saturday evenings. He and Philip were thick as thieves on those nights out.'

'So let me get this straight,' said Connie. 'Andrew and Philip would go out drinking in Bampton together and pick up girls.'

Geoff Bradley looked between the two of them. 'It was only a bit of youthful fun.'

'And more recently?' asked Connie.

'Andrew settled down with Lena. I never heard of anything after that. Philip, as I said, I haven't heard about him for years.'

'But as a teenager he regularly left Bampton bars with someone he had picked up?' said Palmer.

'He was a devil,' said Geoff Bradley, a note of pride in his voice.

*

On the way back to the station, Palmer put his foot hard on the accelerator.

'Slow down for God's sake. If you get caught, we'll both be in trouble.'

'The two of them were as bad as each other, that's what Sadler meant, wasn't it?'

'What do you mean?'

'He told us to look at the definition of aggravated assault, remember? I thought he was talking about the photographs but there are other possible scenarios too. There's a category, "more than one offender acting together". It's not just the photographs. They were working as a team.'

'You think?'

He clenched his hands on the steering wheel. 'I'm sure of it.'

77

Kat sat on the bed with her head on Lena's shoulder. The fear that she'd felt a moment earlier had been replaced by the familiar longing to regain the sister she'd once known. Sitting here with Lena, she could have been thirteen again. Except she could feel her sister removing herself once more. There were so many questions, and she didn't want to fracture the brittle truce they'd reached. She still needed to get at the heart of the deception. 'Andrew was in the photos too?'

Lena nodded. 'He was in the ones on Philip's phone. As well as the girls. There were pictures of the pair of them with the victims. Just before the attacks, I suppose. Larking around and posing for the camera, you could call it, if you didn't see the one where Andrew was holding down the girl. Philip must have taken the photo and maybe the girl didn't make it easy to photograph her. In any case, Andrew was holding her down and she looked terrified. It was obvious they were working together. Prowling as a pair. The thought makes me sick even now.'

'And you confronted him, Andrew, I mean, with what you found?'

'He was in London. It was a Sunday evening, and he'd gone back down to the flat ready for work the next day. It was why I was so confident that Philip could use my bed.'

'So you called him and told him to come home.'

Lena wiped a hand across her face. 'You'd never believe that conversation. I never want to think about it again. But he came back and saw his dead friend in our bed. So I told him why I'd killed him.'

'What did he say?'

'He didn't even try to deny it. He just stood there with a strange look on his face. Told me it was Philip who was the instigator. He just went along with things out of a misplaced loyalty to a teenage friend. So we did a deal. He would leave Bampton, and I would admit to the murder that I'd committed but I'd pretend it was him.'

'But why pretend that Philip was Andrew?'

'I half believed him. That Philip was the instigator, I mean. Philip did have a dominant personality. Everything was about him. So, in order for Andrew to disappear, to get away from Bampton, I needed to pretend that it was him I'd killed. If I'd confessed to Philip's murder it might have come out. About the girls, I mean. It seemed the best way.'

'You came up with this plan? By yourself?'

Lena hesitated. 'Yes.'

'You were prepared to let him off scot-free?'

'Kat, I wasn't thinking properly. I thought about ringing the police and telling them what I'd done, but then it would have all come out. I tell you, the police were horrible to me. I bet nothing has changed either.'

'I wouldn't be so sure of that, Lena. There have been huge leaps in how victims of sexual assaults are dealt with by police. There are even dedicated units you can go to who will support you even if you don't want to press charges.'

'That's now. But in 2004? I don't think things had changed that much. Some of those officers who had treated me like dirt in the eighties were probably still serving in the force.'

'I don't know. Maybe you could have ...'

'I wasn't going through that again and I wasn't going to drag any of their victims into it either. All those other women he'd assaulted. Including you, I thought, at the time. The way you acted. I just thought ...'

Kat shook her head. 'I don't really remember the night you were talking about. I'd probably been dumped, again, and wasn't very happy about it. Given that we weren't close any more, I wouldn't have confided in you.'

'Bampton was a nightmare for teenage girls at that time. I suspected then and I know now. It didn't take much for me to think you'd been a victim too.'

'So you decided to protect us? How could you be so idiotic?'

'Andrew was convincing when he told me that Philip was the architect of those assaults,' said Lena. 'So I began to formulate a plan. To get him away from Bampton without the real story coming out.'

'You paid a terrible price for someone else's actions. Remember how long you spent in prison?'

'Kat! I deserved it. I killed someone. In cold blood as well.'

'I don't think a jury would have considered it to be in cold blood if the evidence of the photos had come out.'

Lena's face took on the familiar closed look. 'That was never going to happen.'

'And now Andrew's dead too. Did you kill him?'

Lena turned to her. 'You've got to believe me. What I've just told you is everything. I didn't kill Andrew. We agreed that we'd never see each other again. But he came back and now he's actually dead. So what happens next?'

78

While Palmer was driving, Connie took the opportunity to call the station and retrieve the details of Andrew Fisher's first wife. Throughout this investigation they'd treated Lena's dead husband as a victim – in 2004 and more recently. Now he was shaping up to be a sexual predator in the Philip Staley mould, and they needed to go back into the past.

Gail Fisher lived in a terraced house to the west of Bampton. They had been workers' cottages built for the employees of the cotton mill that still stood on the bank of the river. The mill had been turned into apartments, similar to Connie's, but the cottages hadn't yet been gentrified.

There was a haphazard air to the terrace. The window frames of each house were painted a different colour, and the front doors heralded the change in fashion over the past hundred years. Connie banged on the door, and, after a moment, a woman answered. 'Mrs Fisher?'

Both she and Palmer showed their ID, and, with a resigned raise of her eyebrows, Gail Fisher let them into her house and took them into the front room. She didn't offer them coffee.

Connie had been expecting someone similar in appearance to Lena, but this woman was short, barely over five feet tall, and heavily made-up. Her cheeks were rouged with pink, a colour that clashed with the peach of her lipstick. Underneath the gunk she was probably attractive.

'I wondered if you'd be coming to see me. Again.'

'I don't suppose this is easy for you,' Connie told her.

'That's putting it mildly, but then it hasn't been easy from the day I first met Andrew Fisher.'

'You were married to him for three years?'

'Two. Oh, I suppose it was three if you include all the stuff around getting divorced.'

'It wasn't amicable?' Palmer had settled back into the sofa and was taking notes, content to let Connie ask the questions.

'No, it wasn't.'

'You petitioned him for adultery, I believe.'

'Yes, he was sleeping with that slut, Lena Gray.'

Palmer's pen stopped briefly mid-sentence, then he carried on writing.

'Who he eventually married.'

'Eventually? About three months after the Decree Absolute came through.'

'Were you aware that he was having an affair?'

Gail Fisher stared at her hands. 'I suspected there was someone.'

'He came home late at nights?'

Gail's face was dour. 'He'd come home early enough and then he was off out again. He never said where he was going.'

'What did you think when you heard that Lena had killed him in 2004?'

A slow smile spread across Gail's face. 'I thought he'd got his just deserts.'

'Because he'd left you for her?'

'Because he was a pig.'

Palmer had stopped writing again.

'A pig?'

'Andrew Fisher was a pig. I should never have married him. And I never liked his mother either. The pair of them had this I'm-better-than-you attitude. Have you seen where she lives? It's only around five minutes from where I grew up, but you'd never have thought it, the way they both looked down on me.'

We really should have interviewed this woman earlier, thought Connie. 'How did you meet?'

'I was working in the dentist's as a receptionist. Both Andrew and his mother were patients. He used to chat me up when he came in. Which wasn't often. Anyway. One time he had some work done on his teeth. Cosmetic, to straighten them. So over the space of a month or so he was in the surgery quite a lot. Then he asked me out.'

'Did you meet any of his friends?'

'I suppose so. They were a rugby crowd. Not my sort.'

Connie bit on the top of her pen. Gail Fisher was, in her own way, as much of a snob as her husband. 'What about a man called Philip Staley?'

Gail coloured. 'There was someone called Philip at our wedding.'

'Do you have a photograph?' asked Palmer.

'They're up in the attic. I keep meaning to throw them out but there are some pictures of my mum who's not alive any more, so I can't bring myself to get rid of them.'

Connie looked at Palmer, who rolled his eyes.

Five minutes later, he emerged from the attic with a pale-pink photograph album covered in rosebuds. Gail took it from him and flicked through the pages until she found the photo she was looking for. She pulled it out of its holdings and handed it over to him. 'You can keep that one.' She bustled out of the room, photo album in hand.

Connie looked at the image. It was a picture of Andrew Fisher and Philip Staley arm in arm, laughing into the camera. They were both good-looking men. Their hairstyles and suits dated the photo. Andrew Fisher was slightly taller but broader than his friend. He looked confident, trustworthy. Philip Staley, despite the smiles, carried with him an air of anxiety. He looked to one side of the camera. The hand that clutched his friend looked proprietorial.

Palmer looked at the photo. 'Victims or perpetrators?'

She put the picture in her handbag. 'Both.'

79

'What do you mean, what happens next?'

Her sister's voice was muffled. 'Someone worked out that Andrew was alive all this time. They must also have known that I had a part in hiding him. Whoever it was has got their revenge. They might want to extend it to me.'

Kat thought back to her patients over the years. Plenty were victims of trauma, people who had been preyed upon, abused and neglected. She couldn't think of a single one who had forged forward with revenge. That wasn't the way things worked. Victims usually blamed themselves. It took anger and a certain amount of self-belief to embark on a path of revenge.

'What about Steph?' She tensed for her sister's withdrawal.

'Steph?' Lena lifted her head. 'The whole time I was inside, in prison, I never even thought about Steph. She was part of that time. From before.'

'But you got back in touch afterwards?'

Lena exhaled a long deep breath. 'You remember how it was when I first came out. I hardly left the house but I did bump into Steph one day. In the park opposite the house. She was walking with her daughter Mary. She looked like him.'

'Like who?'

'Like Philip.'

'Steph had a child with Philip Staley?'

'Yes and she looked just like him.' Lena's face was a vision of misery. 'Not in build. She's thin like her mother. But her face. It was like looking at the man responsible for everything.'

'So you started to see Steph again?'

'She asked if I was still living in the house and, afterwards, we'd meet occasionally. Maybe once every couple of months.'

'Why did she kill herself? Why now?'

'You're asking if it was anything to do with me? In a way, it was. When I left Providence Villa, I went to stay with Mary. She's got a flat not far from here. I know. Don't look at me like that. I had nowhere else to go. Steph knew, of course.'

'I don't understand.'

'When it came out in the press that it was Andrew who'd been found dead, she came round to find out who I'd killed before.'

'She guessed it was Philip?'

'Yes. It was a shot in the dark. She thought he'd moved to Australia in 2004 and that was the end of that.'

'But was she one of his victims? I thought he was her boyfriend.'

'Not boyfriend. Not casual pick-up. Something in between. She was treated badly. Perhaps not the same as the other women. But still.'

'And when she heard of Andrew's body being found, she wondered if it was Philip you'd killed.'

Lena picked at the duvet cover. 'Not a bad guess, was it? In fact, spot on.'

'But why kill herself now?'

'She killed herself, Kat, because sometimes you just reach the end.'

80

The woman was thin, dressed in grey straight-legged trousers and a black jacket. Her cropped hair was immaculately styled, but she'd made no attempt to hide the passage of time. In a few years it would be completely white. She was wearing make-up. Pale mauve eyeliner and pink lipstick. It softened her masculine hairstyle and clothes.

'This is Superintendent Sioned Rhys. From West Glamorgan Police.'

She held out her hand to Sadler. 'Good to meet you. I've heard a lot about you from the Superintendent here.' She had a soft Welsh accent. Barely noticeable but present under the clipped professional tones. Sadler said nothing because he already had a fair idea what was going on and the thought made him so mad he didn't trust himself to speak.

Llewellyn was looking at him through narrowed eyes. Warning him. Rhys picked up on the tension in the room. 'I don't often play the female card, Sadler. I've got where I am, in my considerable opinion of myself, through hard work and talent. I can cop it against the most able of men, and I've got to Superintendent by rolling my sleeves up and mucking in.'

Llewellyn leant back in his chair with a faint smile on his face.

'However, I am going to say this, and if I'm ever asked about it outside this room, I'll deny I ever said it. But if you think you're pissed off about what we've discovered happened to the reporting of rapes throughout the late eighties and nineties, then, believe me, it's nothing to how I feel. I've read those files. All of them and in depth. There are even some taped interviews. I actually threw up after one of them. Would you like me to go into details?'

Sadler shook his head.

'Okay. So we start from the base line that I'm as pissed off as you are. No, in fact I'm more pissed off than you because, one day, over a drink, I'm going to tell you about some things that have been said to me over the years by policemen like those in the files. But that doesn't help you and your case and that's what you want right at this moment, isn't it?'

Sadler nodded. 'I have two police detectives out there who also deserve some answers. They've been scrabbling around in the dark when actually you have some information that might have helped.'

Rhys shook her head. 'I take the criticism head-on but I had to do my job too. It's only recently that it's come to light that my investigation and yours are connected. I admire your loyalty to your team.' She looked to Llewellyn. 'They might as well hear this too.'

Llewellyn shrugged. 'I have no objection. Bring them in.'

Sadler prayed that they were somewhere in the station. Because, if what he suspected was coming, then he'd rather they heard it from the horse's mouth, so to speak. Especially Connie. It would be unpalatable. And he didn't much fancy defending the indefensible.

A quick call to the incident room revealed they weren't there, and Sadler was just about to call Palmer's mobile when

Margaret rang to say they were on their way in to the station. They arrived at Llewellyn's office a few minutes later, Connie looking flushed, Palmer curious.

The first thing Connie did was give the policewoman the once-over.

Rhys ignored the scrutiny, and, once they'd sat down, plunged straight in. 'Have you heard of the Sapphire Unit?'

Connie looked across to Sadler. 'Of course. It's the sex-crimes unit in London. Reported cases of rape in the Greater London area are referred to that department rather than to CID.'

'Well then, I'm sure you're also aware that there have been complaints made against this unit in relation to the way accusations have been handled.'

Palmer and Connie both nodded. Rhys continued. 'I was one of the senior investigating officers looking at the handling of a number of cases in 2012 by a serving DC who was subsequently dismissed. I'm telling you this because I want you to know my background. I know a lot about these issues, and I'm aware of the sensitivities.'

'I was involved, about five years ago, in the sex-crimes unit in Derbyshire. It was pretty exemplary.' Connie's voice was subdued.

'It still is. I visited the team last week. I have no quibbles with the current set-up.' A short silence. 'This is about policing over two decades,' said Rhys. A faint flush appeared on her cheeks. 'What I'm here to talk to you about is what happened in Derbyshire between the years 1985 and 2004.'

'Any reason those dates have been chosen?' asked Sadler.

She turned to him. 'There was a policy review in 2004 that

led to the setting up of a number of dedicated units to deal with reports of rape and sexual assault. It was later than some forces, and it was in response to the Home Office circular designed to ensure that those reporting rapes would be treated with tact and sympathy. Although it was not perfect, in my opinion women were served much better after the creation of those units.'

'But before then?' Connie asked her.

'I'm here as part of the Independent Police Complaints Commission team looking into practices at that time. It's historic, as I just explained, but I can safely say that Derbyshire Constabulary was significantly behind the times in terms of how it handled these cases.'

'And here in Bampton?'

Rhys looked to Llewellyn. 'There was a complete failure to act in a number of instances. Cases of rape and sexual assault were, for a variety of reasons, classified as "no crimes".'

Connie exhaled rapidly.

No crimes, thought Sadler. The phrase used to fob off Anna. Before the creation of the Crown Prosecution Service in 1986, it had been the police who had taken the decision as to whether there was enough evidence to prosecute. A big mistake that had left vulnerable people at the whim of incompetent and lazy police officers.

'I'm going to open some of those files to you. It's clear that your ongoing investigation into the deaths of Andrew Fisher and Philip Staley is related to that time. However, what we can and can't use in a resulting prosecution is up for debate.'

'Debate?' asked Sadler.

Rhys smoothed down an invisible crease in her trousers.

'You want to find out what happened in 2004. Well, my concern is what went on between 1985 and that time. You read the files first, but I'm telling you, some of the police officers serving at that time are still on the payroll of Her Majesty's constabulary. Even if it's via their pensions.' She smiled at them. 'And I'm going to have their balls for breakfast.'

81

Lena had gone. She'd spilt out her secrets and then left. A confession of sorts, but Kat wasn't the person she should be asking for forgiveness. Kat sat shell-shocked on the bed with a hollow pit in her stomach. Finally, she rang the only person who she really wanted to speak to, the man she'd been avoiding for the past few days.

Mark answered on the first ring. 'Who's Daniel?' His voice was cool.

'A friend of Lena's. He turned up a couple of nights ago. Have you been to the house?'

'This Daniel was leaving when I arrived. He didn't seem to want to talk to me. He said he'd seen you and that you'd let him sleep on the sofa. And that he was looking for Lena. Aren't we all?'

Kat struggled to form a sentence. He picked up on her mood immediately. 'What is it?'

'She's been here. Lena.'

'Lena? When?'

'She got in touch through that boy again.'

'Where are you? Don't move. Are you in danger?'

Even down the phone she could sense his tension. Tears welled up in her eyes. 'Not me. Lena. It's Lena who's in danger.'

It took him twenty minutes to arrive. Kat stood outside Patricia's house waiting on the pavement. There was a north wind blowing, chilly and relentless. She couldn't wait inside the house because she couldn't risk introductions. Patricia was a diligent therapist, and she would be putting her in an impossible position if she introduced her to a former client. She could see that her career was in jeopardy, but Mark was the solid presence that she needed now.

She felt relief wash over her when he came around the corner in the car and drew up beside her. He looked over to the house. 'It belongs to my supervisor. I stayed here last night, but we should go elsewhere.'

She didn't need to explain any further. He put his hand over hers and squeezed it. 'Where to?' He looked like he hadn't slept in days. Dark shadows ringed his eyes, and stubble covered his jaw.

'I have no idea.'

'Right. I do. Hop in.' He drove her onto the moor. She'd once told him it was her favourite place, and he hadn't forgotten. The sand-coloured grassland rippled in a single direction in the soft breeze. Despite everything, Kat felt her spirits lift.

He parked in one of the small gravelled areas used by walkers to leave their vehicles. One couple, returning from a hike, gave a condescending look towards Kat's trainer-clad feet. She felt like shouting that she was a local and could wear what the hell she wanted, but what was the point of adding to the prickle of tension she already felt.

They followed a path, of sorts, for about ten minutes, leaving the traffic behind them. Reaching a hollow, they could have been the last people left on earth. The silence was eerie. Mark sat down and hugged his knees. Kat stood over him but, feeling the balance of power tilt in her favour, sat down next to him. She felt him reach for her, and she leant back into him. *When will*

I ever be able to forget he was my client? she wondered and then shook the thought from her mind. Instead, she told him Lena's story. He listened without interrupting. When she had finished he was silent for a moment, processing what she had told him.

'So Lena killed Philip Staley but says she didn't shoot Andrew Fisher. Who did then? The boy?'

Kat shook her head. 'I don't think so. He seems completely under Lena's control.'

'But he waved a knife at you.'

'Yes, but when I shouted at him, he ran away. It was like I frightened the life out of him. The sense of menace is still there, but it's not coming from him.'

'You sure?'

Kat nodded. 'Pretty sure.'

Mark looked unconvinced. 'Who is he anyway?'

'Someone Lena seems to have picked up along the way. Got him to do her dirty work. Including dropping me all those clues. To try to make me link why she had disappeared to those teenage days. She was trying to explain. She's used him, but . . .'

'He was asking for a gun. Andrew was shot, remember?'

Kat shook her head. 'I don't know. The boy is a bag of nerves. His hand was shaking when he was holding the knife. The policewoman said that whoever shot Andrew had a pretty good aim. It was straight into his chest.'

'That's the easiest part of the body to hit, Kat.'

'Is it?'

'Think about it. In the movies you see someone's head getting blown off, or someone shot in the legs when they're trying to run away. That's actually pretty hard to pull off. Especially when the target is moving. The easiest way to kill someone is to keep them still and aim for the chest. Take it from me.'

Silence.

'Don't ask the question, Kat. I served in Iraq. Of course the answer is yes.'

'Then if it's not the boy who killed Andrew, who?'

'Andrew Fisher was a rapist, and so was Philip Staley. Serial attackers. That gives us a wide pool of suspects if one of his victims saw him in Bampton again after all these years. Or perhaps someone enticed him back from Whitby, where he was hiding out, in order to kill him.'

'But I don't know who the victims are,' wailed Kat. 'I need to see the police and tell them what happened. There will be lots of traumatised women because, let's face it, a leopard never changes its spots.'

Kat felt him tense next to her. 'What? What did you say? Of course. You're right. A leopard never changes its spots. Someone like Andrew Fisher isn't going to change just because he isn't in his home town.'

'You mean when he was in London?'

'Don't be dim, Kat. I mean much more recently than that. Where's Andrew Fisher been the past twelve years?'

'Whitby? He wouldn't be so stupid. Lena said that it was Philip Staley who was the instigator of those attacks.'

'Wake up. You're talking about a serial rapist. You think he stops doing it just because he's been found out? He does what most people would do in that situation. He blames his actions on a person who is no longer in a position to answer back.'

Kat's head was spinning. 'Oh my God.'

'The trouble is that we haven't got any credible leads when it comes to Whitby. We don't know anyone there, do we?'

82

'Why did you ask me to help you? To hide Andrew in Whitby?'

Lena used the ancient sofa to steady herself. She was tired. Exhausted from lack of sleep, from lying on the floor in a strange flat, from running from everyone.

She'd come back to the house one last time before going to the police. Kat hadn't been attacked and her desire to protect her sister had overruled any sense she had once had. What a stupid mistake and yet, if she had her time over again, would she do anything differently? It was only now, according to Kat, that victims were getting the support and understanding they needed. It was time to stop running and let the truth come out. In any case, where could she go? Whitby had been her place of refuge, and she'd given it up to protect Andrew, although God knows he'd deserved nothing from her. In doing so she'd ruined another relationship. Daniel was calm, but she could sense a deeper hurt underneath.

'You were the first person I called. I admired your competence.'

He looked hurt. 'My competence. Is that all?'

'I'd just killed someone, and you were the person I thought of to help me. Doesn't that explain things?'

'You never gave me any reason for what you'd done.

Didn't I at least deserve that?'

Lena turned away from him. 'I'm not sure there was a reason. I was thinking and not thinking at the same time. While I was waiting for you and Andrew to get here, I came up with a way of admitting to the murder so their crimes wouldn't come out. There were all those girls I wanted to protect. You wouldn't understand and, anyway, things were different then. You got no support when you reported a sexual assault and I don't think anything had changed in 2004. I wasn't going to let it all come out. I wanted to preserve the dignity of the victims, which I thought included my sister.'

'Your sister?'

'Don't you see? I wanted to look after my sister.'

'I *do* see that.' He looked at her, his eyes blank. 'So you came to me.'

'It's one of the things I've always liked about you. No need to explain myself.'

'He was a rapist. A violent attacker of women.'

'How did you find out?'

'You asked me to help you, and I did. I looked after him, helped settle him in a house. Introduced him to my friends. To my family.'

'You didn't need to.'

'I did though, didn't I? For you. I went the extra mile. I didn't just hide him, I set him up in a new life. You have to take responsibility for that.'

'For what?'

'For me helping him. Because it's you who introduced the serpent into paradise. You.'

'What do you mean?'

317

'You knew what he was like, and you let me take him into my life. Use your imagination, Lena. What do you think happened?'

83

All three left the meeting subdued. They instinctively gathered in Sadler's office, but he didn't seem keen to pick over what had been said. 'Let's call it a day. You two go home. There's a lot to think about, and I want to review the case from the start in the light of what we now know.'

'What, tonight?' asked Connie.

Sadler shrugged. 'Why not? But don't you two hang around. There's going to be plenty to keep us busy over the next few days. Take the rest of the day off. I want to have a think.'

They left Sadler sitting at his desk. He looked disheartened, which gave Connie a feeling of disquiet. She felt the fragile stability that she'd carved for herself over the past couple of years begin to fray. Instinctively her thoughts turned to Palmer. She wondered if he was going to ask her out for a drink. Despite her reservations, she would have said yes. It really had been one of those days. But he'd been cool with her all day. A change in tune from immediately after their tryst in her flat. It had left her feeling confused and vulnerable. She watched out of the corner of her eye as he put on his jacket and left without saying anything to her.

She waited a couple of minutes, and then she too left the station. Back home, she looked around at her tidy flat. There was nothing she didn't like about being a copper. She'd wanted to join the force since she was fourteen, when a young policewoman had come to give a talk to her school. Most of her friends had been joking both before and after the talk, but, curiously, not while the young officer had spoken, because she had a natural air of authority about her that had subdued even the rowdiest in that large comprehensive school. Being a police officer these days meant having a degree, and Connie had studied sports science at Nottingham Uni simply to get that precious certificate so she could join up after graduation.

One of the first surprises had been the sheer mundanity of some aspects of modern-day policing. Lots of sitting around in cars, dealing with minor infringements, and endless cups of bad coffee. Less surprising was that the young officer who had spoken to her as a teenager was now Chief Superintendent in Derby. Their paths had yet to cross, but when they did, Connie had her speech ready.

The downside was the hours. If truth be known, Connie had few close friends in Bampton. Normally she didn't mind. When she got home from work, all she wanted to do was have a shower, pour a glass of wine and sit in front of the TV. Socialising was the last thing on her mind, but tonight it was company she needed. She took out her mobile, and her finger hovered over a name. He'd asked her to call him, and it hadn't felt like a come-on. She pressed the number.

'Scott here.' His voice had a tentative tone. He clearly didn't recognise the number.

She took a deep breath. 'It's Connie.'

The voice warmed up. 'I only know two people called Connie. One's my great-aunt, and you don't sound like her.'

'Is the other a grumpy copper?'

'That'd be the one. You okay?'

'Fine. How's Bill?'

'Oh, he's all right. Just about getting over his sulk about misidentifying the body in 2004. You never know, he might have regained his good humour by Christmas.'

'Good to hear.' There was a short silence. 'I'm calling because you mentioned going out for a drink sometime. I've had one of those days. You up for something?'

'Yeah.' He sounded surprised but pleased. 'Where were you thinking? I can come to you?'

'Is that okay? I'm a mix of super-hyper and dog-tired. I don't trust myself behind a wheel of a car, to be honest. Meet you in the Glass Room at eight?'

'The Glass Room?' he sounded dubious. 'That's a bit more upmarket than I'm used to.'

'But it's big. We can find a table to ourselves and chat without being overheard.'

'Is this about work?'

Connie hesitated, but, sick of lying, decided that honesty was the best policy. 'No. I just need a drink with a mate, to be honest.'

The warmth came back into his voice. 'Sure. See you in half an hour.'

The Glass House was technically a restaurant with half of the tables reserved for diners. Towards the long windows that had given the place its name were comfortable sofas where you could have a drink and chat. Scott was already waiting for her when she arrived. His piercings were in place, but he had clearly made an effort in the time since the call. She could smell lemon soap and shampoo. His hair, curling around the collar of his polo shirt, was still damp at the ends.

Connie plonked herself down next to him on the sofa and checked to see what he was drinking. Peroni beer.

He saw her looking. 'I'm not used to drinking it out of a glass.'

She smiled. 'I thought Becks would be more your drink.'

He leant forward to pick up the bottle. 'I got used to it on holiday in Italy last year. I always have it if the pub is selling it.'

'Italy? I've always wanted to go there. Where did you go?'

'Rome, Assisi and then Florence. I'm interested in art. I went to as many art galleries as I could. It was wonderful.'

'Art?' Connie turned to face him full on. 'I thought computer games were more your thing.'

'I like gaming, but also art. They're not a million miles from each other, you know. When they're done properly, both can draw you into a world completely different from this one.'

Connie suddenly had an urge to smoke. She touched her pocket to check she'd brought her vape out with her. She hadn't.

He saw her checking. 'I've got some fags if you're desperate.'

She grimaced. 'Couple of drinks and I'll be snatching them out of your hand.'

'I tried to give up once. I lasted about four hours.'

Connie sniggered, feeling suddenly much better. She'd forgotten what it was like to go out for a drink with a mate and just chat. Despite the effort he'd made with his attire, he didn't look like he was expecting anything at the end of the evening. Unlike Palmer.

Reading her thoughts, he put down his bottle. 'Anything in particular you wanted to talk to me about?'

Connie felt sick. 'I've had a hard day.'

'Can't be easy, your job.'

Connie thought to the meeting with Sioned Rhys. Well, she couldn't tell him anything about that. 'It's not just work. I've got a bit of a problem, that's all.'

'Man problems?'

'How'd you guess?'

'You said it wasn't about work. So my second guess was a man. Is it Sadler?'

'Sadler?' Connie coughed over her drink. 'Of course it's not Sadler. He's my boss, for God's sake. Anyway, he's not my type at all.'

Scott shrugged. 'He's good-looking though. A favourite among some of our female staff. Him and Palmer. Everything stops if those two come in together.'

Connie looked at the floor.

'It's not Palmer is it?' Scott sounded shocked.

'I know he's married—'

'It's not that. It's just, well, no offence, but I wouldn't have had you pegged as his type.'

'Why not?' Connie tried to keep the hurt out of her voice.

'Well, you're one of us. You know, normal. Palmer looks like he's come from a fashion shoot. He's never got any dirt on him.'

Connie looked down at her grey trousers and black boots. The trousers were okay but didn't fit her that well. She'd bought them in a sale, and the only ones left were a size too big. She'd bought them anyway because of the price. Her boots were scuffed. Not in an embarrassing way, but they could have done with a polish. She looked, as Scott had gently pointed out, ordinary.

'Is it affecting your job?'

'Not yet. We slept together just the once.'

'And now he feels guilty?'

Connie thought back to Palmer's behaviour towards her that day. 'He didn't seem to. He was relaxed about everything, but he's gone all cold on me.'

'Well, he is married.'

'I know. That's what I keep telling myself. What else did I expect? And the daft thing is that I don't actually want a boy-friend. I'm happy as I am and don't want anyone living with me. So the question I need to ask myself is, what exactly do I want?'

'And what answer do you come up with?'

'I wish that I'd never gone anywhere near him.'

84

Mark raced across a darkening Bampton, his foot hard on the accelerator. Kat hunched in the seat and prayed that Lena hadn't made her way back to Providence Villa. She hadn't said where she was going. Surely the house was the last place she would go given that she was still wanted by the police. The problem was, if Lena had decided to go to the house, Daniel might still be there.

'Should I call the police?'

She thought he'd say no, but Mark looked grim. 'I don't think we've got any choice. I don't like the sound of this man at all. Lena was convinced that someone was trying to kill her. You have to choose your battles, and I don't fancy my chances against him.'

Kat pulled out her mobile phone from her bag, but Mark put his hand to stay hers. 'If there's trouble, they're the people to call but I think we deserve at least a head start. Let's see what we find when we get there.'

When they arrived at the house, dusk had fallen despite the summer hours. They'd spent longer on the moors than she realised, and she felt chilled to the bone. The place looked dark and forbidding. A too-large house falling to bits. It needed selling. 'I hate this place,' she said, getting out of the car.

'You've got to wait here. I'd never forgive myself if something happened to you.'

'Not a chance. This is my house and my family. It's time some ghosts were put to rest.'

'This man could be a danger. You're not going to help Lena if she's not there but he is. Think about it. Let me go in first.'

Kat halted. 'What are you going to do?'

'Do you have your keys with you?'

She pulled out the bunch from her pocket.

'Which one is for the front door?' She showed him, and he pulled it off the ring. 'I know the layout of the house. Give me five minutes. If I'm not back by then, there's a problem. Call the police.' As soon as he passed through the gate she could no longer see him. The wait was interminable. After six minutes had passed, she got out her mobile and rang the number Connie had given her in the café.

There were was a loud hubbub of voices. It sounded like Connie was in a bar.

'It's Kat Gray.'

'Are you okay?' The voice was immediately on alert.

'I'm not sure, actually. I've seen Lena . . . look, I can't go into that now but I think she may be in danger. We think the person trying to kill her isn't from Bampton but Whitby.'

'Whitby?'

'It's a long story, and there's not the time now. I'm at our house, and I'm worried about going in there by myself.' An instinct to protect Mark prevented her from giving out his name or saying that he was already there.

Kat heard a sharp intake of breath down the line.

'If there's danger, you shouldn't go inside. I'm on my way. I'm going to call for support. For God's sake, stay put, Kat.'

Kat clicked off the phone. The temptation to go to the

front door was excruciating, but she didn't have a key. The path around to the back of the house was overgrown, of course. She'd probably end up breaking her neck if she went that way. As she waited for the sound of the first siren, she heard a movement through the front gate, and Mark appeared. He took her hand. 'I know I was longer than I said. Did you call them?'

Kat nodded.

'It's just as well, but I want you to follow me first. There's something I want you to see before they get here.' He took her by the hand and brought her up to the front door, sliding her key into the lock.

The house was silent. It was not the stillness of absence but a deathly hush. Kat backed away. Mark's hand was on her back. 'There's no one here now. There's something you need to see before the police arrive. I'm really sorry, Kat, but this is important.'

He gently steered her into the living room and drew back the curtains. The light from the spring moon threw a pale light onto the long room. Kat's eyes took a moment to adjust to the gloom. Mark took her arm again and guided her to the back of the sofa. There, on the floor, was a huddle of clothes.

'Lena!' Kat broke away from him and crouched down beside her sister. She was cold with the chill of the recently departed. Lying on her side Lena looked like she was sleeping, her face calm. Only the unusual angle of her sister's head gave Kat the horrified realisation that this couldn't be the posture of the living.

She looked up at Mark.

'You need to see her. Once the police get here, this room, this house, will be sealed off. I want you to see her before they all get here.'

Kat stroked the top of her sister's head as she'd done as a teenager, all those years ago before the chain of events had started. 'Why? Why did you want me to see her?'

'Because I want you to see what she looked like. I've known violent death. It preys on your mind. Sometimes the thought of what might have happened can drive you insane. I want you to see what she looks like. Have you seen anyone dead before?'

'My parents.' Kat could feel a weight of nausea behind her nose. She was about to be sick.

'And now your sister. But despite the violence, this is what she looked like. She's in the house she loved and felt safe in. I want you to try to hold on to the image in the days ahead.'

Kat could hear the sirens, getting louder and louder. 'We need to leave. The police are here.'

'We need to stay. You called them. They're expecting you to be here. If you leave, they might think that you're in danger. Or perhaps that you were in some way responsible for Lena's death. We need to stay here and meet them.'

'We?'

Mark crouched down beside her and lifted her up. 'Both of us.'

85

At the station, Connie watched Kat compose herself, which she was managing to do, sort of. Connie was an only child so she couldn't imagine what it must be like to lose a sibling.

Lena was lying dead, waiting for Bill's ministrations at some point over the next day or so. The strange web of events was untangling. It had its genesis in a drunken night in 1987, but it had started earlier than that, when two rugby players had joined together to prey on the girls of Bampton. Lena had been an early victim. She had closed herself down, thrown herself into her painting and brooded. Marriage to anyone other than Andrew Fisher might have helped. His secret past had remained buried until one day she'd started an affair with her attacker, Philip Staley.

'I think we have to believe Lena's story,' said Connie. Kat opened her mouth to object. 'I know it's hard. This is where I'm able to help you, Kat. Your heart is feeling deceived but it doesn't have to be like that. Let me look at it from an outsider's point of view. Will you bear with me?' Kat nodded. 'If she recognised Philip Staley as her attacker before she started the affair, then it must have taken a huge effort of will to have sex with him. Lena was frozen after her attack. You told me this. Do you really think she could have been so hard-hearted?'

Kat stared at her hands. 'I don't know. You're asking me questions about a person I lost a long time ago. Could she have been so cold-blooded? You know, I think she might have had that in her.'

'Okay. Fair enough. Well, let me put this another way. If she recognised her attacker, Philip Staley, for who he was, then the killing must have been premeditated and I don't think it was. The hustling off of Andrew Fisher to Lena's favourite place, which meant she could no longer visit there. That doesn't sound right. She'd used Whitby as a refuge for years, and then she sends a man she knows to be a predator there. Does that sound like something she would willingly do?'

Connie could see Kat trying to assimilate the information.

It was late, gone one in the morning. She and Palmer had finished questioning the man they had discovered with Kat. Mark Astley. An interesting past, but nothing to suggest that he had anything to do with Lena's killing. He was refusing to go home until they finished with Kat.

Palmer was shifting uncomfortably in his seat next to her. Well, they were all tired. She had downed two beers earlier that evening, which seemed a lifetime ago.

Connie leant forward. 'You need to believe your sister on this one. I think she discovered that Philip Staley was her rapist that night in 2004 and killed him. Without premeditation.'

Kat looked at the table. 'Why? She let that bastard ruin her life even further. Okay, she discovers that he's her attacker from all that time ago but why kill him?'

'That's the point about unpremeditated killing. You don't plan it. It just happens. I don't think Lena was a natural killer. She acted in the heat of the moment.'

'But she came up with a decent plan to let Andrew go free.'

'She wasn't going to kill him in cold blood though, was she?

330

What was much more likely was she'd ring the police and tell us about him. But she didn't want to do that. Partly to protect herself, not to have to relive the details of the assaults, and partly to protect you from everything coming out. She thought you were a victim too.'

Kat groaned. 'But nothing happened to me. What a complete mess.'

Connie shook her head. 'It was a rubbish plan, and yet it worked. Go to prison for murder, which was, in fact, what she had committed. A form of atonement. At the same time remove the man she also knew to be a sexual predator from his hunting ground. I think Lena's motives were far from clear.'

'But she was punishing herself,' wailed Kat. 'She went to prison for a crime with mitigating circumstances that a judge would have taken into account. She might have got off with a manslaughter charge.'

'Was she always so hard on herself?' asked Palmer.

Kat shrugged. 'I thought she was being hard on me but now I'm not so sure. Have you found him? Daniel?'

'Not yet. We're still looking for him. Why didn't you tell us he'd been in your house?'

'He didn't know where Lena was either, so I didn't think it important. He was just another person looking for my sister. And all along she had been staying with Steph Alton.'

'She told you this? Lena?'

'She said she'd met Steph and her daughter one day in the park. And they'd got to know one another again. And Lena told me that's where she'd been staying. With Mary.'

'And what about Daniel? Did he give you a reason why he was looking for Lena?'

'He told me he was in love with Lena. Obsessed with her, in fact. So he came to find her. And he did.' Tears pooled in Kat's eyes. 'I thought he liked Lena. He was calm at the house when I saw him. The same in Whitby. I never suspected a thing. I thought he was trying to protect her.'

'He blamed her as well as Andrew Fisher for what happened to his sister. Andrew might have been the rapist, but Lena got Daniel to help him start a new life in Whitby.'

Kat's eyes widened. 'What happened to his sister?'

'We suspect that she was Andrew Fisher's victim in Whitby. At least one of them. The sister of Daniel Frears, Alison Frears, reported an attack in February this year. We've been in touch with North Yorkshire Police and the description she's given of her attacker matches that of Andrew. She knew the alleged attacker by the name of Peter Murphy, but we believe it's Fisher. Police went to his address but were unable to locate him. The investigation into the assault is still active.'

'So after the attack he came back here. To be killed.'

'He didn't have anywhere else to go. I think, but it's only conjecture until we find Daniel Frears, that Andrew Fisher knew that he was searching for him. So he had to leave Whitby. Where else would he go? Although we haven't yet discovered where he was staying. And you know what, Kat? The sad thing is that things have changed. If you report a sexual assault now, you are dealt with sympathetically. There are things we can do to secure a conviction. It didn't have to end like this.'

'And where is he? Daniel?'

Connie looked at Palmer. 'We don't know. He may be back in Whitby. Or at least travelling back towards there. We're searching for him now.'

'And it was him who killed Andrew at Hale's End?'

Connie looked to Palmer again. He was leaving her to answer all the questions. 'We're not sure. He's a strong suspect, of course. However, until we locate him, we can't be absolutely sure.'

'What?' Kat hissed across the table at them. 'What do you mean, you're not sure?'

'There are too many loose ends in this investigation for us to be sure of anything. The boy who gave you the gun, for example. He's still unaccounted for. Don't forget it was him who handed you the murder weapon. He needs tracing.'

'Do you think he might be in danger?'

'We need to find him and discover what role he played in this. What exactly did Lena tell you again?'

Kat shook her head. 'I asked her about him but she wouldn't tell me much. She was a great keeper of secrets.'

'We all have our secrets,' said Palmer. 'It's how destructive we choose to be with them that makes a difference.'

Is he talking about what happened with me? wondered Connie.

They finished the interview, and Connie walked Kat back to the station reception. Mark was standing outside the station, talking on his mobile.

Kat turned to Connie. 'What the hell was Lena thinking? You get on with life, whatever it throws at you and you might find happiness. Finding happiness with someone makes everything else bearable.'

Connie smiled. 'You talking about that handsome Mark outside?'

'I suppose, although . . .'

There was a defiant air about her. Connie could smell intrigue a mile off. 'How did you meet?'

'It doesn't matter. He's nothing to do with this. He never met Lena. Didn't know Philip or Andrew.'

Connie raised a hand. 'I was only curious. Don't mind me. Romance is in the air, clearly. It will help you. Your grief, I mean. He seems like a nice guy.'

A red blush spread across Kat's face. 'He's much younger than me.'

So that was it. She was mortified that she was seeing someone much younger than her. 'Don't worry,' Connie said in her most cheerful voice. 'Younger? So what? There are worse things that can happen, like seeing a married man. If anyone found out, that would be your career over around here. These things are best avoided.'

Connie smiled across at Kat and was dismayed to see her eyes fill with tears.

86

Three in the morning, and Sadler couldn't sleep. It had been a late night for all of them. Palmer and Connie had interviewed both Mark Astley and Kat Gray and had got some answers. But not enough. Lena Gray was lying dead, and he still felt he was only looking at part of the picture.

He'd spent the evening coordinating the search for Daniel Frears and that had taken time. Two police forces and possibly more if Daniel was en route back to Whitby. He wasn't a car owner, which made things more difficult. He'd arrived in Bampton under his own steam, and Sadler guessed he had probably made his getaway earlier that day, after killing Lena. By train or possibly by coach. Sadler suspected that he would be easy to find. Once he'd exacted revenge, what else was there for him to do?

Llewellyn had been updated. Although grumpy at being woken up, he had got dressed and had come into the station to help out. There weren't many bosses like him any more, and part of the reason why Sadler couldn't sleep was the thought of his earlier anger towards him. Llewellyn had only done what he was told, and what he'd said to Sadler had been correct. You don't always get to hear everything in an investigation.

He thought about opening a bottle of wine, but he needed to be up and driving by eight. It wasn't worth the risk. He wished he was the sort of person to keep camomile tea in his cupboard instead of the builder's variety. He went to the cupboard and opened it anyway. He winced. Never was it more blatantly obvious that he was a single man who spent too little time inside his own home.

In desperation, he boiled himself a cup of hot water and took it through to the living room. He switched on the television. Too many channels and nothing to watch. He flicked idly between them, stopping every once in a while to see if something was worth watching. It never was. He was running out of choices by the time he reached the Horror Channel.

The lurid colours of the film made him pause briefly. He looked at the screen titles to see what the film was. *Brides of Dracula*. Not his thing at all, but he'd caught the opening sequence so he could at least follow the story until he was tired enough to sleep. The film was as bad as he might have expected. Or maybe as good. In any case, there was enough to hold his attention. The source of the evil doings in the village wasn't Dracula, but someone called Count Menster, who was going around vampirising the local villages. In an interesting twist, his mother discovered what he was up to and chained him in the castle to try to stop the killings.

The mother always knows. A pattern of images swam before Sadler's tired eyes. What had Connie said about Janice Staley? That she didn't think the woman held any illusions about her son. But there were other models of motherhood. Like Pamela Fisher. Jane Reynolds, who had originally spotted Andrew in Whitby, had been adamant that his mother would have known that he was hiding out there. But perhaps she had known much, much more.

87

Connie sat at her desk reading through the case files and feeling the visceral heat of raw anger. Case number five: a woman who had turned up at the police station claiming to have been raped, but she refused to give any further details or to be medically examined. Classified as 'no crime'. Case number eight: a woman claimed to have met a man at a nightclub, and he had taken her somewhere in his car and raped her. A doctor's examination the next day declared her injuries to be consistent with the victim having fallen while inebriated. Victim was an alcoholic. Classified 'no crime'. So it went on. Case number twelve: transcript from the police interview, 'Did you, at any time, enjoy the experience?'

Connie put her head in her hands. She briefly looked up to see Palmer walk into the office. He ignored her, which was just as well given that she felt like slapping someone. He would do. She put the files to one side. Despite herself, she couldn't resist glancing over to where he stood. He was more smartly dressed today than his usual attire, which was saying something, given that he was easily the best-dressed man in the place. He had on grey trousers that looked like they could be part of a suit, and a leather jacket. Connie felt her heart lurch. *It's only sexual attraction*, she thought. *A purely physical response*. She saw his compact movements suddenly tense. 'What is it?'

He focused on her. Not as the lovers that they had been nights earlier, but as a colleague. 'These photos from Julia Miles's wall. Have you looked through them?'

'I've not had time. They were only collected yesterday from Shallowford House. What's up?'

Connie got up and crossed the room to him. He froze and moved away from her slightly. *Don't respond*, she willed herself. *Stay calm.*

'Look at this.'

She could do nothing but lean in towards him, although she noticed he moved away from her again.

The picture was poor quality. Probably someone had snapped it on an iPhone and then printed the image off onto cheap paper. It showed Stephanie Alton squinting into the sunlight, wearing cut-off denim shorts and a lemon T-shirt with a logo that Connie couldn't make out. She had her arms wrapped around her daughter, who looked around thirteen. She was smiling into the camera uncertainly, but the arm that she had wrapped around her mother was confident. It was a moment of happiness frozen in time.

'It's her daughter, Mary. I interviewed her after her mother died. She's older now, nineteen.'

Palmer was scrutinising the photograph. He turned the image towards Connie. 'Look at her. Forget about the bobbed hair. Look at her body.'

Connie frowned. 'She's in her early teens there. She hasn't started developing properly yet. Could be a boy or a girl.'

'What does she look like now?'

'Definitely a gi—, bloody hell.' She took the photo from him. 'You know, she cakes on the make-up, but she's built all gawky and angles. You think this is our teenage boy?'

'It's got to be a possibility, hasn't it?'

*

'You knew, didn't you?'

Pamela Fisher opened her mouth to say something and then shut it.

Sadler had eventually managed to get some sleep, but only about three hours in total. His head felt heavy on his shoulders, and he was fighting the urge to call around to his sister's house even if it meant entertaining her boisterous children. He needed normality, of the kind you can only get from your own family. Certainly not from the warped sense of family solidarity that assailed him from all directions in this case.

'You knew that your son attacked women and you shielded him. Is that why you encouraged him to marry Lena? To give him another alibi?'

'I never encouraged him to marry either of his wives. They were his choice. I did want him to settle down, but he never could. It was that Philip Staley. He was a bad influence.' The woman's tone was bitter.

'I don't think it was as simple as that. They fed off each other. They worked as a pair.'

She refused to look at him.

'Is this where he stayed? When he came back from Whitby? Did he stay with you? Or did he go to Lena?'

'Lena? Of course he didn't go to her. When he wanted to come back here, it was me he came to.'

'And you knew he was in Whitby all along?'

The woman shrugged. 'I knew he was alive. I never saw him but I knew where he was.'

Sadler swayed on his feet. He hadn't been invited to sit down, and, in any case, he wanted to get this visit over as quickly as possible. 'Do you know why he had to leave Whitby?'

The woman stayed silent.

'Can you guess?'

Silence.

'Did he leave anything here?'

The woman looked like she was debating whether to say something. 'Andrew? Only the clothes he brought from Whitby. Nothing special.'

'Can I see them?'

Pamela Fisher led him up the stairs to a small back bedroom. Whatever her affection for her son, she'd put him in the box room with a view of the neighbour's wall. Sadler shook the contents of a rucksack onto the single bed and looked through them. She was right; there was nothing special. He could feel her eyes on the back of him. What was he missing? 'There's nothing else?'

'From Andrew, no.'

The hairs on the back of his neck began to rise. 'But you have something from someone else?'

She hesitated. 'There's an envelope. It's not from now but from before.'

'Before Andrew went missing?'

'Yes, even before that. He used to come here. When he was married to Lena. Get changed, that sort of thing.'

'Get changed?' Sadler could hear the incredulity in his voice.

She flushed. 'Sometimes Philip came with him. I didn't like the man.' She folded her arms. 'Then, that September . . .'

'In 2004?'

'Yes. Philip came here with a load of stuff. He was supposed to move abroad. I think he said Australia or New Zealand. I can't remember.'

'It doesn't matter.' Sadler was impatient to hear what was coming. 'He left some things.'

Pamela nodded at the rucksack. 'It was like that. Full of stuff.'

'Do you still have it?'

She went over to the built-in wardrobe and opened one of the high cupboards. 'It's there.'

Sadler helped her bring down a scruffy navy-blue rucksack and opened the flap at the top. 'Have you looked through this?' he asked her.

'Just once.'

There was an odd assortment of things. Scrappy notebooks, some clothes. Near the bottom was a large blue envelope folder. Sadler pulled it out and opened it. Photographs. Of women's faces. He felt the bile rise in his chest and gather in his throat. 'Have you seen these?'

'Just once,' she repeated. She sounded like she was on automatic pilot.

'Don't you feel any compassion for the women affected?'

'They were at a club. Wearing God knows what. What do you expect, going out looking like that?'

Thank God Connie's not here, he thought.

88

'I'm going to sell this place.'

Mark looked up briefly from the bag he was helping Kat pack. A policeman had accompanied them upstairs and stood sentry on the door of the bedroom. He'd warned them that he would be itemising everything Kat removed. 'You don't need to do anything rash. Now's not the time to make that sort of decision.'

Kat emptied the rest of the drawer. That was all the T-shirts. She'd leave the thick winter jumpers until another time and make do with a couple of cardigans now the weather was warming up.

'What next?' Mark was looking around her bedroom. 'Take enough to see you through for a couple of weeks. I don't want you to have to come back again until things have settled down.'

Kat thought of Mark's spare bedroom. 'Is there room in the car for one of Lena's pictures?'

'Of course. I'm going to show the copper what we've taken from here.'

She crossed over to the landing, went down the stairs and into Lena's studio. The room smelt stale, the odour of paint that had been there on her last visit now nothing more than a lingering echo. She took in the scene. In the shabby room, the canvases suddenly looked like things of beauty. The hues of blue, which had once appeared lacking in passion to Kat's eyes, now had an icy rigour to them. Stifled emotions, perhaps, but even repression was an emotion of a sort. She wondered which one to take.

She crossed over to the window and looked out into the garden. She could see, over by the ancient fence, a bunch of tulips bowing gently in the breeze. She looked through the canvases, and, sure enough, she found a picture of the blooms. She picked up the painting and put it under her arm as she went downstairs.

A shadow outside the front door caused her heart to miss a beat. The knocker slammed against the door. A man in uniform came quickly out of the kitchen. 'I'll get it.'

Connie stood on the doorstep. 'Can I come in? I need to ask Kat about Stephanie Alton.'

'Steph? I thought we'd discussed all this. I knew her as a teenager.'

Connie stepped into the hall. Kat didn't want her to go into the living room where Lena had been found. It was the room she'd been avoiding, and she didn't want to face it now. The detective looked briefly towards it but remained still. Mark, alerted by the bang on the door, came downstairs.

'It's about her daughter.'

Kat frowned. 'Mary?'

'Do you know what she looks like?'

'I've never met her. It's Lena who'd met up with Steph and Mary. I told you all this.'

'We think there's a possibility, a strong possibility, that the boy who left you those gifts from Lena was Mary.'

Kat opened her mouth and shut it again. The boy was a girl? She thought of the musky masculine sweat emanating from his clothes. 'I'm not so sure about that.'

The detective shrugged. 'Well, we're not positive, either, but I need to check it out. Where did Lena say she'd been staying while she was in Bampton?'

Kat shook her head. 'I told you. She said she'd been staying with Mary. I don't have any more information. A flat some-where in Bampton, I assumed.'

Connie's mobile rang, and Kat watched her answer it. A voice barked down the phone. The detective's features brightened as she cut the call. 'I'm going to go there now. You sure Lena didn't say anything else about Mary?'

Kat heard Mark move behind her and felt him lay a hand on her shoulder. 'Lena told me only what she wanted to tell. That was always the case with her.'

*

They drove in silence back to Mark's house, the car stuffed full of her things. He pulled up outside the house but didn't get out.

'What's the matter?'

'I could almost hear that girl's address. You were closer to that policewoman. Did you hear what they said?'

Kat nodded. '12b River Terrace.'

He looked behind him.

'I want to come with you.'

He shook his head. 'I'll take the car. We can unpack it later. I know where River Terrace is.'

'But—'

'I'm worried that if Mary is the boy who's been leaving you

the things, then she's still a danger to you, or to someone else. He was carrying a knife when you last saw him.'

'But Connie's going to see Mary. Why can't we just leave it to the police?'

'I'm going to help someone I understand. Someone whose position is not a million miles away from my own. You know who's to blame for that.'

'Lena?'

'Your sister screwed up someone's life. No, don't protest. Whatever happened in 1987, it doesn't justify her manipulating someone just out of childhood. That young girl will be grieving for her mother.'

'She was traumatised.'

'I know all about trauma and about feeling helpless, but the question, Kat, is how many people are you prepared to make pay for someone else's crime? And where does it stop?'

'I don't know.'

'I didn't make anyone pay. Neither did Stephanie Alton. But Lena did. And it's time to stop things. I do understand. I really do, but not everything can be condoned, and not all is forgivable. You know that as well as me.'

After he had gone. Kat stood in the road for a moment then pulled out her mobile from her bag. She flicked through her contacts until she found the number. Theresa, who had endured years of counselling in an attempt to come to terms with her own experiences at the hands of her attackers. Probably either of those two men. She needed to know that there were others out there. The call went to voicemail. Kat thought about leaving a brief message but instead clicked off. Almost immediately, the phone rang.

'Did you just call? I'm sorry I didn't get to the phone in time.'

'It's Kat Gray.'

'Is everything all right?'

Kat took a deep breath. 'Theresa, I really do think you should go to the police.'

89

Sioned Rhys sat in front of Llewellyn, holding her cup on her knee. She'd turned down Margaret's offer of coffee from the shop across the road, preferring instead a cup of mint tea from a packet she kept in her handbag. She spotted Llewellyn looking at the pale-green liquid.

'I drink two glasses of red every evening. In case you think I'm one of those goody two-shoes. I've just got sick of drinking crap coffee in the stations I visit.'

Llewellyn grunted. 'I'm spending a fortune at that new place. Three quid for a cup of coffee. It's daylight robbery.'

Rhys looked down at her cup. 'Sign of the times. You've got to move with them. Talking of which . . .'

Llewellyn picked up the bound document in front of him. 'So this is your report.'

'You've read it? What do you think?'

'I think it makes depressing reading.' Llewellyn flicked to a page. 'Complaint number one,' he read out, 'Failure to show understanding or knowledge of the CPS policy with regard to prosecuting rape cases. The Rape Investigating Officer openly admitted in interview that he had no knowledge of the CPS Policy for Prosecuting Rape Cases at the time of this investigation.' He looked up at Rhys, who was watching him calmly. 'Finding, therefore,' he continued, 'that I consider there to be sufficient evidence to substantiate this complaint.'

Rhys put the cup on his desk. 'I'm sure you've got the gist. In the vast majority of the cases that were examined, the behaviour of the detective sergeants and constables involved fell well below the standard expected of them.'

'And your recommendation is . . . ?'

'That the officers involved are subject to disciplinary proceedings.'

'You mention individual *and* organisational failings though.'

'As part of the recommendations, I'm going to ask that the policy and procedures of the treatment of women who make allegations of sexual assault are reviewed. But from what I can gather, the current system works much better. Significantly better.' She looked across to Llewellyn. 'Do you know the officers involved?'

'Of course I know them. I'm so old, I think I know everyone here.'

'It wasn't just lack of training, you know.' She made a face. 'I seriously wonder how some of the individuals involved got through the recruitment process.'

Llewellyn put the report down on the desk with a bang. 'The thing I'm worried about, what's keeping me awake at night, is did we damage the investigation into the murder of Andrew Fisher by keeping quiet about this one?'

'I don't think so. Andrew Fisher and Philip Staley were allowed to continue their attacks because of our failure to treat the reports seriously. But nothing we did has impacted on the investigation into their murders.'

Llewellyn grimaced. 'But it's connected, isn't it? What happened now. Mistakes from our past are coming back to haunt us.'

Rhys smoothed her skirt. 'Mistakes usually do.'

90

The station was boiling as usual. Sadler had rolled his shirtsleeves up to above his elbows and made a mental note to ask the facilities manager to turn down the heating. Palmer also appeared to be sweating slightly. His usually neat appearance was tempered by a five o'clock shadow that shouldn't have been there at eleven in the morning. Sadler thought about asking if everything was all right but baulked at the potential consequences. Connie had also been looking down recently, and if the reason for this was what Sadler suspected, then he really didn't want to get involved, even though he knew, eventually, that's what he would be doing.

Palmer was flicking through the notes that they had spread around the table. 'I can't believe it went this far and no one picked it up. We've got a mixture of unreported attacks that Connie discovered through finding old patrons of that bar, and ten or so clear reports of rape that absolutely nothing was done about.' His voice was shaking with anger.

Sadler picked up a file. Case number nine had been particularly badly treated, in his opinion. The victim had drunk four blue Bols and lemonade. She had said in her statement that she was drunk but had not particularly responded to the man's advances and had been leaving the bar when he pounced. The officer who took the statement had reported it in the standard way, but the dismissal of her claims, mainly due to the amount of alcohol she had drunk, made Sadler hot with an anger to match Palmer's.

He wondered what the victim was doing. Was she a Stephanie Alton or a Rebecca Hardy? Because it was the Rebecca Hardys of this world that you had to hold on to. She'd gone on to make a decent life for herself. A happy marriage and three children. Just that one lingering resentment, a prickle of unhappiness in the life she had made. That an unprovoked attack made years earlier had not been investigated with the vigour it had warranted. Sadler thought about Connie's righteous indignation regarding everything that happened. Surely things had changed. And Stephanie Alton. What made someone a survivor and another not? The eternal question.

Palmer was looking at Stephanie's picture. 'Do you think everything that happened is down to us? The life she had in the end? If we'd given her more support, do you think things might have turned out differently?'

'I don't know. I always shy away from simple explanations, but one thing's for sure: we did things wrong. When I started this case, I thought the outcome would be greater scrutiny for the way we identify recent deaths, but I would personally welcome anything that improves the way we treat these women. The victims.'

'And yet, our focus is on the perpetrators. We're spending all our time and resources on finding who killed them.'

Sadler felt suddenly tired. 'We're bringers of justice. Whatever form it takes. Whatever we feel about the people in question.'

'You think Lena Gray was culpable too?'

'In her own way. For killing Philip Staley. There are a lot of women being denied justice because she administered her own particular brand of it.'

'You still think it was unpremeditated.'

'Probably. I don't always understand people's motives. I'm not endowed with extra gifts of insight, even after years in the job. I don't know why Lena decided to help her husband when she knew him to be an associate of the man who raped her.'

Palmer was back at his computer scrolling through his emails. One caught his attention. He squinted at the screen. 'What the—'

Sadler looked up. 'What is it?'

Palmer picked up a sheet of paper from the printer. 'This can't be right.'

'What? What is it?'

Palmer laid the paper down on the table and ran his finger down numbers.

Sadler joined him. 'What's the matter?'

'I've got Daniel Frears' mobile-phone records here. Andrew Fisher was shot at Hale's End on the ninth of May.'

'Right.'

'Well, according to these records, Daniel was using his mobile at regular intervals around the Whitby area.'

Sadler picked up the paper and looked at the dates. 'He could have lent his mobile phone to someone.'

'It's possible, I suppose. But why would you travel from Whitby to Bampton without your mobile phone? When you go on a journey you would usually take your mobile with you, wouldn't you?'

'Perhaps he was trying to confuse us. In case of an arrest, his mobile would be being used by someone else.'

'I don't think he was thinking like that. If he's angry about his sister, would he be thinking that clearly?'

They glanced at each other. 'So if he was in Whitby, he can't have been in Bampton murdering Andrew Fisher.'

'But he definitely killed Lena.'

'He was in the house around the time of her murder. Kat confirms this and he's now missing. That certainly makes him our prime suspect.'

'And if he wanted to kill Andrew Fisher, then Lena would also have been in his sights. It was she who sent Andrew to Whitby in the first place.'

'Unless someone beat him to it.'

'Where's Connie?'

Palmer shrugged.

Sadler lost his temper. 'What the hell's that shrug for? Where's Connie?'

'She went out. Talking about tying up loose ends. We think the boy who left the gifts for Kat Gray was Stephanie Alton's daughter.'

Sadler slammed the paper down on the table. 'Get her on the phone.'

91

Mary Alton lived in a newly built housing-association flat close to the river. The street jutted up at right angles from the water's edge. Those living at the top of the row were furthest away from the scenic view. It was a prime Bampton location, but Connie wondered how it must have felt living there given that Mary's mother had willingly filled her pockets with stones and entered the water further along its bank.

Flat 12b was about halfway down the row. Connie pulled up her car close to the front door and got out, thrusting her keys into her trouser pocket. She rang the bell and clattered the letterbox. One of the doors further along the row opened. 'Can't you keep the noise down?' A tousle-haired face peered out her.

Connie nodded towards the flat. 'Do you know who lives here?'

The man opened the door fully. He was wearing a blue dressing gown. 'Who's asking?'

Connie thought about showing him her warrant card but this looked like a small community. Mary Alton clearly had a problem with authority, and she'd hardly welcome her neighbours' knowing she'd been visited by the police. 'I'm a friend. I've not heard from her the past couple of days, and I'm worried. After what happened to her mum.'

The man looked Connie up and down but seemed to accept

her explanation. 'She's probably in. She just never answers the door. It doesn't matter who knocks. I'm always being woken up. Try around the back and tap at the window so she can see who's knocking. She might answer if she knows you.' He turned around, and Connie saw a large 'S' on the back of his dressing gown. Superman.

She headed down towards the water's edge, counting the number of the doors she passed. She needn't have bothered. At the back of the development the wheelie bins were all numbered with their owners' address. Out of curiosity, Connie peered inside 12b's to see the contents, but it was empty. She opened the gate, walked up to the back window and rapped again hard. This time she could sense movement. 'Are you in there, Mary? Your neighbour suggested coming around the back.'

'Who is it?'

'It's DC Childs. We met at the station recently. I talked to you about your mum.'

'I can't come to the door. I'm not dressed.'

'I'll wait. I wanted to see if you were okay.'

There was silence. Connie patted her pockets for her electronic cigarette, but she must have left it at the station. She was craving nicotine, and it was typical she had nothing on her.

After five minutes, she wondered if Mary had done a bunk out the front when, with a click, the kitchen door opened. Instead of inviting her in, Mary pulled the door to behind her. Her face was heavily made-up, like the first time Connie saw her. She was wearing a pinafore dress, lightly sprigged with pale flowers, over a pair of jeans. Her bare arms were thin but muscular with thin sinews winding up her forearms. On her feet were a pair of trainers. It was these that Connie focused on.

'When I interviewed Kat Gray, she told me a boy had been leaving gifts for her. She couldn't give me a very good description because of the hood he was wearing. Just that he was medium height and wearing Converse trainers.'

Mary dug deep into her pockets and pulled out a packet of cigarettes. She carefully lit one, not offering one to Connie. 'So?'

'I keep forgetting that Kat is tall for a woman. Medium height for a boy might mean tall for a girl. Someone like you, for example.'

'Me? Do I look like a boy?'

'Do you know what? I think you could pass for one. You're tall and thin. Okay, you're wearing make-up, but without it I don't think your features are girlish. You could be the boy who was passing gifts to Kat. If you are, I want you to tell me why.'

Mary shrugged. 'I don't know what you're talking about.'

Connie took a step forward. 'Mary, you're the victim here. Talk to me and tell me what's been going on.'

Mary threw the cigarette on the floor. 'Come inside. I'll tell you what I know.'

Connie followed the girl through a small kitchen into a tiny living room furnished with just one sofa and a small square pine table. The table was covered with cheap women's magazines, an ashtray overflowing with cigarette butts and cups containing half-finished brews.

'Take a pew.'

Connie looked at the sofa and rejected it. It was too low down, and she didn't want to be stuck there if the girl got agitated. Instead she picked up the chair by the pine table and sat down with her back to the wall, near the front door. The girl shrugged and pulled out the other chair and sat down opposite her.

'You think I'm really a boy.' She sounded amused.

' I think you've been impersonating one.'

'Me? Why would I do that? I like being a girl.'

'Tell me, do you know Kat Gray?'

Mary examined the tip of her cigarette. 'She's the woman whose sister was killed yesterday.'

'You know that then.'

'It's all over the news. It says you're looking for a man in connection with the killing. That was on the news too.'

'Let's talk about her sister, Lena. Did you know *her*?'

'Never heard of her.'

'Your mum knew her.'

At the mention of her mother, Mary froze. 'My mother killed herself. What's she got to do with anything?'

Connie was trying to formulate thoughts in her head. To make connections. 'I think your mother was involved with a man, your father, who was involved in an assault that traumatised Lena. I think Lena may have played on that, exploited you even, to get you to help her.'

Mary was still sitting stock still, her eyes on Connie. She made an effort to smile. She got her packet of cigarettes out of her pocket and threw them across at Connie. 'Go on, have one. I can see you're dying to.'

'Am I that obvious?'

Connie reached into the packet and, as she did so, became aware of Mary standing up suddenly and swinging the pine chair above her head.

92

Kat was stuffing what she could of her clothes into the tiny chest of drawers in Mark's spare bedroom when the phone rang. She thought it might be Theresa calling back to say that she couldn't go through with it, that everything they had discussed would have to wait. Kat wouldn't have blamed her. But it was Mark. She looked at her watch. He's only been gone fifteen minutes. He was breathing hard down the phone.

'We've got a problem. I've come to River Terrace. The front door was open when I arrived.'

'Is the girl there?'

'There's no one here.'

Kat exhaled with relief. 'Are you going to wait for her?'

'We've got a big problem, Kat. The living room's a mess, and there's blood on the floor. Not much, but some.'

'Do you think DC Childs has already been there?'

'I don't know but it doesn't look good. It's where she told us she was going.'

'Good God.'

'Call the police for me, will you? I'm going out to Hale's End.'

'Hale's End!'

'I've been in the bedroom. There's stuff there about that disused morgue. Maps and old black-and-white photos. The girl seems to have been obsessed with the place.'

'But what about you?'

'Call the police but don't come. You'll be putting me in danger. I can't look after you and myself. Do you understand? You need to stay there.'

The connection was cut.

Christ, thought Kat. She dialled 999.

93

The girl held the knife across her throat, and Connie felt suddenly calm. So this was how it would end. At the hands of someone young enough, nearly, to be her daughter. She could feel the girl's thin strength through her sweat-drenched T-shirt and knew she was no match for it. The blade was touching her skin, and she felt small drops of blood trickle down her neck. Her mouth had closed up, and she could only breathe heavily through her nose.

The bang from the chair had stunned her. *Stupid.*

She'd remembered her training up to a point. Had sat near a door as a means of escape if necessary but hadn't really seen Mary as a threat. When she'd come to, Mary had been half carrying, half dragging her outside to a car. Her car. She threw Connie onto the back seat and tied her hands behind her. She must have taken her car keys from her pocket.

And now she was here, at Hale's End, where it had all begun, in dense woods with a girl damaged by her past and her heritage. She was the offspring of a night so indelibly etched in her mother's memory that it had tainted her life and that of her child's. Some smart-arsed sergeant had once quoted her a line from Confucius: *If you embark on a journey of revenge, dig two graves.* Now here she was, contemplating her own destruction by someone anxious to prevent her mother's shame being paraded for all to hear and her own tainted blood picked over with the same embarrassed attention.

It doesn't have to end like this. This is what she wanted to tell the girl but her throat remained closed, paralysed in fear. She shut her eyes and leant back against her assailant. She could feel Mary's body tense in surprise. She thought of Palmer's hands on her. Would he be sorry that she was gone? Or would she remain forever that niggle of guilt on nights out with Joanne when she was regaling him with mutual friends' stories.

The girl leaned forward and whispered in her ear. 'I don't want to kill you.' Her voice sounded strong but not sorry. Simply stating a fact.

'Then don't.' At last she got the words out. Mary wrapped her arms around Connie's body, her forearms across her breasts. The touch was not sexual but still reminded her of Palmer.

Mary's mouth remained by her ear. 'I've got to, you see. I've started a train of events, and this is how it ends. Lena thought she was playing me. Giving Kat presents from the past to try to make her remember but I'd already started everything off. Because it was me who killed him. Andrew Fisher.'

'But it was Philip Staley—'

'—who was my dad. I know that. But they worked as a pair. Did you know that? I found out because Andrew came back. He was hiding at his mother's. Lena told me. I went looking for a gun, but I didn't need to find one because Lena had one all along. She showed it me because I told her I was scared. Told me where to find it if there was a problem.'

Connie closed her eyes. *What a stupid thing to do.* It was Lena who'd unleashed the chain of events again.

'Where did you get the bullets?'

Mary smiled. 'It was easier than you imagine. Easier than

finding a gun. I carried on asking around Bampton and someone sold me some.'

'But why kill Andrew? It was Philip who ruined your mother's life.'

Mary pulled her closer. 'Because, I told you, they worked as a pair. Don't you see? They were as bad as each other. And my father lies dead in Lena's bed and Andrew is sent away. Where's the justice in that?'

'It doesn't have to end like this.' Connie shouted it across the dank building. It was a mistake. Mary grabbed the top of her hair, causing her to cry out in pain, and spun Connie around to face her. Connie was smaller than her, and, looking up, she could see a pair of furious brown eyes.

'How else can it end?' Mary's breath was sharp. She leaned into Connie's face. 'How . . . else?' She hauled Connie towards the side of the room and smacked her face against the stone wall. Connie felt the impact of the cold granite and then a stream of blood from her nose that met the pool that had gathered at her collar. Mary gripped her hair, and slammed Connie's head at the wall again and again.

It'll end like this, she thought. The pain from the final blow was so great she was unable even to scream. Then, finally, nothing.

94

It's all Palmer's bloody fault, thought Sadler. *I'll have him up in front of the disciplinary committee for this.* If he hadn't been so busy playing it cool about Connie's whereabouts, they might have realised the danger before now. Because Sadler had no doubt that Connie's life was in peril. Blood in Mary Alton's house was a bad omen. Blood anywhere usually was. Connie had clearly been taken somewhere against her will.

Connie's phone was ringing on to voicemail. 'Do you think . . . ' Palmer was ashen-faced.

Sadler ignored him and walked to his car. Palmer got into the passenger seat, and, as Sadler pulled his seat belt across his body, opened the door and vomited onto the tarmac. After the final heave, he shut the door and sat in silence as Sadler reversed and drove quickly away.

'Where are we going?'

Sadler ignored him and accelerated hard, forcing Palmer to hold onto the dashboard. It had just stopped raining, and, through the weak sunshine, Sadler could see the beginnings of a rainbow. The town sped past them, and messages on the communications system informed them of the progress of the support vehicles also hurrying towards Hale's End Mortuary.

'You think she's there?' Palmer sounded as if he had a mouth full of cotton wool.

'I don't know. A patrol car got to Mary's flat quickly after

Kat Gray's call. Connie's not there, and Hale's End is a definite possibility. There are newspaper cuttings and maps in the bedroom. Brought him back to the scene of his and Philip's past crimes. So it makes sense that it's where she's taken Connie. It's a guess, of course, but it's all we have at the moment.'

'Oh God.' Palmer looked like he was going to be sick again.

Sadler felt the rage boil over him. 'What the hell have you been playing at? You should have gone with her to Mary Alton's flat. Never mind what's going on in your private lives.'

Palmer shrank into the seat. 'It's a consenting relationship.'

'Relationship? I couldn't care less about that. It's the secrecy that might kill the best detective I've ever had. Don't look at me like that. She's a damn sight better than you are. I'd rather have her brave-faced passion than your indecision any day.' From the corner of his eye, Sadler saw Palmer put his face in his hands. His mood darkened, and he took the corner too quickly, the back wheels sliding for a second on the still wet tarmac.

As they neared the entrance to the narrow track that would take them to the mortuary, he slowed right down and pulled into the nearby verge. He got out of the car and opened the rear door.

'Shouldn't we wait for Armed Response?' asked Palmer.

For a moment, Sadler thought about hitting him. Instead, he pulled his coat from the back seat and strode ahead up the path. He was listening for the approaching sirens in the distance. He needed to get to the building before they arrived. According to Julia Miles, Mary Alton had a deep-seated mistrust of anyone in authority. The best chance they had of rescuing Connie was to get there first.

Sadler's hunch was that Mary Alton wasn't armed. They had

the gun that she had used to kill Andrew Fisher in their possession. It had been given to her by Lena, who had, through manipulation, eventually had a hand in the crime of which she'd been convicted.

At the entrance to the building, he stopped and called into the doorway. 'Mary!'

No answer. Palmer came up behind and pushed past him. Sadler swore and followed. The single room was empty. Palmer was examining the ground and knelt down, his hands sweeping across the stone floor in an arc. He stood up, and crimson glistened on his fingertips.

Their eyes met. They ran out of the building and went in opposite directions around the back. The grass was more overgrown here, and the recent rains had made the soil soft underfoot. Sadler heard a shout and arrived to see Palmer sprinting towards the field behind the building where a tall figure stood.

Sadler also started running, but Palmer had halted suddenly about ten or so metres from the girl. As he joined him, he could see what had made him stop. In front of them stood the girl. She had her hood low over her forehead and from underneath he could see her eyes blazing at them in the spring glare. By her feet was a figure, curled up into a ball. Sadler saw, with a sickening glance, that the body on the ground was Connie. He could smell petrol, the pungent tang infusing the air.

The girl held a cigarette lighter in her outstretched hand. 'Don't come near me. I'll set it off. Don't think I won't. I know I'm responsible. Mum started drinking again and then walked into the river because she guessed what I'd done. She asked Lena if she'd killed Philip all those years ago. But all the time she was talking to Lena she was looking at me. She didn't care that that bastard Philip Staley was dead. It was what I'd done that killed her.'

Sadler could see the wildness in the girl's eyes. Now her hood had moved, he could see her angular face, her gaunt features showing tension and determination. 'Did you know that the ancient Britons used to celebrate the end of winter with fire? It was called Beltane, and they'd light a fire to burn their winter straw beds but they also had human sacrifices. To promise a fruitful harvest.' The girl glanced down at Connie. 'She's not the sacrifice. She's already gone.' She kicked at the inert figure. 'Or if she hasn't, she's nearly.' Again she kicked her.

'You little bastard.' Palmer covered the remaining distance in a flash and threw himself at the girl. In terror, she flicked at the light. It sparked and sparked again, but nothing caught. At last, a whoosh of light travelled from her hand and up her sleeve. Sadler pulled off his coat and moved towards the blaze. He pushed Palmer out of the way and saw that the front of his jacket was also alight.

A man appeared out of nowhere. Short and stocky, he ran to Sadler. 'Throw her on the ground. The grass is wet but be careful not to burn yourself.' Palmer had managed to rid himself of the burning jacket but was clutching his arm. Mary was in a much worse state. The petrol flames were licking up her body. The smell of burning flesh was overpowering, and steam rose from where the body came into contact with the ground.

The man was deftly rolling her in the grass, and eventually the flames were extinguished. He leant over the thin figure and looked up at Sadler. He shook his head. Sadler turned to look for Palmer, who had slid over to Connie. With shaking hands he was feeling her neck for a pulse. 'Help me.'

Sadler was immediately at his side and also laid his hands against Connie's neck. 'There's still a pulse.' As he pulled out his phone he could hear the approach of the sirens in the distance but he didn't look towards the sounds. Instead, he watched his sergeant lie down beside Connie and put his arms around her.

95

'She will be okay, won't she?' Where had the note of desperation come from? He had a sergeant in the serious-burns unit despite the fact that the consultant had assured him less than an hour ago that Palmer's injuries weren't, in fact, serious. Not life-threatening anyway. His expensive jacket had taken much of the flame, and its natural wool fabric had ensured that the material hadn't stuck to his skin. Palmer would be okay, although, at the moment, no one was allowed see him. Not even his wife Joanne, who Sadler had left anxiously pacing the corridor outside Palmer's room.

He had been glad to leave the burns unit. The complexity of Palmer's private life made his head ache, and he had more pressing concerns. Connie was in the high-dependency unit, and she wasn't allowed any visitors either. Her father was holidaying in Scotland and would be driving down first thing in the morning. There seemed to be no other relatives. Friends? She must have some but not many, it seemed. This damn job got in the way of the casual relationships that the normal person would make.

He was standing opposite another doctor, a woman this time, wearing a hijab and thick black spectacles. She was competent and not very encouraging. 'Ms Childs has received a number of severe blows to the head. She has a fractured skull and a subdural haematoma. We'll be taking her into surgery shortly to remove the clot. It's not routine. These things never are. I'm sorry I can't give you any more news at the moment. I can update you after the surgery.' The woman touched him lightly on the arm, and he watched her disappearing figure, feeling helpless.

He heard footsteps approaching and turned to see Llewellyn walking up the corridor. He was so surprised to see his boss outside the station that he was momentarily lost for words.

'Any news?'

Sadler shook his head and sat heavily into one of the chairs in the corridor. 'They're operating soon.'

Llewellyn rubbed his face with his hands but said nothing.

'Palmer's upstairs. He has burns on his arms and chest. Not life-threatening. He should be back at work soon enough.'

'Do you think that's why I'm here?' Llewellyn's voice was gentle.

Sadler shook his head. Llewellyn sat down next to him. It was the first time that Sadler had seen him not wearing a suit. He had brown corduroy trousers and a black fleece with deep pockets. It was into one of these that his hand delved, and he pulled out a silver hip flask. 'Have a sip, man. Go on. It's brandy. Good for shock.'

Sadler lifted it to his lips. It was cold but fierce.

'Metaxa Five Stars. Hits the spot every time.' Llewellyn took the bottle back off him and wiped it with his sleeve. Then he took a long swig himself.

'Who's this Mark Astley?'

'He's a friend of Kat Gray.'

'Sounds like it's just as well he turned up when he did to

help you. I could've lost the lot of you. We couldn't get the Land Rovers along that bloody track quick enough to get to you.'

Llewellyn wasn't stupid enough to ask what had caused him to go there without back-up. It had been an emergency. A colleague's life in danger. Connie's life. They'd got there only just in time. 'When will we know more?'

Sadler shrugged. 'They're going to update me after the operation but I don't know how long these things take.'

They sat in silence for a moment. Llewellyn screwed the top back onto the hip flask. 'It's probably not the right time for me to be telling you this, but it looks like we're going to be in for a long night. They found Daniel Frears. He was staying at his sister's house. He didn't try very hard not to be found, if you ask me.'

'And?'

'He's been charged with the murder of Lena Gray. That's the extent of his role in this drama.'

'According to Kat Gray's interview, he didn't seem desperate when she saw him in Whitby and at her house.'

'Revenge isn't always hotheaded. I've seen a few cold-blooded murders in my time too. Let's not lose sight of that. But it'll be for Daniel and his lawyers to explain the Whitby side of the drama to the courts. The rest is a Bampton story, and we have all the answers, don't we? We know what happened in 2004 and why.'

Sadler reached out for the flask. He unscrewed the top and took a long swig of the fiery liquid. 'It was all about what men do to women. Again.'

96

Bill Shields perched on the edge of Connie's bed. 'I won't have the pleasure of seeing your innards for the time being.'

Connie tried a laugh, but it felt like her head was about to explode. She put her hands up towards the bandage but then stopped short. Any pressure, however slight, brought a pain so exquisite in its agony that she thought she was, in fact, dead. Instead, she pointed to the sign that sternly instructed all visitors to refrain from sitting on patients' beds.

Bill made himself more comfortable. 'I've heard about your trouble.'

Connie closed her eyes.

'Scott told me. For a moment we thought you were a goner, and he was pretty cut up about it. He told me what you'd been talking about in the pub. It's no good, you know. He won't leave his wife for you.'

Connie could feel tears beginning to well up under her eyelids and felt one escape from underneath her eyelashes. There was silence from the bottom of the bed although she could still feel the pathologist's weight next to her.

She felt it shift slightly. 'You're still young enough. Don't fret about it. We all make mistakes, but take a piece of advice from an old hand like me.' She sensed him lean towards her and felt his breath on her ear. 'You're worth ten of Damian Palmer. Don't set your sights so low next time.'

'What about you? Your job, I mean?'

Bill grinned at her. 'Oh, don't worry about me. There's going to be an investigation. I'm still waiting to be even contacted about it. I'll take whatever they throw at me. That's the point, isn't it? You take responsibility for whatever you do.'

*

'How's Connie?' Sioned Rhys snapped her briefcase shut and put her raincoat over her arm. Llewellyn got the impression she wanted a swift leave-taking, which was fine by him.

'Not brilliant. But better.'

'Out of danger?'

'Yes, but she suffered serious head wounds. I don't expect her back at work for a few months. She'll be in hospital for a few weeks more.'

'Has she said much? About what happened, I mean?'

'Not much. We've got the sequence of events that led her to go to where Mary Alton was living, but about anything else, she's clammed up like an oyster. She won't see Palmer. I went to see her to assure her that both he and Sadler did their best to get to her in time. She doesn't seem to blame either of them for what happened but, at the same time, she'll see Sadler but not Palmer. Very strange.' He saw Rhys frown. 'What is it?'

'Nothing. You men can be so obtuse sometimes. How is Palmer?'

'Back at work next week. Feeling sorry for himself, I would have thought. He has a nasty burn mark on his arm. That's not going to go away. Doctors mentioned the possibility of a skin graft, but he didn't seem that interested.'

Rhys put her briefcase on her lap. 'It's been quite a mess here. You've got your work cut out.'

Llewellyn sighed. 'I'm thinking of retiring.'

'That'd be a shame.'

'Would it? That's very kind of you to say, but I doubt I'll be missed. I've been in charge of an embarrassment of blunders.'

'None of which, I'd say, were personally down to you. What's happening about the original misidentification of Andrew Fisher?'

'I referred to your lot as soon as I found about it. At the beginning of the case. You'll know more about it than me.'

'It doesn't work like that and, anyway, I'm just a humble superintendent.' They both smiled. 'What I will say is if they thought you were seriously culpable at this stage they'd already have suspended you.'

Llewellyn stood up and crossed to the window. 'I'm going to think about it anyway. If I don't go now, I might be pushed. Even if there's no comeback from that original mistake, not going now means staying on for another couple of years. I'm not sure I've got the stomach for it.'

'Case get to you?'

'Everything got to me. Lying to my team. The policing methods of thirty years ago. I was a copper then. Part of the problem.'

'But we've seen the changes, haven't we? Rung them in. Let's hold on to that.'

Llewellyn grunted.

'Anyway, I need to you to stay on for a bit.'

He looked surprised. 'I thought you'd concluded everything.'

'Philip Staley took photographs of his victims. The team have managed to match some of them to the reported cases. They form part of the case files.'

'And the others?'

'I have photos that haven't been reconciled with any reports, allegations or whatever. We both know there'll be women out there who haven't come forward.'

'What are you going to do with them?'

'I've a press conference at two o'clock today. I'm going to get asked that same question.'

'And?'

'There'll be a community consultation. With women's groups and so on. It's the best we can do. No one's prepared to let those photographs languish in the police files. Some of the women we *have* identified want them destroyed.'

'Will you be able to do that?'

'Once upon a time, I would've said no, but public opinion is a powerful force these days. The police commissioner is involved. This force could well be setting the standard for how these cases are dealt with in the future.'

Llewellyn smiled. 'Don't tell Connie. She'll want to be back at work in weeks at this rate.'

'It might be what she needs. In any case, I think you're what's needed. A safe pair of hands. Think it over. The reverberations don't all have to be negative.'

Llewellyn nodded.

97

Kat felt the brazier surge with heat as Mark added the photographs to the flames. She watched the images of the curly-haired child he'd been vanish as the paper shrank and puckered with the heat. An acrid chemical smoke turned the air black.

She pulled her cardigan around her, shivering despite the warmth of the day and the flames. 'You don't have to destroy everything.'

'Are you talking as my therapist or my girlfriend?' He turned to her, the smile in his eyes softening the words.

'Former therapist,' she corrected. 'And it's too soon for us to be using the word "girlfriend".'

Mark was silent, watching the flames.

'We need to have a proper talk about this. According to the code of practice, I'm not supposed to enter a relationship with an ex-client for at least two years.'

'But these things happen.'

It was Kat's turn to be silent. There was a lot of soul-searching still to be done but perhaps now wasn't the time for it. At some point, sometime soon, choices would need to be made.

'Let's focus on the photographs for the moment. I'm simply asking you whether or not you need to destroy everything. You can hold on to the photos if you want. Or even some of them. Not everything is ever completely bad. You must have had some good times with your mother.'

'You're wrong on that one, I'm afraid.'

'I'm just saying, you could keep some.'

'What for? I'm not going to look at them again. Don't credit me with a sentimentality I don't have.'

'How come you have so many? Photographs, I mean? Did you take them with you when you left your mother?'

Mark snorted. 'She sent them all to my uncle's a few weeks after I'd left. Once she knew that I'd gone for good, that was it. Obliterated out of her life.'

'Well, not quite. She got in touch recently, remember?'

'Not likely to forget, am I?'

'You didn't reply to her email?'

'No.' He threw another couple of photographs onto the fire. He was older in this batch. Early teens, Kat guessed. Not long before he made the break. His mother had still cared enough to take some photographs of her son. *Families*, she thought. *As long as they continue to exist, the world will need therapists.* She leant forward to pick up one of the images from the flames.

'Leave it, Kat. I'm not keeping any, and I don't want you to have any either. You take me as the adult I am, not the child I once was.' Reinforcing his point, he picked up the remaining photos and threw them into the blaze.

They stared into the orange glow. 'Does it bother you? That there's a photo of Lena out there? Possibly in the police files or maybe somewhere else?'

'Yes.'

He didn't say anything. There was nothing to say. But he moved closer to her and slipped an arm around her waist. Together they watched the flames consume the kaleidoscope of images that swam before their eyes.

Acknowledgements

Huge thanks to everyone at Faber & Faber for their hard work on this book and for the fantastic job they did in promoting *In Bitter Chill*: Hannah Griffiths, Sophie Portas, Samantha Matthews and to Katherine Armstrong. Also many thanks to Anne Brewer, Jennifer Letwack and Shailyn Tavella at Minotaur Books in the US.

Kirsty McLachlan is my fantastic agent, first reader of my books and my port of call for sensible advice. Also grateful thanks to Alison Baillie-Taylor and Kathy Durkin for their comments on early drafts of this book.

So many bloggers and fellow crime authors have been huge supporters of my writing and there's not room to thank everyone individually here. You know who you are! Thanks too to everyone at Iceland Noir and my fellow Petrona Award judges, especially Kat Hall for the use of her first name for one of my characters.

Thanks to Peter Westlake for the police help and Andy Thomas for chatting through therapy practice. Thanks to Mike Linane and Maura Lynch for being such enthusiastic supporters and Tweeters and to Neil Smith for the DM chat and advice. Also to Karen Meek for being a great pal and another sensible crime-y friend. Thanks to Tony Butler for his eagle eyes.

Ευχαριστώ, as usual, to the Greek contingent especially

Chris, Jill and Carol.

Finally, love to my family – Dad, Adrian, Ed and Katie – and to Andy Lawrence whose presence, support and emergency cake supplies have made the writing of this book so much more special.